when the creator moves me

A Story about Music, Resistance, and Creative Activism

By Shelley Muniz

with Mark Dyken and Bear Dyken

Word Project Press
Sonora, CA

© 2018 Shelley Muniz. All rights reserved.

When the Creator Moves Me

No part of this publication may be reproduced or transmitted in any form or by any means, electronic or mechanical, including photocopy, recording, or any information storage and retrieval system, without permission in writing from the publisher.

Published in the United States
by the Word Project Press of Sonora, CA

Requests for permission to make copies of any part of this work should be submitted online at
info@wordprojectpress.com

Credits:
Cover and Interior Design:
Melody W. Young, Graphic Designs by Melody

Cover Photo:
Joel Grimes, photographer

Noted interior photos:
Dan Budnik, photojournalist

Additional photo credits: Daniel Harrison, Shelley Muniz, Jim Lundeen, Kerry Rice, and Catherine Lambie

Word Project Press, Long Barn, CA

ISBN 13: 978-1-7328691-1-0

Also by Shelley Muniz:

Eagle Feathers and Angel Wings: Micah's Story
Tunneling, One Great Tribe

For the Dineh at Black Mesa—the Earth Protectors
And in memory of Corbin Harney
Shoshone Medicine Man, and Spiritual Leader

We are not speaking for a group of people,
nor are we trying to represent the views of a group of people.
The issues facing the Dineh and Hopi are complex and not easily
understood, especially by outsiders like us. Everyone who visits Big
Mountain comes away with a unique perspective. This book is a
collection of what we have seen, heard, experienced, and researched.
It is with great respect and regard that we present these stories.
We hope there is a place for them in your heart.

–Shelley, Mark, and Bear

"I drove from sea to shining sea with Clan Dyken during the 1992 Nobody for President Tour. The band and I did many Whole Earths together as well, and Mark and Bear play music and work the Kid Zone at Katestock, as I call the Kate Wolf Music Festival. Mark and Bear do so many good things to help people and our earth, but I especially honor their work with children. That kind of effort warms the cockles of this old clown's heart."

—Wavy Gravy

"This book is a blessing. The things that happened on Black Mesa are a part of our history and a part of our future as well. To teach is to grow. To learn is to remember. The skills and stories of our elders are important to share."

—Jonathan Yazzi, Youth Coordinator at Tó Łání Lake Enterprises

"The lyrics cry out for us to care a little more about our fellow man and our planet, the music lifts our spirits to a state of joyous celebration. There's just no sitting still when the Clan weaves its spell."

—Kim Angelis, The Violin Voyager

"This powerful book weaves together many stories to create a tapestry that is equally devastating and hopeful. Its portrayal of the links between creativity and activism is a gift to the world."

—Kate Evans, author of *Call it Wonder*

"Trying to pick out my favorite memory of playing and traveling with Clan Dyken is like gazing into the Milky Way and choosing the best star. I'm grateful for every moment of music, laughter, and friendship."

—Kris Osward, bassist/vocalist - Clan Dyken, Mirth & Glee Carolers, New Christy Minstrels, Drifters, Coasters, Shirelles.

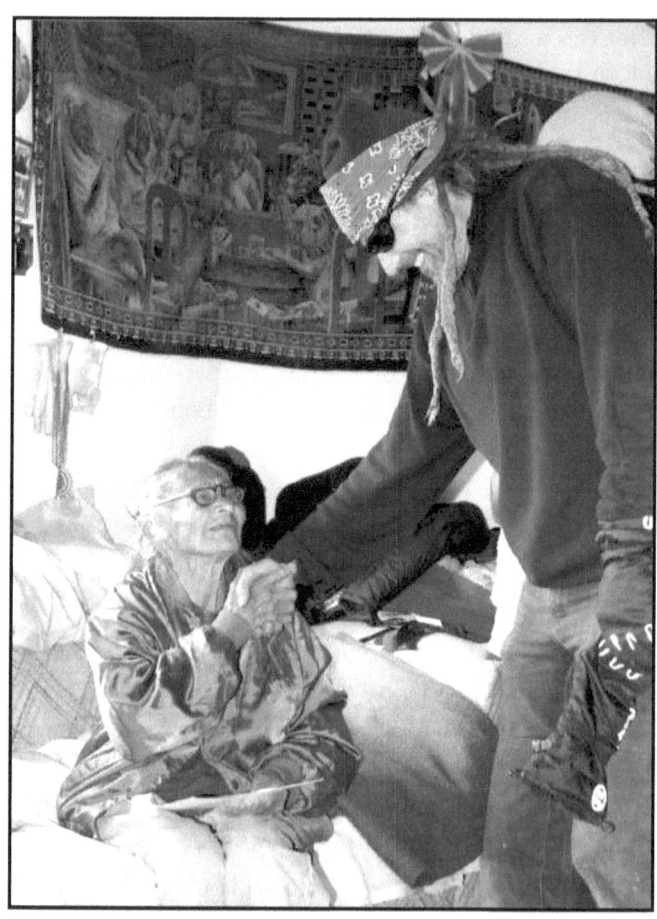

Anna Begay and Bear Dyken

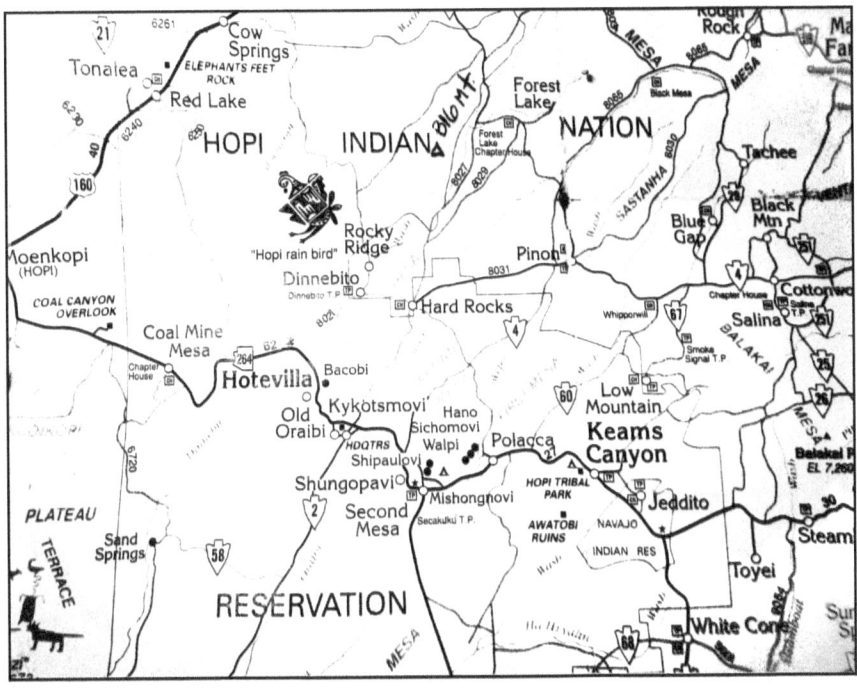

Navajo and Hopi Reservations, Black Mesa, Arizona

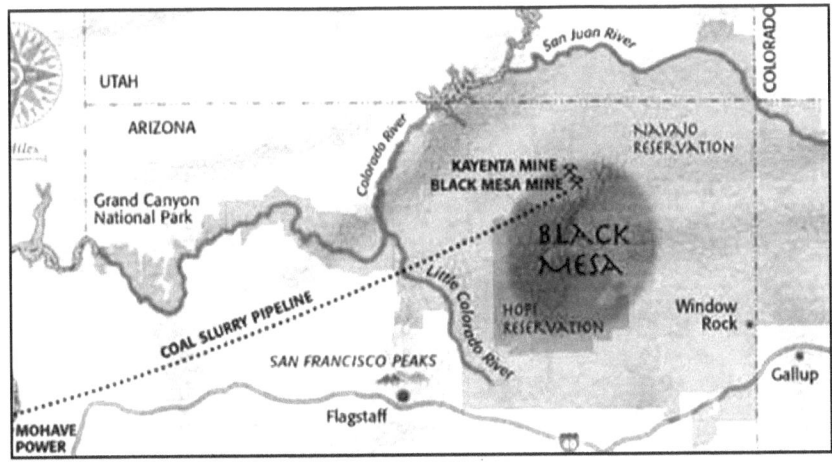

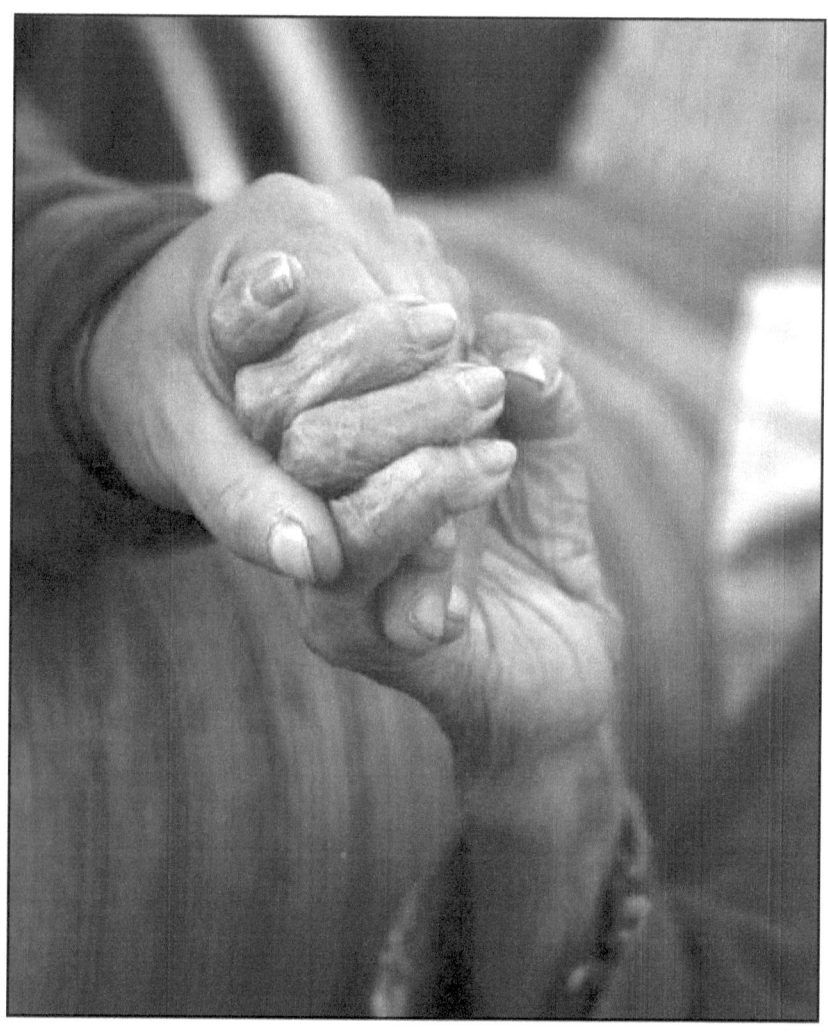

Joining hands with Grandmother
Photo by Daniel Harrison

# 1

I Want To Help You Bear Your Load[1]

And should the winds blow cold, and all our friends grow old
If we're traveling that same old road, I want to help you bear your load

Hooghan haz'ą́ = Family

The 1977 Silver Eagle Tour Bus slugs its way up the Siskiyou Pass near Ashland, Oregon. The old coach does pretty well on flat ground, but hills of any consequence are an effort. With one hand on the wheel and the other on the leather pull cord that activates the horn, Mark Dyken double honks at a blue Honda Prelude to acknowledge the peace sign the driver flashed as he passed by. Dressed in denim, wearing sunglasses and a short-brimmed cap, Mark fits the part of a cool nonconformist: bus driver, drummer, storyteller, radio programmer, school board member, and foster care liaison, to name a few.

Bear Dyken, leaning over his guitar, sits behind his brother Mark. Bear's black fedora is perched on top of a turquoise bandana and long curly hair. The salt and pepper in his braided beard intermix as fluidly as his musical range. Stylistically diverse and lyrically adept, this singer-songwriter is a human jukebox. Whether playing guitar, flute, har-

---

1 Clan Dyken. And should the winds blow cold. "Help You Bear Your Load." *Clan Dyken*. CD. Track 4.

monica, or accordion, his rich musicality produces everything from blues to rock 'n roll, rap to reggae, and folk ballads to world music.

Beside Bear is his son, Silas Dyken. Si plays bass guitar with the family band and performs solo using his stage name, S-One Freshperception. Today, Si has spent the last hour creating an original beat, rapping freestyle, head rocking, dreadlocks popping, meshing lyrics and sound into quick-witted hip-hop.

Though members of the band have rotated in and out, and collaborations with other musicians throughout their careers have been a constant, Mark, and Bear, and Silas, remain the mainstays of the group called Clan Dyken. The band's core mission is to help people create a better world through music and nonviolent activism.

We are headed for Williams, Oregon, the last stop on the annual Beauty Way Tour, a multi-legged venture beginning in Sonora, California, on into Oakland and then to Nevada City, Junction City, Arcata, Crescent City and ending in Williams. Since 1992, people from all around the world have joined the band on this trek, so the bus crew continually changes. This year, the group consists of Bear Dyken, Mark Dyken, Silas Dyken, Daniel Harrison, Catherine Lambie, and me. Daniel and Catherine are fellow activists, longtime friends of the Dykens and both are primary supporters of this fundraising effort. Daniel sets up and stows the band's equipment, assists with bus repairs, and logistical issues while on tour. Catherine helps with all stages of the trip, from ordering supplies to working the delivery runs.

Even in the early November chill, the tour bus is toasty warm. Maroon curtains hang in the single-pane windows, and solar-power batteries provide soothing ambient light. We sprawl comfortably on couches covered with native themed blankets, sharing organic raw cashews and apple slices. Catherine says a few words in French (her native language) while offering a plate of brie and crackers to each of us.

Conversations ebb and flow. The self-proclaimed "rebel rock band," Clan Dyken tells stories about family, the sequence of activism that led them to the Navajo people at Big Mountain, Arizona, and their relationship with a Shoshone man named Corbin Harney. Comradery teases the discussion forward, sometimes haphazardly, sometimes in a more orderly progression. My pen, journal, and voice recorder are handy. "We've often thought of having a writer come along," Mark had told me months earlier. "Knowing a bit about your passions, I can tell you right now, this trip will affect you—it may change your life."

This trip will affect me. It may change my life. Those words intrigue me. From my first meeting with Mark and Bear in Sonora to every venue along the way, this band has proved that they are not the average musical group—and their Beauty Way Tour, named after the Navajo Beauty Way ceremony and prayer, is far from the typical concert tour. *Beauty Way,* for the Navajo, teaches balance and harmony with all things, earthy and divine—a natural order and respect. There is action behind the Dykens' commitment to this fundraising effort, and then there is follow-through—both qualities that I admire.

Mark flips the turn signal, swinging the bus wide to make a left toward Williams. The growl of the bus's engine and the refrain of an old Dylan song streaming from his laptop competes with Si's beat, adding a raspy, folksy vibe to the mix. Bear is picking at his guitar strings. He plays some Dylan tunes and Woody Guthrie. His thoughts, at times, seem driven by the lyrics.

"In 1990, the AIM[2] people were airlifting food and supplies to the Black Hills in South Dakota and Big Mountain in Northern Arizona. We did this fundraiser with AIM activist Dennis Banks and some other people. Buffy Sainte-Marie was supposed to play that gig, but she canceled, so Dennis called us." Bear smiles at the recollection.

"Yeah," Mark chuckles, his eyes pinned to the road. "We filled in for Buffy."

"After Buffy canceled," says Bear, "Dennis asked a friend of ours, 'Who can we get?' And he said, 'Call these yayhoos. They'll do anything.'"

It isn't unusual for the band to accept gigs at the last minute or to fill in for other groups. They have played music together in one form or another since childhood. Clan Dyken has been through many incarnations, but right now it is Bear, singer, songwriter, lead guitar; Mark, drummer/percussionist; and Silas, bass guitar. After thirteen CDs and over 150 original songs—no one can say these guys aren't tenacious. As

---

2 AIM: American Indian Movement Native American civil-rights activist organization, founded in 1968.

a family/activist band, they continue to crank out tribal/world-beat/folky/funky rock 'n' roll tunes that energize and unite their audience into a common cause.

"We started out as environmental activists, anti-nuclear activists," Mark says, speaking over the persistent bus rattles and road hum. His gloved hands grip the steering wheel, as at home there as anywhere. "So then we go to San Francisco and do this benefit with Dennis Banks. That was our first involvement with Big Mountain."

"We were touring and playing music," says Bear, "doing shows and anti-nuclear actions at the Nevada Nuclear Test Site, right in the middle of Shoshone country alongside the Shoshone medicine man, Corbin Harney. Corbin was a spiritual leader, a healer, and guide, and he helped us understand about cultural genocide." Bear's voice softens; his strumming stills. "He was an internationally known indigenous rights and anti-nuclear weapons activist and performed his songs all over the world, including at the United Nations and in Kazakhstan, Russia, and the Russian nuclear bombing range. Corbin taught us how to use the big drum as a tool for drawing people into a story, and that music comes from all life forms, including the land, and the air, and the water. Through him, we came to realize that Native rights were at the forefront of most of the causes we supported."

"At one of those test site actions, where we met Corbin," Mark says, "there was this guy who was talking about the forced relocation of the Navajo at Big Mountain, Arizona. The Navajo, or Dineh, as they call themselves, live right next to the world's largest coal strip mine."

When *Siri* spouts directions to the nearest Love's Truck Stop via Mark's iPhone, he merges onto an off-ramp. "This guy was a part of the group, Veterans for Peace," he continues, while on his hunt for diesel fuel. "For several years, they had been making Thanksgiving supply runs, taking food and other necessities to people, primarily elderly Grandmothers who were resisting the relocation effort."

The first explanations of events told to Mark and Bear were simplified but on point. Big Mountain is part of Black Mesa, a tableland located in Northern Arizona. The oldest continuously inhabited places in North America are the Hopi mesas in the midst of a giant swath of Navajo territory throughout this region. In 1966, a secret land lease deal developed between Peabody Western Coal Company[3] and the Hopi and Navajo Tribal Councils. In the 1970s, Robert L. Bennett, an Indian agent assigned by the government, and a well-connected lawyer named John Boyden, negotiated a land deal, redistributing a massive amount of Navajo land to the Hopi and opening up Black Mesa to mining.

"Boyden seized an opportunity to gain possession of the land where the coal was located by dealing with progressive Hopi," Mark explains, "who were more willing to negotiate this deal than the traditional Navajo and Hopi elders. Navajo residents became trespassers on this newly designated Hopi land."

Mark's voice rises; this issue moves him. It has become part of him and part of Bear. What happens at Big Mountain deeply matters to them. "There had been minor disputes between the tribes over grazing rights, things like that, but with this redistribution of land, things got bad," Mark says. "In the 1970s, a public relations firm hired by Boyden created a phony range war, a *land dispute*, and in 1974, a law was passed to forcibly relocate all of the Navajo people from this region now in conflict, the area Peabody Coal wanted to mine."

Catherine is sitting in the passenger seat across from Mark. She adjusts her seatbelt and turns just enough so that we can hear her. "I made my first trip to Big Mountain in 1998," she shares. "It was an unforgettable moment for me. I was shocked to discover that a brutal injustice was taking place here in the United States and that the plight of these people was little known and mostly ignored. The people I met were extraordinary, and the respectful connections that Mark and Bear had developed with the Dineh were so touching. I loved the fluidity and immediacy of the fundraising efforts. The money raised through music and joyous gatherings, the humility and trust involved from the beginning of the fundraising effort to the end, inspired me."

The story is beginning to gel. The how and why of Clan Dyken's role in activism at Big Mountain feels substantial. Their years of support have a purpose, and the reasons behind their annual trips mesh as a part of their past. Though there are many questions left to answer, this starting point feels instrumental in explaining their growth as a group and as

---

3 Francis Peabody founded the Peabody Western Coal Company as Peabody, Daniels & Company in 1883. Peabody Coal is the largest private-sector coal company in the world.

a force within California's activist community.

"So how we give," says Bear, leaning forward, elbows on his knees, "is that we carry on the tradition started by the Veterans for Peace. Every fall leading up to Thanksgiving, we do this concert tour. Communities throughout Northern California and Oregon pitch in, and we raise money to buy food and firewood and bring what the Grandmothers need to get through the winter. That's what we're shooting to do, anyway. The Dineh call this supply run their Clan Dyken Christmas. But it doesn't belong to us."

"Yeah, there are a lot of other activists out there, so speaking only of our small effort—we're backed by a lot of people," Mark says, circling one hand in a wide arc. "We are a channel for it and maybe a bridge for connection. We get support in all the communities we visit and from an online community and the people who go out and help us do the work, but no way can you say that this is us."

"Many activists follow the 'journey' and appreciate the work that we do," says Daniel, as he closes the curtain over a drafty bus window. "It's not just the music. It goes way beyond that. The music is the medium to share the message. The message is that there is a Third World country right here in our backyard."

"The *Dineh feel* something most of us will never understand," Mark says. "They have the power and the *presence* of the earth in their bones, and their efforts to protect it are done for all of us, seven generations out."

"And by now," says Bear, his graying beard framing his face, "we are the elders. People our age are the elders we originally went out there hoping to help."

Williams, Oregon is a rural community of around 2,200 people. Located in Josephine County just two miles inland from the Pacific Ocean, this hidden valley town harbors abundant emerald grasslands and numerous organic farms. Each year families in Williams celebrate Clan Dyken's return. This is not a haphazard affair. The effort put into hosting this Beauty Way event is notable. The entrance ticket includes a vegetarian meal of local organic food: lentil soup, green salad, homemade bread, and dessert. Practiced dancers perform a traditional corn dance, moving in synchronized patterns around a tipi of corn stalks, their choreographed dance a prayer offering to harvest and light and another bountiful season. Donated items are up for bid in a silent auction: jewelry, paintings, local coffees and wines, plants, all to raise funds for the Navajo at Big Mountain—the fundraising effort this community annually supports.

What inspires people to put out this kind of effort?

What brings them back every year?

Liz Tree, an organic farmer, is one of the fundraiser organizers. We talk during dinner. She is engaged in the conversation, but her focus is on her young son, Jamie, playing with another child near the food service line. The kitchen in the old Grange Hall is bustling with cooks, servers, and fundraiser guests and performers. The tables are full, as are the chairs lining the perimeter. Liz swishes her long brown hair off her face and adjusts her glasses. "Clan Dyken's songs are relevant, positive and political in a progressive way," she says. "I've known Mark and Bear for many years. Their music is uplifting and environmentally significant, with a beat you can dance to as well."

As Thanksgiving nears, people in Williams, Grass Valley, and other small towns along the tour route secure the event site, work on publicity, and gather items for auctions and raffles. Donation deliveries such as organic pumpkins and squash, apples, pears, coffee, dried beans and lentils, cedar boughs, and gently-used clothing are gratefully accepted. Money made by selling tickets for the event will purchase more food, firewood, dog food, and other supplies to be carried and delivered to Big Mountain.

"It's more than the music," Liz says. "It's the vibe and the feeling. Mark and Bear are like brothers to all of us. When they come, they bring the 'news' along with their music. Their songs are a part of our bones, like preparing for Thanksgiving each year and cooking a traditional holiday meal. This fundraiser brings Williams together as a group. We know that all the money we raise is going straight to the people who need it. We trust Clan Dyken. That's what it comes down to—and knowing that the Native people who are being screwed by big oil and big coal are feeling our love in some small way."

I think about how, regardless of the venue, when the band plays, people dance, absorbed by the feeling of community and a purposeful gathering. Like Liz, many of these people have followed Clan Dyken for years. They trust these brothers as they trust family.

Family. That word comes to mind as I watch the crowd mill about, sharing a meal, visiting with each other and with Mark, Bear, Silas, and the others. Something magical happens at these fundraisers. From Sonora to Nevada City, Arcata, to Crescent City, the energy raised is magnetic.

The lights in the Williams Grange Hall dim. Center-floor, Grandmother Drum sits and waits. The drum measures two-and-one-half feet across and eighteen inches deep. The large round shell is made of recycled cedar wood; the drum skin of cowhide tightened and laced into place, made ready for the songs, stories, and fundraisers that will carry the love and support of activists to the people of Big Mountain, Arizona. Grandmother Drum has traveled the country, the world, with the band Clan Dyken and provides the heartbeat for their Blanket Dance—the climax for each performance on the Beauty Way Tour.

Wisps of gray hair hang below a multicolored beanie, the announcer on stage giving his introduction. "These guys continue to keep it real," he says. "They are legendary town favorites and seasoned musical healers, here tonight to celebrate and rise in spirit our Navajo brothers and sisters. Please welcome Clan Dyken!"

There is a burst of applause. On stage, Mark wears a Beauty Way tour t-shirt, Bear a tomato-red pullover and turquoise Converse tennis shoes, and Si, a black t-shirt adorned with a cannabis leaf. Mark sets the beat on his bass drum as Bear welcomes friends and thanks the audience for coming. He starts out slowly, building the tempo on his electric guitar.

As the band begins to play, people rise to their feet, swaying, swirling, wrist bobbles jangling—old and young, baby boomers to millennials with children in tow. Most wear jeans and t-shirts, casual clothes, hippie-style streetwear. Some are barefoot, some wear shoes, but all groove to the beat of Clan Dyken's song, "Revive the Beauty Way."

Woke up this morning, wondering what kind of tracks we'll make today, running food and supplies out to the resistance, people clinging to their Native ways, sings Bear.

Once the music enters the bodies of those dancing, it's hard to stand still—one earth, one air, one water, one people, channeling the spirits of the ancestors, the bones of Mother Earth through the second song, and the third, and the fourth.

The voices of the band float through the room. While Clan Dyken plays, those who know the words sing along:

> *Good morning, Grandmother, thank you for this healing*
> *Thank you for this blessing, thank you for this cleansing*
> *Good morning, Grandmother, thank you for this teaching*
> *Thank you for this day, and thank you for this healing.*

Mark talks between songs. "The elders at Big Mountain don't speak English," he says, eyebrows rising with the pitch of his voice. "Many of them use little or no money. They don't have running water. There are longtime activists out there, these old Grandmothers, who live this struggle day to day. We go out there a couple of times a year. It's on our minds, but these people *live* it."

"This misuse of native land was a set-up from way back," Bear says. "In 1882, the government created a reservation for the Indians of this region, knowing that the area was rich in mineral resources and that if white settlers claimed ownership, they could claim the mineral rights as well."

The next song is a cover of "Stolen Land" by fellow musician, Bruce Cockburn.

> *From Tierra del Fuego to Ungava Bay*
> *The history of betrayal continues to today*
> *The spirit of Almighty Voice, the ghost of Anna Mae*
> *Call like thunder from the mountain, you can hear them say*
> *"It's a stolen land, stolen land."*

Though they often play "Stolen Land" during the Beauty Way Tour, Clan Dyken's songs are usually original; many are topical songs relating to the cause, drawing those gathered into the purpose of the fundraiser. Throughout the concert, a slide show depicting previous trips to Big Mountain projects a landscape as hauntingly beautiful as are the faces of the people pictured. Elders with weathered brown skin, their faces and eyes determined; children with long black hair and almond eyes, smiling, shaping miniature hogans out of mud and sticks.

Healing day, healing day, healing day
Go to the altar and give it up
Surrender, surrender
It is what it is, surrender.

A few people sit in chairs around the perimeter of the room, but the majority are still dancing as the song ends, as longtime friend Daniel Harrison strides across the dance floor and removes a turquoise Navajo print blanket that has covered Grandmother Drum until now. His practiced movements are purposeful; he knows the routine. At many events, Daniel carries a sign that reads FREE HUGS, but at these fundraiser gigs, he is all business, watching for signals from Mark or Bear that the sound on an amplifier needs adjusting, or that the slideshow projector needs attention. He might dance. He may drum on occasion but is ever-present.

"Grandmother Drum brings the ritual of the music to life," Daniel said to me earlier in the evening. "I feel a strong responsibility to see that all of the band's instruments are accounted for and that everything is in its place when packed on the bus. But there's something special about Grandmother Drum. The sound and the songs that come out of her change the atmosphere in a room, no matter the venue. When we carry her out onto the floor, people know that something big, something important is going to happen. She has a life of her own. She's a member of the band."

Bear steps off the stage and he and Daniel carry the drum further into the center of the room. From a bag, Bear pulls out two handmade drumsticks with wooden shafts and double-sided beater heads wrapped in soft white leather. Daniel rejoins the crowd as subtly as he first appeared.

Mark stands near the front of the stage, his demeanor serious, his stance grounded. He takes the mic as several audience members choose a drumstick from the bag and kneel with Bear around Grandmother Drum. These drummers can be random (no one is turned down) though the majority know the songs and have participated before.

Bear sets the mood.

Here we go dancing around the world
Here we go dancing around the world.

In a fluid wave of movement, people gather, awaiting instructions. "Get your hands together, make a circle around that drum," Mark tells them. "We want your toes pointed toward that drum, your hands together in a giving and receiving position. We need all the folks in the circle."

Here we go dancing around the world, sings Bear, along with the other drummers.

"This is how we raise the energy," Mark says. "This is how it happens, and we need everybody to get out here and get your hands together. Listen to that rhythm. It's like a little heartbeat, right?"

Ba bum, ba bum, ba bum

"Take a step to the left every time you hear the beat—one two, one two, move to that rhythm. One two, one two—you got it. If somebody comes up behind you, let them join in, just make the circle a little bigger. That's it. That's it."

Ba bum, ba bum, ba bum

The drumbeat can be felt in the bounce of the floorboards, the sway of each person, the rocking of the drummers, the constant shimmy of Grandmother Drum at the pounding of the sticks. The vibration in the room swells. If one welcomes their imagination, the walls of the Grange Hall could appear as Black Mesa's limestone cliffs, the ceiling a bed of clouds and a vast bowl of stars.

"You heard people talking earlier in the evening," Mark continues, "about the faith that comes with prayer and intention, about love going out to the people at Big Mountain."

Hey ha, hey ha, hey ha, hey yo, sings Bear, still pounding a heartbeat on Grandmother Drum.

"This dance is the prayer for this evening," Mark says. "Every one of these heartbeats is part of your prayer, and every one of these heartbeats is part of that prayer that lets you have a connection to every other person you know. There is a power working right here in the middle of your body. Right here in your heart."

The whoops and hollers intensify. Synchronized feet move to the rhythm of the drumbeat as the room fills with song. The slideshow sends shadows to the walls, transporting the faces of the Navajo into the center of the dance. As the dancers stomp and sway, Mark's story carries us to Big Mountain, a journey we all are ready to take.

"Our friend, a Shoshone healer and medicine man, Corbin Harney, taught us how to use the big drum," Mark says, "and that the drum is the heartbeat of the people."

Mark's voice grows louder and then softer, his words pulling and pushing the audience with the rhythm of his inflections. "*Unity* is a root word of *community,* and the circle is the symbol of unity. And we raise this energy *right now,*" he shouts, "and we send it to Big Mountain, where people are standing firm, right now, for our Mother Earth. Because we only have *one earth—one air—one water—one people,* and when we move together we'll bring that spirit up to support those earth defenders, those protectors out there on land at Big Mountain. It's like a great healing that we're all doing together; when our hearts move and our bodies move together that makes us stronger than we are as individuals."

Here we go dancing around the world, hey ha hey ha hey ha hey ho. Here we go dancing around the world, sings Bear, eyes closed, still kneeling.

"Look at the people around you," Mark says, scanning the room, "and know that they are family. We come together out of love, and as you see people walk in the door, just grab them by the hand and pull them into the dance circle, and as we do that, the bond gets stronger by the minute, by the second. When we feel that heartbeat, it goes through our whole body, and we're sending that out right this minute to Big Mountain where the Grandmothers have been holding fast. You know that's who holds on in this indigenous world are the Grandmothers, and those are the people to whom we bring food and firewood, supplies of all kinds so they can stand there for us. Grandmother is out there now, weaving a blanket—she's lighting a fire, trying to preserve a way of life that is her birthright."

Here we go dancing around the world
Hey ha hey ha hey ha ho...

"We move that circle in a sunrise direction," Mark continues. "We keep it moving and get all of our heartbeats pumping and matching that drumbeat right now. Oh yeah, do you feel that beat beneath your feet? We're not done yet, we're not done yet—so now, we have another dance that goes to one beat, one, one, one, one."

The dancers drive at a steady pace. Some have their eyes closed. Others concentrate on their feet, the movement of the body next to them. Sweat runs down brows; smiles flicker across faces. Near rhythmically, they slow to the new beat. "Stand in one place and move your feet up and down. Let go of the hands of the people standing next to you. Reach into your pockets and grab whatever cash is in there. Drop it into the blanket as it goes by you," instructs Mark.

From near the stage, Catherine and a helper appear, carrying the turquoise drum blanket open-faced, one woman to each side, a hand grasping each corner. Sidestepping to the beat of the drum, they round the circle between the drummers and the dancers, participants depositing cash donations in the belly of the blanket.

"Money turns into food, it turns into firewood, supplies, gasoline, and this is your opportunity to reach out to Big Mountain," Mark says, his voice louder again, faster. "Everything you put in the blanket will come back to you *many, many* times over. Over the years, Grandmother has been *working* for you. She's been out there fighting the world. She's standing her ground! She's fighting with fire! Over the years, Grandmother has been saying her prayers for you. She's been standing out there on the front lines—she's had her heart ripped open, she's had her house torn down. We've seen the site of the Sundance ceremony bulldozed. We've seen sacred sites desecrated."

As the blanket rounds the circle, it grows heavier, swaying with the footsteps of the women carrying it until it reaches the last person—until it is back up front and placed on the stage.

One beat, one beat, one beat, *ba bum, ba bum, ba bum,* and Mark joins the dance now, moving people around the room, slowly at first with spirit and grace. The drummers beat their drumsticks faster, harder, and Mark picks up the pace, spiraling the dancers closer to Bear and Grandmother Drum. He drops the hand of the person to his left, instructing the person on his right to keep moving, inward toward the center of the room.

Mark kneels beside Bear, and Bear passes him a drumstick.

And the drum talks in a single beat: *Ba, bum, ba, bum, ba, bum.*

I wanna be ready, I wanna be ready, I wanna be ready
Walking to Jerusalem just like John.[4]

Let the food I eat give me strength
To do the work of the one great spirit
Who animates all the universe
From the smallest creature to the farthest star
Heal, heal, heal these wounds
Heal these global wounds.[5]

---

4 Sam Hogin and Mark D. Sanders. I wanna be ready. "Walking to Jerusalem."

5 Clan Dyken. Let the air I breathe. "Heal These Global Wounds." *Retrospective*. CD. Disc III, Track 11

Grandmother Drum

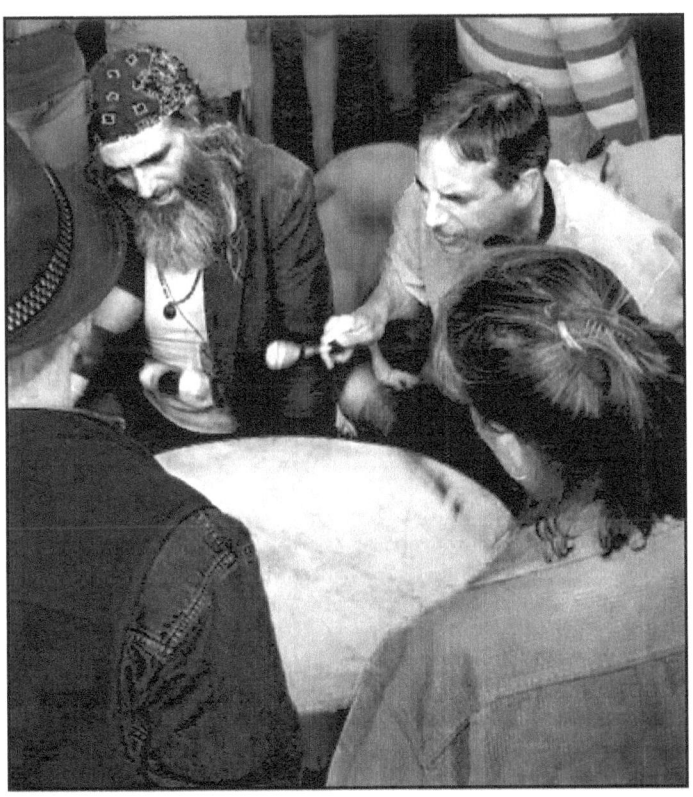

Bear Dyken, Mark Dyken, Kris Osward, Shelley Muniz,
and Grandmother Drum

Corn Dance, Williams, Oregon/Beauty Way Tour

Beauty Way Tour Fundraiser, Ukiah, CA

Mark Dyken

Bear Dyken

Silas Dyken

Clan Dyken, Beauty Way Tour (2016)

Daniel Harrison installing bunks in the Silver Eagle (2016)

Mark Dyken, on the way to Big Mountain

2

GOOD MORNING GRANDMOTHER[6]

Good morning Grandmother, thank you for this healing

Yá'át'ééh = Hello

It had been twelve hours since we rolled back into Calaveras County. Mark was installing extra bunks in the bus: two-by-two frameworks covered with plywood, each fitted around windows and above the existing pull-out beds. He had this way of doing carpentry—measuring each piece of wood, then standing back and pondering a bit before going at it again. He had a plan in mind and from the outside never appeared to get flustered when an idea needed a bit of reorganization. "We're good. Remember, we're on hippie time," he said.

Under the thin November sun, it was hard to reacclimate. For the past few weeks, we'd been following the route set for the Beauty Way Tour on narrow residential streets in Oakland, up highways and down country lanes from Central California to Williams, Oregon. We'd gone on tour and come home, and gone and come home again, the last leg of the trip lasting nearly a week. "Boldly go where no bus has gone before. That's my motto," Mark often teased.

Soon we would be back on the bus and headed for the Grand-

---

[6] Clan Dyken. Good morning Grandmother. "Good Morning Grandmother." *Water, Fire, and Other Relatives*. CD. Track 2.

mothers in Northern Arizona. All but Silas and Daniel, who had other commitments, would be going to Big Mountain. But some new crew members would meet us along our planned route.

As Mark finished the bunks, I sorted donated clothing, separating it into storage bags, stuffing those between boxes of squash and pumpkins in the exterior cargo compartments. Two hours later, we were on the road again. We picked up Catherine near the foothill town of San Andreas and would be stopping for the others along the way. Bear would follow the bus in his truck. It was the first trip to Big Mountain for all but Bear, Mark, and Catherine—and we each came for our own reasons.

Jim Lundeen, a local physical therapist, avid rock climber, and outdoor enthusiast, had heard about this trip several times before he met Mark through friends. Mark had encouraged him to come—so now he would meet us in Jamestown, near the Family Resource Center where Mark worked.

Kimberly Bass, a stylish musician from Grass Valley, had a long-time musical connection with Mark and Bear. As an accomplished guitarist and vocalist, Kimberly had accompanied Clan Dyken at the Grass Valley fundraising event for Beauty Way. After the gig, she shared how honored she felt to be invited on the trip. She looked forward to visiting with the Dineh, and being of service, she said.

Curiosity drove Lotus Allen, who first visited the Southwest in 1981 with an anthropology class from St. Louis Community College. The students went to Mesa Verde National Park and other sites where the Hopi and Navajo lived. This past year, Lotus heard about the supply run to the Navajo elders from people at Sandhill Farm in Missouri, who had made a trip to Big Mountain with a support group other than Clan Dyken. When she learned about the Beauty Way Tour, she connected with Bear and let him know that she was interested. Lotus was an artist and designed the Big Mountain logo for the 2016 Beauty Way poster and t-shirts.

My connection came through a mutual friend. "Blame it on Kris Osward," Mark often said when referring to our friendship. Kris had known Mark and Bear for years and was a stand-in bass player for Clan Dyken. He and I were colleagues at Columbia College in Sonora, where I worked as a library specialist. "You *have* to meet these guys," he often told me. "You are going to hit it off." Kris and I frequently talked about Native issues. He knew of my Choctaw heritage, and that I had long-standing concerns about the consequences of living in areas that had been affected by heavy mining, and more recently, fracking. As a geology student in college, I took trips to Northern Arizona, first to the Grand Canyon and then on my own to the Navajo reservation around Big Mountain. I was drawn there by a longing to understand not only specific events in my Choctaw family history but the far-reaching effects of the Navajo and Hopi experience. I wandered somewhat aimlessly along the high desert roads in my 1967 Ford station wagon, windows rolled down, my long brown hair tangling in the wind. I was twenty-two years old and had no idea where I was going, no idea what I was looking for, just needing to see and be present. I journaled daily and drew pictures of what I saw: plants, animals, and in my scrawled unconventional way, the faces of the people I encountered. After I was invited by an anthropology instructor to intern at the reservation on Black Mesa but was unable to take the trip, the thought was planted in my head that I would accomplish that dream in the future. So now here I was, on a bus headed to Arizona, ready to live out that missed opportunity and to write about it.

"Creatives tend to feel deeply about such things," Bear once said, referring to anyone who expressed environmental/societal concerns through artistic means of self-expression.

We were a rag-tag group, with a variety of genetic and cultural diversity. Unique, but bonded and with a shared sense of purpose. The bus was the vehicle, the road the conduit. It was a natural fit. From Central California, we headed south on Hwy 99 to Bakersfield, east over the Tehachapis through Barstow to Needles, through Kingman, Arizona, and toward Flagstaff, stopping for gas, dinner, and to sleep one night in a parking space at a Love's Traffic Stop: the crew of the Silver Eagle, and Jim Lundeen in his Toyota pickup. As the driver of the bus, Mark had time commitments, and people were awaiting our arrival, but Bear, driving his Ford diesel, took a detour, visiting a friend and a hot spring along the way. We would meet up with him later.

Jim's pickup and Bear's 1989 Ford F250 truck, aptly named the Blue Pearl, were valuable commodities. They would be used to haul the food and firewood we needed to deliver once we reached the reservation. In the bus, we talked politics and drought, love and loss. We wondered over the sunrise sounds of the Arizona desert: whistling wind, the chorus of birdsong, a raven calling, a coyote yip-howling—a drum, a flute, worldly music that raised more questions than answers. Occasionally Mark would purse his lips like he does when drumming; sometimes he would round and stretch his neck and shoulders, but other than bathroom breaks and stops for gas and meals, his hands rarely left the wheel during the sixteen hours it took to reach the Colorado Plateau. The lingering smell of vanilla past its peak summer pungency (the contribution of Ponderosa Pine forests) and the mild temperature spurred our readiness to arrive.

The high desert landscape near Flagstaff brought back memories of my earlier trips with friends and classmates to Monument Valley and the Grand Canyon: the pine and aspen trees, cholla and Saguaro cactus—mountain peaks and sandstone plateaus, and the majesty of the canyonlands. In Flagstaff, we stopped at the Whole Foods Market to pick up preordered organic chickens and more fruit and vegetables to flesh out the food boxes that would be delivered on the reservation. By now food and clothing donations filled the vehicles, the underbelly of the bus, and all available interior space, on beds, under seats, and over much of the floor.

Ninety minutes past Flagstaff we drove into Tuba City, the largest community on the Navajo Reservation. The translated Navajo name for *Tuba* means "tangled waters." But there is also a story about a Hopi Chief named Tuuvi which suggests that Mormon settlers called the area *Tuuvi* then changed it to *Tuba* because they found it difficult to pronounce the name.

From Tuba City, we traveled southeast through the Hopi village of Moenkopi, meaning "place of running water." It was 8:30 p.m. We drove past the sporadic clusters of homes, a dimly lit gas station, a grocery store, and a post office, and then toward Hotevilla and north onto Dinnebito Wash Road. Even in the dark, however, "running water" seemed a paradox, as no springs, no creeks—no water could be seen. Soon barbed-wire fences blackened by nightfall marred the open desert. We were driving on a two-lane asphalt road heading from Hopi Partitioned Land onto Navajo Partitioned Land, and back onto Hopi Partitioned Land—the center of the dispute.

"This is our turnoff to Dove Springs," Mark said, swinging a wide left onto a narrow dirt road. For the next several minutes the bus bumped along a series of ruts and ripples and through a dry wash, slipping sideways while Mark negotiated a hairpin curve.

In the distance, the muted dome lights inside a cab-over camper appeared like a mirage. There were no streetlights at Dove Springs and no storefront neon to invade the solitude. Stars stretched across the night sky, a vast openness that spanned a horizon framed by monuments of stone. Over a short rise, the single dome light multiplied into two, and then three, and then four—like the sudden bioluminescence of a cluster of fireflies. A kerosene lantern twinkled, and a campfire blazed announcing the presence of other activists, friends who had arrived a few days earlier to prepare camp, pick up the dog and cat food and the Blue Bird Flour—responsibilities that were crucial to starting the deliveries on time.

Mark parked the bus on a flat spot across the wash from the main camp. The "phhst" of the air brakes trailed the silencing of the engine, the sudden calm magnifying the riders' moans and groans as we readjusted after sitting for so long. When ready, we walked over to say hello but cut the evening short. Tomorrow would be our first workday. Maps were drawn. Routes were planned out, and the boxes were assembled and ready for packing. Under the immensity of the Navajo sky, our presence seemed paltry, mere flashes in time compared to the generations of ancestors in whose footsteps we walked, those ancestors who looked up at the same sparkling extravaganza and wondered what tomorrow would bring.

Six a.m. give or take. One by one, we rolled out of our bunks and traveled to the outhouse, or not. Across the wash, people moved through the makeshift outdoor kitchen and around the fire pit. Scattered about were the trucks with their cab-over campers, Bear's shift-pod tent, and the Dykens' tour bus set up with the new bunks. Eighty boxes covered the ground outside our supply tent—a geodesic dome designed to keep the winter cold from freezing the food we had brought.

Ice covered the tarps and bags of donated clothing. The air was crisp, cold and dry, no snow, no rain. Stories of previous trips told of bitter weather and mud so thick it stuck like cement to the tires and wheel wells of the activists' vehicles. "The first year I came out here," Mark said, gripping his cup of tea with glove-covered hands, "I drove Bear's red Toyota pickup. It was raining like crazy, as it had been for days. The truck side-slipped along the reservation roads, sliding, skidding, mud flying everywhere. By the time I left Big Mountain, the entire vehicle was brown. I couldn't see an inch of red paint anywhere."

It was hard to imagine the kind of rain or heavy snow that made winter on the reservation so challenging, but minor indicators were evident: the rugged conditions of the roads, the outhouse so many yards from any dwelling, and the lack of easily accessible heat—even firewood, according to Mark, was not easy to come by. The wood we purchased was trucked in from Flagstaff.

At the work scene, twelve-year-old Jaia assigned me my duties. "Put those apples here," he told me. "Two in each box to start. We'll see how many we end up with, and we can always add more." Strands of Jaia's hair poked out of his hooded parka, and he smiled as he talked, even while working. Jaia was a veteran here, having come with his parents, Brian Hannigan and Michelle Bienick, since he was three. This family had persisted in their support of the Dineh for many years, and they were friends of Mark and Bear. Brian and Michelle were organic farmers from Williams, Oregon and had participated in the Beauty Way fundraiser, then afterward made the trek to Big Mountain. Together with Mike Patterson, another supporter from Williams, and Darlene Markey, a businesswoman from Nevada City, we filled boxes with packages of dried beans and lentils, organic apples and oranges, squash, pumpkins, potatoes, and onions as well as coffee, canned goods, boxed cereal, bread, and baggies filled with fresh cedar cuttings that we had brought from our homes in the Sierra Nevada.

Michelle and Karen, who was a nurse by profession, sorted and separated clothes into sizes for men, women, and children, then packed them into bags in some semblance of order so that at each stop we could distribute according to need. Both women wore long skirts—a sign of respect for the Navajo Grandmothers, and work boots, heavy gloves, wool hats, and scarves. "This jacket will be great for Anna," Michelle said. "And this," said Karen, tossing a blue shawl beside the jacket.

Trucks were loaded. Maps checked, locations verified, and directions carefully plotted. Tzaddi, hatted and gloved, wearing jeans and a light jacket, traced with his finger the different delivery runs and locations of family homesteads. Tzaddi was a child when he made his first trip here with Mark and Bear. Since then he'd come by himself many times and had lived with a host family for extended periods. He knew the reservation and the people who lived here. He and Karen would go one way with his truck; Brian, Michelle, Jaia, and Mike, in their vehicles, would go another. The rest of us would divide up between Bear's Blue Pearl and Jim's Toyota.

Each delivery to every family would include the box of food, a frozen organic chicken, a twenty-pound sack of Blue Bird flour, a fifty-pound bag of dog food, and a load of firewood. Our crew now numbered fourteen: the original group, plus those who had gathered before we arrived, including Dar, Tzaddi, Karen, Michelle, Brian, Jaia, and Mike. We would have our cell phones, but the reception was spotty. Most likely, we would not see or hear from the other groups until we returned to camp late in the evening.

As we worked, we talked about the history of the Navajo. This present situation was not the first government-imposed relocation of the Dineh from Navajo land. In the winter of 1864, 8,500 Navajos were forced to walk the "Long Walk" (400 miles) to the Bosque Redondo—a barren forty-square-mile reservation in eastern New Mexico near the newly established Fort Sumner. These people were starved into submission and rounded up at gunpoint. With only their hand-woven blankets to keep them warm, they trudged through rain and snow, men, women, children, and elders, disheveled and confused, on an unfamiliar trail leading further and further from home. With their backs bent under the weight of their belongings, they walked on. The old ones covered their ears as the soldiers guarding them shouted words in English that they didn't understand. Along the way, some who were pregnant, elderly or malnourished could no longer keep up and, at the soldiers' insistence, were left behind to die.

More than 200 Navajos died of starvation and exposure to the elements. Some escaped, finding sanctuary in the depths of the Grand Canyon, on top of Black Mesa, north of the San Juan River, and in other areas where the soldiers did not penetrate. The ones who made it to the Bosque lived in crude shelters constructed of branches and canvas. Legend says that today, when men and women talk about "Hwéeldi," as they call the Bosque Redondo, they speak in broken words. It is something they can't talk about or would rather not. The memories are too painful.

In an article for *Smithsonian Magazine* in December of 1997, mountain climber and author David Roberts wrote: "Officials called it a reservation, but to the conquered and exiled Navajos it was a wretched prison camp."

The injustice of the Long Walk was hard to fathom. I could relate to it in my way because of stories my mother told my sisters and me when we were children, true stories about our Choctaw ancestors, and how they were forced to walk the Trail of Tears in 1838. Different tribe, same story: broken treaties, false promises, displaced families—lost hope and dignity. Neighbors in Filer, Idaho called my great-grandfather "Squawman," a slur that rang in my ears many times as I fell asleep at night.

"It's easy to cry here," Bear said, warming his hands over the morning fire. "Just feeling for a moment what life is like on the reservation changes your perspective on everything." He gazed out across the landscape to an animal pen tucked against a wall of rock. The pen housed six sheep, their cream-colored wool blending with the bleached ocher sandstone.

As I looked across the wash, I understood what he meant. These sheep once roamed free, as did the people who lived here. Each of us in the camp that day handled the truth of the past and the anguish of the present in a manner appropriate to our life experience: by reflecting, meditating, or working—slipping a gift into the hands of a new friend.

Helena, a Navajo child, stood staring at the activity before her. She was about Jaia's age, shy but curious about the food delivery crew. She walked to the edge of the wash and circled the camp, watching from afar. I waved, inviting her over, and together we inspected the boxes of clothing, choosing a couple of t-shirts and a pair of tennis shoes that might fit her. In my pocket was a heart-shaped rock, a worry-stone from home. I gave it to her, and she grinned, cupping it in her small hands. Soon she was playing with Jaia, racing along the trails and laughing. Her bright smile, long dark hair, and deep-brown eyes—the solidarity of her heritage braided into the outside world by way of her bright pink parka, blue jeans, and tennis shoes.

Helena's grandparents, Tim and Belinda Johnson, came to greet us, offering hugs and handshakes to their longtime friends, Mark, Bear, and Catherine. Tim and Belinda were our hosts at their homestead called Dove Springs. As is tradition, Tim and Belinda kept a hogan as well as a home, both minutes from our campsite. The hogan, an eight-sided dwelling with the door facing east, is sacred to people practicing traditional Navajo religion. Every family, even if they live in a newer house, must have a hogan for ceremonies, spiritual renewal, and balance.

Dressed in denim, long hair tied back, Tim Johnson, spoke slowly, a greeting and then prayer. This particular morning, we gathered in a circle arranged in birth order, youngest to oldest. The sun was up, not yet hot but offering a prelude to clear skies—the seventy-degree temperatures promised by weather forecasters earlier that week. Tim's blessing was casual at first, and he thanked us for coming, recognizing the continuity of this group who had become family. I stood in awe, not only of the strength of the dialect but the beauty and flow of the message. Tim's words reflected the history of the Navajo, and though he sometimes spoke in his native tongue, the message transcended linguistic boundaries. As a tribal elder and chapter president, he voiced his truth. The language of his people rolled from his throat, a welcoming, an explanation of circumstances, a prayer, a song. "Think, plan, do, reflect," he told us in English. "Begin your day with intention. That is the Navajo way."

The silence around Tim's words was palpable. Time slowed, and bodies emanated warmth. Outside of this place cars careened down highways and chain-store baristas served up coffee, but here there was only the crackle of the fire, the quiet of singular speech, the cry of a hawk, and the shuffle of feet against the earth.

Shadows of the ancients inhabit this land. Their whisperings can be heard as the wind whips over Big Mountain and through the myriad of mesas and low-lying plateaus within the Navajo reservation. For hundreds of years, the Navajo have lived in this vast stretch of canyon land—dry, desolate, and hauntingly beautiful with its rugged sandstone, limestone, and igneous rock formations. They are sheepherders. They have raised their families here. They have lived and died in the shadows of the San Francisco Peaks. The area around Black Mesa wears its history well: the red rock and water-parched sandstone, the buttes, spires, and rock arches that straddle the land; bone-dry creek beds and washes framed by junipers and pinyon pines. Change is palpable here. It is a landscape dotted with sage and ephedra plants, gray in color, much of it dying due to pollution and drought. Roads are in disrepair, and the rutted washboards are challenging to drive. Wide-open spaces, partitioned now by a crisscross of fences, restrict movement of both the people and their herds of animals that once roamed free: sheep, horses, cattle, and goats.

Lizards skitter into shadowy cracks in the limestone as the sun heats the sky. Petroglyphs speak without talking, whispering reminders from the mouths of caves, the ancient artistry carved on boulders and vertical walls describing a way of life, memories of the people and animals who once roamed the rocky escarpments. These remnants of the ancestors tease the imagination.

On a bluff near our campsite, I saw a woman in full Navajo dress: a skirt of blues, oranges, and reds, a red blouse, a blanket around her shoulders. Cross-legged, she sat silently watching our camp. *Oh*, I thought. *Where's my camera?* I turned away, checking my pocket, then thought better of it. There was no way to ask permission to take her picture, and to photograph her without asking would be disrespectful. I turned back for another glimpse, but she was gone. That fast. She was there, and then she was not. Later, I asked others in our group if they had seen her. No one else had.

Was she a vision? Perhaps. A blending of faces ran through my mind, the first resisters, the Grandmothers I admired but had not met: Pauline Whitesinger, Katherine Smith, Alice Benally, Anna Begay, Glenna Begay, Roberta Blackgoat, Ida Clinton, Lidia Watchman, Jennie Manybeads, and so many others.

It was easy to picture these proud and protective women following the paths their ancestors had walked for hundreds of years. Tending their sheep and goats; planting vast gardens of corn, squash, beans, and pumpkins; stringing bead necklaces; weaving blankets with the wool sheared from their sheep, using yarns they dyed by hand; dyes they made from local plants, fruits, and berries.

Earlier that morning, Bear had told me a story about a time he had visited the home of a respected elder, Anna Begay: "The woman was in her eighties," he said. "We drove up, and she was wearing her usual long skirt and blouse, squatting in the engine compartment of her pickup with a wrench in her hand, fixing her truck, way out there, deep in the reservation."

Living alone, miles from her nearest neighbor, the only noises this Grandmother hears each day are the bleats of her sheep, the neigh of her horses, a coyote yip-howling at the moon. "She has a family," Bear said, "people who check on her, but she, like so many others, is fiercely independent." Somewhere on the bus there was a picture of Anna riding her horse, on her way to buy supplies in Tuba City, another example of her tenacity.

"We'll visit Anna," Bear said, "when we go to Coal Mine Mesa."

As we started our morning runs, the reason for the map became obvious. The first stop was made together, but from there, each driver would veer off in different directions, better assurance that we could cover the day's necessary stops. The sun shone bright, the small pinyon pines and juniper trees providing minimal shade to the houses we encountered. Dogs barked, leery of our approach. Some were friendlier than others, but all were reservation dogs: scruffy, thin, and raised to do a job—guarding property and herding sheep.

The trek to homesteads at Jeddito and Low Mountain took hours, the roads twisted and bumpy, consisting of dirt and bedrock. In Bear's four-by-four, we bucked and bounced, the tires kicking up rocks as we drove, our train of vehicles appearing like a dust cloud traversing the high desert. In the early afternoon, we came to the home of a silversmith by trade. Monroe's house was stick-built, and there was a solar panel in the yard. "This family has signed the Relocation Agreement," Mark explained, as we drove up. "That's why the conditions here are slightly better than at other places we'll stop. The Hopi gave them money to remodel and upgrade in trade for a lease agreement stating that in seventy-five years their land will revert to the Hopi tribe."

Bear and Mark opened the doors of the truck and stepped out, work gloves in hand. Elder Monroe, his son, and daughter-in-law greeted us, both nodding, and shaking hands. "Yá'át'ééh," hello, they said, smiling. The family's dogs barked, wary of visitors but happy with the treats we gave them. The older dogs pulled hard on their tethers, maneuvering around sage and mesquite, while the younger, smaller ones ran free, sniffing at our feet, hungry for more biscuits.

We unloaded and offered a box of food, a bag of dog food, the sack of flour and a frozen chicken. We stacked firewood alongside the house where Monroe indicated it should go. Inside, his daughter-in-law carried his handmade jewelry to the kitchen table, silver rings, bracelets, and necklaces available for purchase. Palms up, she indicated that we could look the pieces over, try them on if we wished, and she gave prices for the items we chose. "Twenty dollars," she simply stated, as we held up a ring or bracelet. Monroe watched the transactions, talking a little with Mark and Jim. Pliers, stamps, gravers, and other tools lay on a worktable by the front window. Beside the worktable, a wooden stump, marred by many years of use as a hammering surface, bore witness to the time and energy Monroe spent at his craft. Holding his jewelry was like cradling a gift, each piece unique but traditional—silver beading, squash blossom designs, and turquoise inlay. The women lingered around the kitchen table, purchasing finery for friends and family back home. No need for talking, other than simplicities, as the appreciation was universal and expressed by the smattering of words we knew in Navajo. "Ahéhee'." Thank you. "Nizhóní." Beautiful.

There were two bedrooms in this house, plus a living room and small kitchen. Living room furniture was minimal: a television, a bookshelf filled with mementos, and a couple of chairs. A painting and banner depicting a peyote ceremony hung on the wall, along with framed family photographs. As at Dove Springs, the outhouse stood apart from the main house. While we readied to leave, three small puppies ran to greet us, ribs prominent, eyes budging and matted with yellow goo. Michelle and Kim opened a bag of dog food and scattered kibble about the ground, which the puppies swallowed without chewing.

"These guys were dumped on the road and in the ditch," Monroe's son told us. "Dogs are left abandoned all the time out here. We try to save the ones we can, but many die before we get to them."

As we drove away from Monroe's place and on to the next, the ditches seemed more noticeable, as did any dumped box or random movement. Puppies need food and water—excesses hard to justify when you can barely provide these necessities for your children. Spaying and neutering? Both expensive, though, according to Mark, there have been instances where veterinarians traveled to Big Mountain to offer spay and neuter clinics—a noble endeavor with logistical difficulties. Driving long distances to get animals to a clinic is a big stretch for people living on Black Mesa.

By the time we reached the next stop, we were shedding coats and sweaters. Even in November, the air was dry, the temperature averaging in the seventies. This house was also stick-built, small and rectangular, and painted gray. We knocked on the door, but no one was home. As we unloaded supplies, a goat bleated in the distance, the animal's cry—weak and airy. Following the sound, we found him and four sheep in a small enclosure made of tree limbs and corrugated tin. They had no food, and their water trough was empty. The goat's cries grew in intensity, sounding more frantic and desperate. The sheep stood apart from each other, heads down, barely moving. We searched the property for water, but there was none, other than a couple of rusty and rancid smelling inches in the bottom of a large blue barrel stowed in a pickup truck. We dumped the water in our thermoses into a metal pan and the trough, sharing what we had with the dogs, the goat, and the sheep. The sheep tumbled over one another, eyes bulging as they fought their way to the trough. The goat lost his footing, his quivering tongue lapping at the air, his smaller body fighting for ground among the larger, heavier ram and ewes. The tears Bear promised would come ran down our cheeks as we forced ourselves to leave.

"It's tough," Bear said. "As you can see, these people have no water for themselves, let alone their animals. Maybe that's where this family is now—on a water run. Let's hope."

We arrived back in camp well past dark, tired and hungry but satisfied with the work we had done. Two caravans of vehicles had delivered supplies to families separated by miles of unpaved roads. The day inspired as many questions as it answered. There was interest in adopting puppies and discussion about which family might make a deal to sell or trade for the dogs that they considered a valued commodity—sheep protectors, with a job to do. The *idea* of rescuing one or two from a homestead where multiple dogs lived seemed appropriate enough, but perhaps not to the owners of the animals. This endeavor could be touchy, involving a cultural variance of opinion.

We ate meagerly and communally: baked squash and warm tortillas heated on the campfire grill. The warmth from the fire felt good as the chill of the evening set in. We sat on logs and in camp chairs, talking a bit. How was this Grandmother or that Grandmother? Did she seem healthy? Her sheep, how many? Was she warm? Was she still weaving? We were so tired; all we could do was wipe off the dishes and use the outhouse, then head for our beds.

Settled snugly on the bus, I closed my eyes, repeating a word I'd learned that afternoon: Amá sání, a Navajo name for a maternal grandmother. The jet-black sky and the infinite quiet were a tonic, peaceful, no sirens, and no horns honking. As dreams filtered in, a day in the life of a Dineh Grandmother played out in my mind, my writer's imagination working overtime and in story form, complete with a protagonist, an antagonist, and a plotline inspired by what we'd seen throughout the day.

Amá sání rose while stars stretched across the heavens in the predawn sky. Darkness moved slowly on the reservation, and in the night she had dreamed of her family, of the six children she bore and of the grandchild sleeping now in her daughter's womb. The hogan was cold, but she had wood. Her oldest son had brought it to her along with enough water to last several days. She said a blessing to him, to the earth and the sky and the natural spring that fed her thirst.

Amá sání's hogan, the eight-sided dwelling that had belonged to her mother and her Grandmother before, was in need of repair: wind whistled through cracks in the siding, and although the hole in the ceiling remained stuffed with wool, cold permeated the dwelling. She bent over and fed the fire, stirring a pot of stew that was cooking on the woodstove. She glanced at her loom and the new rug she was weaving. Her fingers itched to work the yarn, but that would come later. She poked at a fresh sack of wool that hung with other treasures from hooks and nails in the wooden beams and wall braces: strands of tobacco, pouches filled with dried corn, pine nuts, herbs and tonics, baskets, utensils, clothing. Her husband's wool shirt hung on a peg beside the door. She lifted the material to her nose and breathed in the smell of him. Though she missed him, a small part of her was still angry with him for leaving.

Alongside the shirt hung an ornament her great-great-grandfather once traded for a turquoise brooch. According to the storytellers, the gold and crimson sash belonged to a Spanish soldier. He was among the first to bring sheep and goats to the tribe. The sheep were of a particularly good bloodline and produced many rams and ewes, providing meat, wool, and status. Amá sání's family was well respected. Their herd now numbered twenty, and she cared for them well. Her mother taught her that their sheep were a gift from the Holy People. In return for watching over and protecting them, the Holy People provided rain to nourish the earth.

Everything depended on the sheep.

Amá sání pulled a blanket around her shoulders and opened the door, walking out into the crisp fall air. When she whistled to her dogs, they came running, circling wide around her and back to the sheep, huddling together in a log pen built against the sandstone near her hogan. She opened the gate, and in a ripple of movement, the sheep poured out, heading down a path as familiar to them as to her. The dogs circled again, keeping the herd tight while Amá sání followed with her walking stick. For a mile or more, the sheep moved slowly, feeding on saltbush, winterfat, and bunch grass. In the distance, Amá sání could see the gray outline of a Hopi pueblo. She didn't interact with the Hopi much, but there was a woman in the pueblo who liked to trade, exchanging baskets for hand-woven blankets, knives for mutton, and piki bread for peaches. The man in the nearest dwelling, she didn't like at all. He often sent his dogs after her sheep. Sometimes he came running at her with his arms spread wide, shouting and chasing her sheep away.

Amá sání knew she herded her sheep too close to the pueblo, but this was where her mother had herded, and her mother before her as well. Amá sání climbed a sandstone cliff and settled herself, rubbing the same rock her Grandmother touched, nesting her bottom into the same indentation where her mother sat, acknowledging their light, their energy and strength, as always. Herding was in her blood, as was walking on the mesa that was her home—had been her family home now for hundreds of years. She pulled a piece of fry bread from the pocket in her skirt. She often brought food, sometimes extra in case the herd wandered too far or in case she didn't make it back to her hogan by nightfall. The dome of stars above her head was as vast as the landscape. The only sounds came from her sheep, munching and chewing the grass. She was used to the quiet. Even her children knew to use their words sparingly—to speak only when spoken to—to use language as a gift. She closed her eyes and remembered the Beauty Way Ceremony she'd recently attended. The songs. The storytelling.

Telling tales was a way of life, the same stories retold for generations around a campfire. Ceremonies were a time for learning, for teaching, and for laughing. As a child, her uncle taught her this blessing, and she remembered it still:

> *In beauty may I walk*
> *All day long may I walk*
> *With beauty before me may I walk*
> *With beauty behind me may I walk*
> *With beauty above me may I walk*
> *With beauty all around me may I walk*
> *In old age, wandering on a trail of beauty, lively*
> *In old age, wandering on a trail of beauty, living again*
> *It is finished in beauty*
> *It is finished in beauty*

Dreams, dreams as long as night, ribboning from fiction to truth. I woke before first light, thinking of all I had heard that day from Bear and Mark and the others. Interference by the Spanish and then the United States government made the disputes between the Navajo and the Hopi worse over the years. Treaties were signed and then broken. Land boundaries were established and then changed. Once the United States government discovered the vast mineral deposits on the Navajo reservation, economic gain became part of the equation. Uranium and coal, in particular, were sought-after commodities and the Navajo now stood in the way of progress.

The internment at Bosque Redondo (the Long Walk to Fort Sumner) was a fiasco. The army's original plan, or excuse, was to end the "bickering" between the Hopi and the Navajo and to put a stop to the raiding practices the Navajo used to increase their herds. Major General James H. Carleton hired Colonel Christopher "Kit" Carson to "round up" the Navajo and transport them to the Bosque. Said Kit Carson, "I have come to kill Indians, and I believe it is right and honorable to use any means under God's Heaven."

True to his word, Colonel Carson and the U.S. Cavalry killed thousands of Navajo. The ultimate plan for the Bosque was to civilize and retrain the "relocated" Indians and to discourage their herding way of life. The attempt to teach them "modern" farming techniques failed miserably, however. Parasites ravaged the corn crops, and alkaline water caused an outbreak of dysentery among the captives. People were angry. Depressed. Many of them died. General Tecumseh Sherman eventually offered the Navajo a new treaty, naming 3.5 million acres straddling the New Mexico-Arizona border as reservation land. On the morning of June 1, 1868, twenty-nine Navajo headmen and former war chiefs signed the treaty with X marks, and the Navajos were soon on their way home, walking in a column and escorted by Army troops.

While Navajos were recovering from wounds inflicted at the Bosque, events were unfolding that would set the stage for the Navajo-Hopi land dispute and the Navajo Relocation Program a century later. Although the 1868 treaty set aside some of the Navajo homelands as a reservation for the tribe, it also relinquished much of the best Navajo land in western New Mexico to the United States. The Navajos returning from Fort Sumner had no idea that the land they had occupied was no longer theirs and that the boundaries had changed—*boundaries* being a concept that was unfathomable to the elders in particular. Also, when the initial roundup occurred, the army's effort to keep the Navajo from re-inhabiting their land had been an all-out search-and-destroy mission. Vast herds of animals were slaughtered, fruit trees were cut down, gardens and crops burned or stomped to the ground. When the Navajo returned to their homeland, they had no tools or clothing, no gardens, and no sheep, other than one or two granted to each family as a condition of the treaty.

Despite these conditions, the Navajo population grew. Less than twenty years later, the land set aside by the 1868 treaty could no longer sustain them. In 1882, President Arthur issued an executive order setting aside 2.5 million acres around most, though not all, of the Hopi villages in the Black Mesa area. The parcel of land, known as the 1882 Executive Order Reservation, designated this region for the "use and occupancy of such other Indians" as the Secretary of the Interior saw fit, which confused tribal boundaries even more. Since before the inception of the executive order, both Navajo and Hopi had lived on and around Black Mesa. Despite overcrowding, the tribes coexisted amicably, other than occasional disagreements over land and water usage. Though historically, the U.S. Government kept a foothold on reservation lands, it showed no special interest in the Black Mesa region until the early 1900s, when the discovery of fossil fuel reserves prompted a significant monetary incentive. By the 1920s, when the first oil companies attempted to lease Navajo land for oil resource development, the Navajo had a familial and cultural foothold, and many traditional leaders refused the deal, citing their stance on "defiling Mother Earth." Sadly, these tribal leaders faced a future they might have foretold, patterned by land disputes, relocation efforts, and disparaging tribal disagreements.

As for the woman, vision or no, sitting above our camp on the sandstone bluff: did her family walk the Long Walk? Did she know the pain of forced relocation? Were her sheep healthy? Were they thirsty? Did her roof leak? Did she have sufficient heat? Food? Did she have someone to care for her through the long, dark winters? These questions and more pulled me from my warm bed and into the brisk early morning air. Outside, by the makeshift kitchen, Bear made a cup of tea. Jim tended the fire. Lotus practiced her yoga. No one said a thing, but I knew that their sleep had been as restless as mine. Their dreams as filled with the truth.

3

Voices of Wisconsin[7]

The voices of Wisconsin are whispering to me

Áłchíní = Children

During the Beauty Way Tour, music and laughter, stories and song had echoed off the metal walls of the Silver Eagle. Above the windshield hung a picture of Buddha with the words *Suffering Sucks* printed across his belly. On the dashboard were remnants of past trips with family and friends: a few photos, a chunk of rose quartz, Yellow Submarine and Blue Meanie figurines and a small replica of Sgt. Pepper's bass drum. Buttons picked up somewhere along the way, a piece of Pipestone, sage smudge sticks, and a sprig of fresh lavender were reflections of Dyken family history.

Beyond the keepsakes lay the soul of the music. Bear's eyes reflected his passion, the importance of *getting it right*, as he contemplated the sounds of the just-received rough tracks of Clan Dyken's CD, *Water, Fire, and Other Relatives*. Mark tapped the beat as the two brothers reviewed and discussed each vocal, guitar, bass, and drum track. Together they listened for tonal quality, integration, and placement in each song's mix noting changes they might make before the release.

As the soundtrack played, heads bobbed, and bodies rocked. To an

---

[7] Clan Dyken. The voices of Wisconsin, are whispering to me. "Voices of Wisconsin." *Water, Fire, and Other Relatives.* CD. Track 7.

untrained ear, the CD was perfect, lyrics sweetly reminiscent of parental love and childhood adventures—others soulfully reflective about the destruction caused by wildfire, and the tragedy of losing a child. Bear and Mark carry the past in their songs. For instance, "The Voices of Wisconsin" is a tribute to their family.

> *Where the voices of Wisconsin were whispering to me*
> *Sayin' something about life long ago*
> *An old red barn with a weather vane*
> *A different time in the Kettle Moraine*
> *In Wisconsin, where she was born.*

In 1955, in the small town of West Bend, Wisconsin, Mark and Bear's parents, Richard and Dorothy, met. Richard's father was the inventor of the Dyken Rolling Machine—a device meant to ease the process of rolling sheet materials such as paper, rugs, and insulation. His parents' success was a classic rags-to-riches story: chasing an idea and creating an opportunity within the post-war boom period. As a young man, Richard could easily have staked his future alongside his father, but like other teenagers, he questioned that choice.

"The family business offered a great opportunity but was not one my dad chose to take," Mark explained, his dark eyes mirroring his father's. "Dad had his own ideas and passions."

As a child, Richard contracted rheumatic fever, an inflammatory infection that can affect the joints and other organs, including the heart. The family's physician prescribed quarantine, followed by months of bedrest, minimal walking, or even talking. Richard read books and kept up his studies. He watched from his bedroom window as kids in his neighborhood played games of kick-the-can, stick-ball, and hide-and-seek. In times of stress, his eyes would turn skyward, imagining life as a pilot flying in the vast blue wild untethered by illness. Perhaps, in the deep of night, he kicked off his blankets and imagined himself in the cockpit of a Boeing Stratoliner or a Douglas DC-3, engaging his flight fantasy, soaring miles above the ground with the sun on his face, and the light tickling his skin. Though Richard's illness was a hindrance, it never held him back, and as he grew up, his sturdiness through adversity became a model for his life. He thought things through before reacting and said what he had to say, but was never one to expound or chatter—perhaps the result of the hours he spent in alone-time contemplation, nursed and cared for by his parents and with little contact with children his age.

Dorothy Breit was a farmer's daughter, one of ten kids. After school let out each afternoon, she worked at home with her brothers, supervising the younger boys and tending the family's dairy farm: sixty-two milk cows, pigs, chickens, and honeybees—fields of feed corn and green beans. "Every day her father worked the farm," Mark said, "and then worked the night shift at Gehl Implement Factory assembling farm equipment—often blowing his paycheck on alcohol at the local bars. Her mother got pregnant at age eighteen and was chronically depressed.

"We have this family picture of our grandparents' wedding day," he added. "Grandma Breit's dress was maroon, rather than the traditional white, and she's standing in the vestibule of the Catholic Church. They wouldn't allow her to get married in the nave (or chapel), so instead, they were married in the hall. Back in those days, getting pregnant out of wedlock was a disgrace, and she lived with that internal shame all her life."

Descendants of German immigrants, the Breit family felt the importance of nostalgia, ritual, and tradition. Keeping a rein on the children seemed a part of old country values, but with her mother's depression and her father's drinking, that responsibility often fell to Dorothy, the oldest of Agatha's children. Not only did Dorothy care for her siblings, but she also got up each morning, got herself ready and went to school, came home and did her chores and her homework.

After graduating from high school, Dorothy attended college in Oshkosh and was the first in her family to pursue a degree. She shared a room with seven other women, returning home during school breaks to work and earn her tuition money. The summer of her freshman year, she took a job waitressing at the Beacon Restaurant in West Bend. One evening, during a dinner shift, Richard wandered in, hungry and looking for something to eat. The checkerboard linoleum, rounded countertops with bar stools, tables along the outside wall, soda machine and tabletop jukebox exemplified the post-war style of the 1950s. Dressed in his collared shirt and pants, Richard seated himself and searched the menu. "What can I get for you?" Dorothy asked as her dark brown eyes drew and held his gaze.

"Night after night, Dad returned to the Beacon for dinner but was too shy to ask Mom for a date," Bear said, grinning.

The story, as Dorothy later told it, gave credit to a traveling salesman, *a stranger in the corner—an angel*—who frequented the restaurant and was no doubt charmed by Richard and Dorothy's timidity and youth. As he watched from his stool, it would have been easy to observe their smiles and sideways glances, the extra time Dorothy took when making Richard's malt and serving his meal. "Aren't you going to ask her out?" the stranger finally asked, smiling, tipping his hat. "If you don't—I will," he teased, as he paid his bill and walked out the door, never to return.

"On the last night of Mom's summer job, Dad offered her a ride to the train station, and she said yes," Bear said. "He ended up driving her all the way to school, just to get more time with her," he chuckled. "Mom didn't know why, but she trusted him. Dad's dry humor made her laugh, and her laugh made him smile, and so they made plans to see each other again."

On their second date, Richard took Dorothy to a movie. "Their third date? He probably dragged her to an airshow," Bear teased, plunking on his guitar.

Had Richard taken his mother's advice, however, the story would have ended there. In the small town of West Bend, with its barbershops, and beauty parlors, corner grocery stores and friendly gatherings, it was easy to spot a family's struggles. Gertrude Dyken knew about Agatha's depression, about her husband's fondness for alcohol, and the family's financial woes. The Breit family literally lived "across the tracks," outside the comforts of town and Gertrude's recently acquired wealth and status. Gertrude was sure that Richard could "do better" than to settle for a woman with a background such as Dorothy's, and just as the romance blossomed, she pushed him to break off the relationship.

"But Dad persisted," Bear said. "My mom was something special, and he felt that right off. She had this glow about her and kindness that ran so deep." Bear's smile reflected Dorothy's smile, as shown in family pictures. His curly hair hung shoulder-length, the same as hers had at the time she met Richard.

"I remember one of Mom's childhood stories in particular," said Mark, "and this describes her pretty well. It was late summer, and she was out working on a neighboring farm with a crew of other kids. One girl among them was of Mexican heritage, shy, and she spoke little English. The older boys liked to tease her, and on this particular day inside that barn, there were no adults to supervise."

In Wisconsin, thunderstorms can shatter records. Rural roads can become impassable due to flooding. This day, while the group picked green beans, cracks of thunder shook the sky and lightning bit the ground, illuminating the fields and surrounding forest. The field boss called the kids to his flatbed truck and drove them to the barn. "Stay in here until the storm passes," he instructed, before leaving. Once inside, the older boys circled the shy Mexican girl, taunting her and calling her names. Straw dust roiled in the air as their feet scuffed about, rounding closer and closer still. The girl's dark hair hung limp and her shoulders slumped, arms pressed to her sides.

"Mom couldn't stand it," Mark said. "'Stop bothering this girl right now!' she told those boys. When you think about it, in those days, farm boys were a tough bunch," he said. "To be a twelve-year-old girl, and to stand up and tell them to stop it—that defines our mom pretty well."

> *It must have been an angel, must have been an angel,*
> *must have been an angel*
> *Talked to Dick that day*
> *It must have been an angel, must have been an angel*
> *Introduced him to Dorothy*
> *They were on their way.*[8]

After Dorothy and Richard were married, they moved to the small town of Cedarville, just miles from where they were both born. Six years later, they moved to Saukville and bought their first home. Their extended family included grandparents and parents, aunts, uncles, and cousins. Within the family dynamics and aside from the issues that played out in their youth, it was easy to remain close to their heritage when grounded by all that was familiar. Land and lineage mattered. There was a sense of place, of belonging. "There's nothing like knowing where your home is," Mark said. "That security, that familiarity with the land you grew up on is something that we should never take for granted."

Like most immigrants, the Dyken and Breit families found comfort in the people who knew and understood their heritage and the history of their country of origin. Their roots remained entrenched in the old

---

8 Clan Dyken. It must have been an angel. "Must Have Been An Angel." *Water, Fire, and Other Relatives.* CD. Track 8.

country culture, but their feet trod the modernized American ground. Typically, though, the older people held tight to their traditions and customs. Great-grandmother Katherine Breit never learned to speak English, preferring the Germanic language of her homeland. Stories about the past and the family's reasons for leaving Germany were a part of life, their history forever bound to a revolution and a man named Friedrich Franz Karl Hecker.

"Our people came over from Europe by boat in the 1840s and 1850s, carrying all their belongings in big steamer trunks," Bear said. "They were part of an uprising, The German Socialist Democratic Revolution, and after a long struggle, their side lost. For many of the 48ers who left Germany at this time, the decision to pack up was not by choice. Their country, their government, kicked them out, and so they left for America."

Friedrich Franz Karl Hecker[9] was a lawyer, a politician, and a revolutionary, the primary agitator in the 1848 Revolution in Germany. Hecker's political program had as its goal a form of a social republic with constitutionally guaranteed academic freedom, freedom of the press and personal choice. "This revolution was about trying to get some representation for the peasants and merchants," Bear said, "but the revolutionaries lost to the armies of the autocracy." Hecker believed in a democratic republic and led like-minded comrades in a revolt, known as the Hecker Uprising, or the Baden Uprising. After moving to the United States, he served as a brigade commander in the Union Army during the Civil War, supporting the preservation of the Union and abolition of slavery. He assembled an entire regiment of German-Americans and became commander first of the 24th and later of the 82nd Illinois Regiment. In both countries, he fought for freedom, civil rights, and for the rights of the working class.

After Richard married Dorothy, Gertrude kept her distance, tolerating her daughter-in-law but remaining aloof and indifferent, until the birth of her first grandchild. Gertrude was enamored by baby Mark and impressed by the way Dorothy mothered him, attending to his needs and Richard's as well. There were no tears or complaints, only soft words

---

9 "Hecker, Friedrich Karl Franz (1811-1881) - Germanheritage.com." Web. 25 Sep. 2018 <http://www.germanheritage.com/biographies/atol/hecker.html>.

and comforting cuddles. Soon Gertrude was helping out, often visiting, talking and laughing with Dorothy while growing to love her and each of the eight children she bore.

Richard and Dorothy worked hard, supporting and parenting their growing family. Richard went to flight school to become a pilot, graduating at the top of his class. Even with his accolades, however, he found it difficult to get a job. At that time, trained pilots returning from WWII secured most of the positions offered by the airline industry. As desire alone does not pay the bills, Richard took a job working as a machinist at a local factory. In the early years of their marriage, Dorothy stayed at home to care for the children but eventually finished school and received her teaching credential.

"She was always involved in something," Mark said. "She worked on the school board for twenty-five years and even signed my high school diploma. She volunteered at COPE, a suicide hotline, for ten years, taking phone calls. Eventually, she became the executive director and expanded the operation, in both size and scope. That's how my mom was. She had these kinds of passions. For as long as I can remember, my mom was an activist, whether she was participating in church or doing things around town, she was always standing up for the underdog."

"No telling how many people she saved," said Bear. "Mom was just like that. She cared so deeply and helped so many."

Saukville is a small village in Ozaukee County nestled on the Milwaukee River. Surrounding Saukville are long stretches of open cornfields, hills and mountains, hardwood, pine and cedar forests, large rivers and flowing creeks, and the expansive beach at Lake Michigan five miles to the east. Saukville itself is a residential community with neighborhood parks and tree-lined streets, excellent schools and numerous churches. In the 1960s, at the time the Dyken children were growing up, Saukville was also the home of Freeman Chemical Company.

"Across the street from our house were other houses, and behind those houses was a gigantic chemical plant," Mark said. "It took up several blocks. You could walk up the street, down another, around and around, and arrive at our Catholic Church and school. That plant, Freeman Chemical, filled up the whole area behind those places. When we were little kids, the factory workers would fire off incinerators, and we'd be out on the playground, and there would be toxic ash falling on everybody."

"The smell, the weird things that oozed into the water," said Bear, "were frightening. We didn't know what they were making in that plant, but we knew the residue was toxic."

Mark was thirteen, and Bear was twelve. Along with their brothers, sisters, and friends, they rode bikes on roads and trails, skateboarded, and sledded. The parks and fields and trees were a part of the scenery, but factory walls were a backdrop, smoke billowing in the sky. There were days when they would rub their eyes, and their noses would run, irritated by the contaminants in the air. With one foot on the asphalt and the other on a bike pedal, they would stop and glance skyward, feeling an ache in their lungs when they breathed.

"We knew that factory shouldn't be making that kind of pollution," said Bear. "Even at our young ages, we knew this just wasn't right."

The situation at Freeman Chemical led to the first feat of activism for Mark and Bear. Every morning for four years, they delivered newspapers throughout Saukville. The boys would get up at 4 a.m. and start their route. Every part of town was familiar; there was no yard or alley left unexplored. Their familiarity with the neighborhood was how they came to know about Freeman Chemical's habit of dumping sludge into the drainage ditch near their house and of incinerating the waste products created by their production of plastics.

"Our street was a dead end street. Between the dead end and the Milwaukee Road railroad tracks there was this drainage ditch," said Bear. "In Wisconsin, the land is all glacial till. That whole area used to be a big ice mass, and so the groundwater is close to the surface. People have to use sump pumps to keep their basements from flooding. The chemical plant was dumping their overage right into that drainage ditch. We could see this scum of little plastic stuff and chunks of plastic. There was no concern about the shallow water table and the sludge from the plant mixing."

The factory brought industry to Saukville. They paid taxes. They helped to build the lovely parks and good schools and other things funded by the monies that came in from their production of plastic. Many people throughout the area worked there. "So you see," continued Bear, "the economy played a role in people's reaction to this mess, plus plastics were a relatively new industry. People didn't talk about the negatives. Then the water started tasting like the air smelled. We knew something was wrong and, on our own, decided to do something about it. It was Mark's idea. He got little medicine jars, and we took samples of that water and sent it to the Wisconsin Department of Natural Resources."

"The postal service wasn't happy," Mark said, smiling, "because the jars leaked on everything."

Bear laughed. "That's right," he said. "The net result was that the Department of Natural Resources must have talked to Freeman Chemical because the plant sent representatives to our school to speak to the kids about how safe their manufacturing process was and explain that the stuff they were dumping into the ditch was noncontact cooling water. Mark and I knew better, though. The water that we were drinking tasted like crap."

"So that was our first real act of activism," Mark said.

"My dad used to joke," said Bear. "He called our tap water 'Freeman Cocktail.' The plant was mixing rosin and catalyst, which produces polychlorides so that stuff was in the air and in the water."

Aside from their concerns as they grew older, the Dyken children enjoyed the familiarity and freedom of small-town life. Parents weren't afraid to let kids play outside, and the kids never worried about someone causing them harm. No matter the season, creativity and games were the cry of the day: hide-and-seek, kick-the-can, basketball, football, snowball fights, and sledding. They built tree forts, rode bikes, went camping in the surrounding woods and played in and around the Milwaukee River.

"You hear kids talking about how their parents fight about money and other life issues. Our parents kept all of that from us," Mark said. "I mean, we knew things weren't always perfect, but we never heard about any of that. My parents never cursed. They never raised their voices. They didn't do any of that. My mom might get after us kids for something we did, but never did my parents yell at each other or act out in anger.

"We were wild," Mark said, his voice pitching upward. "Especially by the time we got to high school, we were just uncontrollable. We would stay out late, and Mom would say, 'I'm worried about you,' and we would say, 'What are you worried about?' We'd be out drinking, smoking pot—

driving around with other kids, going to Milwaukee—that was a big city to us. At that time, there were no cell phones, mind you, and we sure as heck weren't going to stop and call Mom and say, 'Hey, we're okay.' We'd be gone for days sometimes. Even when we were younger, we'd go out on our bicycles, on bike hikes, and we'd go camping. There were these woods not too far from our house, and we'd go out there, build tree houses, and stay overnight. We were very active. Bear and I were the worst."

There were eight kids by then: six boys and two girls. They each had a schedule for basketball practices and choir and other activities, which they kept without a reminder. They played hard but maintained some semblance of a routine at home, particularly at mealtime. Eating together and sharing food around the table was family time, happy time. Dorothy laughed at Richard's jokes. All those years later, she still loved his dry wit.

"So we would all be sitting down at the table for dinner," Bear said while speaking of his parents. "And I don't know, whatever my dad would say, my mom would laugh so hard that she'd lose her breath. Tears would be coming down her face, and we'd all be laughing just because she was laughing—we had no idea what was so funny. She interrupted dinner for, like, twenty minutes sometimes because she couldn't stop."

"We played in a cemetery," Mark said. "Behind the cemetery, there was this massive public landfill. This was back in the day when you could throw anything in there—batteries, refrigerators, used oil—whatever, and we used to love to go over there and pull stuff out. Freeman Chemical had a dump as well, and that's where we got the FCC Van—this big wagon we rode up and down the hills around there."

The winding, hilly asphalt roads and wide grassy slopes of St. Mary's Cemetery were the perfect venue for neighborhood kids to test their skills. Whether it be snowball fights, bike races, tobogganing, or skateboarding, the cemetery was a happening hang out. Well-tended graves with granite headstones marked family histories dating back to the 1800s. Laughter and squeals were often heard as children careened down the hills past pine trees and flower-decorated plots—whispers, too, and ghoulish stories inspired by a barely legible cryptic epitaph, and nighttime vigils and the excitement of first kisses received within the hidden tangle of lilac bushes.

"There was this long hill," said Bear, "and our street was a hill as well. So all of us kids would get on the FCC Van and fly down the roads. We got to where we could steer that little wagon pretty well."

"Then one day our next-door neighbor, Ernie Maynard, asked for a ride," Mark said. "There were four of us kids on that wagon, plus the old man. We made the first corner, but with the extra weight, it was much harder to turn. We realized pretty quickly that we were doomed."

"So one at a time," said Bear, "we started jumping off, and Ernie went sailing on his own, right into a neighbor, Mrs. Pavlowich's, yard."

"We just bailed on him," Mark said, "and let him ride it out to the end."

"It was something else," said Bear, laughing.

"Bear gives a very accurate telling of that in his song, *The FCC Van*,"[10] Mark said.

> *I'm going to tell you a story, about a 4-wheeled glory*
> *Made out of wood and steel*
> *Had a big metal push bar on the back*
> *Hard rubber caster wheels*
> *Rough cut 2 x 6 running boards*
> *Where you could sit or stand*
> *A little tin plate, stamped in caps*
> *FCC Van.*

Music, as well as laughter, filled the Dyken household. Grandfather Dyken played the organ. While visiting his house, it was common to hear old-time Tin-Pan Alley tunes played by ear. In the old Breit farmhouse, the "uncles" would play accordion music as well. Dorothy's family had little in the way of extras, but in later years, after losing the farm and moving to town, her mother purchased a stereo console and acquired an extensive collection of records—everything from show tunes to jazz, to the classics and more modern country. The kids grew up listening to Johnny Cash, Ray Price, Hank Williams, and Johnny Paycheck. They were entranced by their grandmother's collection of records and spent hours sprawled on the floor of the new ranch house, spindling up those old albums.

"My grandmother loved Elvis Presley," Mark said. "She was awe-

---

10 Clan Dyken. I'm going to tell you a story, about a 4-wheeled glory. "FCC Van." *Water, Fire, and Other Relatives*. CD. Track 9.

some. She had quite eclectic tastes for someone her age."

"My dad was really into jazz. He would listen to public radio at night and record his jazz onto cassette tapes," said Bear. "Dixieland stuff, Duke Ellington, and Glenn Miller. He would do this in their bedroom. It was his little corner of the world, and there you did not tread," he joked.

"My mom loved country and old-timey music," Mark said. "Her favorite song was 'You Are My Sunshine.' She also loved all the Catholic hymns, but she listened mostly to country."

Mark started pounding on his first set of drums when he was in fifth grade, but before that he remembered beating on things around the house: pots and pans, whatever. He joined middle school band in the sixth grade and played in the orchestra. "I was always doing this kind of thing, tapping out rhythms. Still do. It doesn't matter—when I'm out—if I'm riding my bike or if I'm running—I see the world in rhythmic patterns. I see it in the way people walk, I see it in how cars flow, how wheels turn, and I have a thing I do with my teeth. I do it all the time. I don't remember not doing that, not measuring time and space by rhythmic patterns."

As in their parents' generation, the Dykens' exposure to a variety of music gained momentum with the addition of new sounds and genres. "Like a lot of us," said Bear, "it started with the Beatles. We saw them on Ed Sullivan, and we just took off with it. Grandpa Dyken gave me my first harmonica. He showed me a few chords on the keyboard. Artistically, he informed me. He wasn't trained at all and did everything by ear. He had a vast repertoire of songs, and he played them all in the key of C. He'd listen to similarities and figure it out, all in the key of C. So there was that base, and then we saw the Beatles on Ed Sullivan."

The time and place set Bear's story. On February 9, 1964, families all over America were watching the Ed Sullivan Show on television. Girls swooned. Boys watched in awe. Everyone had their favorite Beatle. Kids began listening to music with a different ear. Rock musicians became rock idols. John, Paul, George, and Ringo set the pace for a new genre of entertainment, and Baby Boomers, young people all over the world, were ready to grab hold for the ride.

"We got little transistor radios," Bear said, "and would bring those on our bikes and deliver our newspapers while listening to the Dave Clark

Five, Crosby, Stills, Nash, and Young. It was the 1960s, these musicians were talking about important stuff in their music, and they were reaching the youth. A lot of the older generation was hearing the music but not listening to the words, not understanding the words, and this was affecting us. I think the song 'Four Dead in Ohio,' pretty much displays that, for me." Bear paused, strumming a few bars on his guitar. "Neil Young used music to tell his story in a way that, you could dance to it, it was a great piece of music, but it was a weapon against the military-industrial complex as well. Then there was John Lennon and *Imagine*. John Lennon just relentlessly hammered away."

No small town, including Saukville, was immune to the sounds of the 1960s. The happenings of Woodstock and the horrors of the Vietnam War hit the homes of residents via television, radio, and newspaper. The young people, in particular, reacted to the beats and lyrics—a whole new level of musical influence. It was more than sound and danceability that drew teenagers. As Bear said, the songs of the times became a passionate call to action.

"The money we made on those paper routes empowered us to get the first stereo system in our neighborhood," Bear said. "We started collecting records, and my mom and dad let us do whatever we wanted in our little basement in the house. We painted a mural on the wall and had lights. It was epic."

"The guy I took drum lessons from was a serious jazz drummer," said Mark. "He smoked cigarettes the entire time I was in for my lesson. He was one of these guys who played nightclubs and then to earn money on the side, worked out of a music store."

"Serious jazz though. Jazz grip," Bear said. "Early on, I played the viola. I liked the way it looked and the way it smelled, but it wasn't a guitar. I remember during that time I got a Sears and Roebuck guitar that came in a cardboard box, and I used to drive Mark crazy with that thing. He'd throw a pillow at me, and yell, 'Stop playing that…'"

"He was playing, like, 'Aura Lee,' a hundred times over," Mark teased.

"Dude, you had to do that to learn…"

"Single notes, over and over."

"I remember doing a Pete Townsend on that guitar," Bear said, "smashing it against the basement wall. Then we had a friend whose mom was a guitar player, and she had a hollow-box electric guitar that she wanted to rebuild. This friend gave me that guitar, and I sanded it down and put a finish on it. It never would tune up or even get close. I made a lot of rude noises with that thing, plugging it in every-which-way into the stereo system…blowing all kinds of stuff up.

"We had this little posse of kids," Bear continued. "There was a foreign exchange student from France who was enamored with the Rolling Stones, and a there were a couple of older kids who played pretty good guitar and would show me a few things here and there."

"Somewhere around there we met Virgil," said Mark. "He was in his thirties and played in some bar bands. We were just teenagers, but he could play songs like 'Mustang Sally.'"

"The blues," Bear said.

"The blues, basic three-chord rock songs," added Mark.

"Meanwhile," Bear said, "our brother Gary started playing the stand-up bass, which weighed about four times more than him, and he used to carry it on the school bus and would play in the orchestra. The guy was a genius, whether it was learning an instrument or figuring something out mechanically. Schoolwork was nothing to him. I'd be struggling to get through algebra class, and he didn't even have to open a book. He was good at playing bass. I was like, 'Oh, I need him to play blues with me,' and I showed him some blues progressions. At one point, my dad came down to the basement with a camera and made a little movie of us playing that Steve Miller song, 'Living in the USA.' All of this happened in the closet, so to speak, in high school, and it wasn't until I went to college that it all came around.

"It all happened in the basement. That's where it all started."

Though Richard never bought an airplane, he didn't give up his love for flying. On his own time, he borrowed or rented planes and often took his children with him when cruising the skies. Uncharacteristically, however, there was one thing Richard did that, perhaps, reflected the history of his great-grandparents, the Dyken penchant for rebellion. "Because of my father's childhood illness, his rheumatic fever," Mark shared, "he lived his whole life with a heart condition. His doctors told him that he wouldn't make it past thirty years of age. When he did make it past thirty, they told him he wouldn't make it past forty, and on and on. At age fifty-five, he got all the valves in his heart replaced. I think that part of what allowed him to survive all of that was his calm nature. My mom was the disciplinarian in our household, but my dad was steady and dedicated. He had this big passion for the sky. I have no doubt that he could have purchased his own airplane," Mark said. "But we always came first. That's the kind of man he was."

Mark slowed his story but continued. "That's how Dad died—in a plane crash," he said. "Dad volunteered for this small skydiving outfit. Then after many years, there came a time when he didn't pass his physical—it's the first time I ever saw him do anything like this, but he couldn't *not* fly, so he forged the certificate for his license. I think that's what happened in the end. We think there was an issue with his health up in that plane. He was alone and flying the same field he had taken off from and landed on thousands of times. He aborted the first landing, flew around the circle, came back in and hit telephone wires and crashed the plane. There was no one with him when it happened. He was alone."

Years later, when Dorothy passed, all of her children were present. Leon, one of her youngest, opened the bedroom window and while listening to the voices of her children singing the gospel songs that she loved, she closed her eyes and floated away with the breeze, flying to meet her husband, the man she had lived with and loved for forty-three years.

> *Dick should have been born a bird*
> *That man loved to fly*
> *He was most at home when he was up in the sky*
> *He flew in, and he flew out*
> *I'm sure that's how he planned it*
> *He hated long goodbyes*
> *Dorothy's room was filled with angels*
> *There were angels*
> *Angels everywhere*
> *When the window shade was open, and the sunlight streamed in*
> *She flew away to him.*[11]

---

[11] Clan Dyken. It must have been an angel. "Must Have Been An Angel." *Water, Fire, and Other Relatives*. CD. Track 8

Richard and Dorothy Dyken, 1955

4

INTO THE NIGHT[12]

Mama's calling, children must come home
She will tell you things you need to know.

Tó Éí Ííná = Water is Life

Contrails crisscrossed the dusky, Navajo sky. The visitation of these jets reminded me that we were eighty miles north of Flagstaff and that 330 miles to the west sprawled Las Vegas. In these cities, the resources mined near Big Mountain fueled home heaters and powered the lights for businesses, hotels, and casinos. Yet on this part of the reservation, there were no power poles, other than the ones supplying power to the national energy grid for Southwest Arizona, Nevada, and Southern California. On Big Mountain, electric lights were the exception rather than the norm, and electric floor heaters were rare or nonexistent.

We were making our last run of the day, traveling pocked and rutted roads miles out on Black Mesa. Our caravan of trucks rocked and pitched as we made a U-turn and backtracked to find the homestead where we would make our delivery. Jim Lundeen and I laughed. "You prepared to spend the night out here if they lose us?" he asked. It was a joke, but the possibility existed. At night, in the dark and unfamiliar territory, the sand-

---

12 Clan Dyken. Mama's calling, children must come home. "Into the Night." *Clan Dyken Live.* CD. Track 2.

stone plateaus and mesas blended into a shadowy abstract and even with the abundance of stars, I felt disoriented. We sped up, catching the two trucks ahead of us as they fishtailed and sped along the rocky dirt road.

Twenty minutes later, we noticed a yellow speck further out on the plateau. The light flickered and dimmed, flickered and dimmed, like the embers of a dying fire. We drove faster and bounced harder, going over bumps that propelled me high enough off my seat that I hit my head on the roof of the truck. As we got closer, the source of the light grew into the distinct shape of a kerosene lamp, and it was glowing through the window of a hogan.

There we were greeted by curious goats, including one sizable Nubian doe who was eager to eat my camera. The hogan door opened, and an older man wearing a Colorado Rockies baseball cap waved us into his home. He pointed to a spot beside the house where he would like the wood stacked and gestured to a place on the floor inside where we could set the food. I handed him one of the frozen chickens we had purchased from Whole Foods in Flagstaff, but he seemed hesitant to take it. He had no refrigerator in which to store the chicken and no power to run a fridge, anyway.

In this dimly lit hogan, furniture was sparse: a couch, a recliner chair, and a wooden kitchen table with two wooden chairs. Chunks of coal sat near and fueled the woodstove, so the small living and kitchen area was now toasty warm. Still, this elder was thankful for the wood. "Good," he said, *"Aoo'.* Yes." On the wall opposite the stove hung a small American flag. "It's ironic," Bear said later, "because some of the older men out here are pretty patriotic despite everything, even with their long history of abuse by our government—they fly those flags."

Back in the truck with Jim, Mark, and Catherine, I wrote in my journal. As the Toyota jostled along the reservation roads, my penmanship appeared as scrambled as the thoughts in my head, and the words on the page were as difficult to comprehend as what I was hearing. "American Indians serve in the U.S. military in greater numbers than any other ethnic group and have since the Revolutionary War," Mark told us. "Native Americans have served with distinction in every major U.S. conflict for over 200 years."

I knew about the Navajo Code Talkers who served in World War II. Their contribution to the war effort was well documented. In 1942, the war was not going well for America and her allies. Japanese carrier-borne bombers and fighters had crippled the U.S. Navy's Pacific Fleet at Pearl Harbor on December 7, 1941, attacked American bases in the Philippines and on Guam and were attacking others in different parts of the Pacific as well. In Europe, France had fallen to Germany, and Britain was suffering the effects of Nazi raids and bombings.

The Japanese were adept at breaking U.S. Armed Forces codes until the United States government enlisted the help of the Navajo. The recruits came straight off the reservation and spoke both Navajo and English. These newly recruited Navajo soldiers had limited exposure to other cultures while growing up and had never ridden a bus or train, let alone cross an ocean. They adapted to army life well, however, and took their work seriously, devising the long-awaited code, one that proved unbreakable and which gave the allies the military advantage they were seeking.

The man whose hogan we visited was a Vietnam vet. As I pondered what Mark said, I thought of news stories I'd read about other wars and other veterans: a Hopi woman, Army Private First Class Laurie Piestewa, killed in action in Iraq in 2003. Clifton J. Yazzie, a Navajo soldier and member of the 327th Infantry Regiment, 1st Brigade Combat Team, 101st Airborne Division, killed in 2006 in Huwijah, Iraq—indigenous people serving as soldiers in first one conflict and then another.

As we passed the Rocky Ridge Boarding School, the lights dimmed. By now, the children were in their beds and the dorm aides were resting. "Thankfully, unlike in years past, they're teaching some of the old ways in these schools now," said Catherine, her voice rising to outdo the racket of the engine. "Forgotten practices, traditions and a grounding to the land are part of the curriculum. Still, the kids here are away from family during the school week. They stay and live in these schools and then go home on the weekends."

"The problem is that the families are scattered, said Mark. "Some people live so far out that they have no way to get the kids back and forth each day, so the boarding school provides the best option for schooling.

"Back in the 1800s and into the 1900s children in boarding schools were berated for speaking their language," he added. "The headmasters would shave their heads and scrub them down with lye soap. These 'teachers' would burn their clothes and anything they brought from home."

History books told *parts* of the story. During the nineteenth century, the United States government policies called for Native Americans to be "totally assimilated" into American culture and for any remnants of tribal culture to be "eradicated." A component of this assimilation policy required the United States to build boarding schools and the federal government to set quotas for attendance.[13]

My thoughts returned to the veteran we'd met earlier that evening, how proud he was to fly his American flag. Had he been enlisted directly from a boarding school, like so many others? The disagreements with the Hopi and federal interference continued during the time he served in the military. How must this have felt? Leaving one war to fight another.

The hum of the tires and the rock of the vehicle were like a tranquilizer for my weary body, a smooth draw into quiet reflection. The woman, Amá sání, developed further in my imagination, a story woven from stories I'd heard throughout the day.

The cold penetrated Amá sání's bones, and she felt its sting. She wrapped her blanket tighter around her shoulders, shivering a little, missing for a moment the security of her man's presence, the heat of his body next to hers. If she closed her eyes, she could see Ahiga, smell him, his brown skin lacquered with sweat, alive with the odors of smoke and sheep and mesquite. It had been so long; she had nearly forgotten the feel of him. Nearly, but not quite. It was easier to be mad at him than to miss him. *That* she decided long ago.

The war in South Korea had changed Ahiga, had taken a precious part of his spirit. His decision to enlist was, to this day, perplexing to her. The defilement of their homeland was more important than some faraway war and should have demanded his full attention, but those recruiters, the men in uniforms who visited the reservation, were convincing, making promises, telling lies. Navajo and Hopi went together to this war and drove away in a bus, side-by-side. The People's unity was good to see, but strange as well, what with the mounting tension between the tribes.

---

13 "The Hopi Reservation | Native American Netroots." Web. 25 Sep. 2018 <http://nativeamericannetroots.net/diary/1202>.

For as long as Amá sání could remember there were disagreements with the Hopi, disputes over rangeland, mostly, like now, as with the man in the nearby pueblo, waving his arms, sending his dogs to harass her sheep again. Amá sání waved back and yelled: "Kodjį'! Go away!" She turned her back on him, showing her contempt, but kept one eye trained in his direction. She reached for the rifle at her side and pulled it closer, just in case she'd need to fire a warning shot. She was not afraid to do this. She had done it before and would do it again, if necessary.

The words of the Hopi man were like those scratched on treaties. He was one of the progressive thinkers, those who talked up the benefits of resource extraction, first uranium and now coal. Not all Hopi were like this though. Her friend Kaiah, who was Hopi, was a good woman, wise, learned in the old ways, grounded to the earth and the sun and the moon.

In a wooden box in her hogan were copies of the old treaties— words on paper written in a jumble of ink. "Do-ya-sho-da," she often said. "No good." Ahiga (Albert was his English name) was a medicine man and knew tribal history better than most. She didn't know how he'd come by such old papers or the knowledge that bubbled from him like the water from their spring. He'd spent nights by the fire, laying out the pages, rubbing his fingers over promises that died. What was he searching for, she wondered? Did he think he could find some truth buried there? Something missed, or overlooked, or maybe a sign, a premonition of what was to come?

Amá sání was proud of her man's knowledge, but more so of his skill with plants and animals, his ability to understand them and their importance to the tribe. He made medicines to cure bloat and hoof rot and to help a sheep through a painful labor. He had a relationship with horses like none she'd ever seen. His hand was gentle, his voice soothing. His white mare followed him everywhere; even when she was too old to ride, that biddy tailed him like a pet, her muzzle to his back like a pup to its mother.

A large ewe, well past her birthing time, wandered too far from the flock, and Amá sání whistled, drawing the dogs' attention. She slid off the rock where she'd been sitting, stretching the kinks in her back while her dogs gathered the wayward sheep. To her left were the first of the fences. She cursed them and cursed her dead husband for coming home broken by the Korean War. Despite the cleansing ceremonies, the healing ceremonies, the peyote ceremonies in his honor, despite all of that—the war had ruined him. He returned to her alive, but his spirit was injured by the fighting and killing and nameless atrocities. He drank every day and wrapped his truck around a tree one night upon returning from Tuba City. He was good at many things, but even he couldn't overcome the power of whiskey. Along with the ghosts, that drink came from Korea with him, and a bottle was beside him the day he died in that pickup truck.

The ewe ran toward the barbed wire fence, but the dogs turned her, guiding her back to the safety of the herd. This fence was the first of many to come. She knew this because the BIA rangers told her it did no good to fight. They laughed in her face. Spat at her. These men would build their fences, regardless of her resistance, the rocks she threw, the fence posts she pulled out of the ground. She thought again of the bundled up papers in the old wooden box. She couldn't read the scribbled talk, but after the war, to Ahiga, they became an obsession. Drunk or sober, he would drag the old box from under their bed, nursing the documents as one would a cherished relic.

On cold winter nights when the air was still and white snow fell upon the yucca, Ahiga told her of a peace treaty signed in 1868, giving the Navajo 3.5 million acres in reservation land. This was after the Long Walk *(like an atonement could make up for the horrors her people suffered at Bosque Redondo,* she thought, as he read). In 1882, that agreement was changed by the federal government. Hopi were given reservation land and told they "could use it" but did not own it. The *arrangement* did not please the Hopi, Amá sání knew. This new Hopi land was surrounded by the Navajo reservation and excluded the Hopi village of Moenkopi. Navajo lived there—on land now designated as Hopi. Three hundred people at least, including Amá sání's family. What good could come of this, she wondered, while Ahiga explained the treaty's meaning. She thought of the petroglyphs down in the canyon, drawn by her mother and her aunts, and of petroglyphs carved by Hopi, and of the many religious shrines up on the plateau. Neither tribe would give up claim to land marked by the ancestors in such a way. Not amicably.

Some nights the readings went on for so long it felt as if Amá sání's head would burst. If Ahiga felt like she wasn't listening, he only talked louder: "Reservation boundaries changed again in 1934, and in 1936 nearly 500,000 acres of open reservation land was now recognized as Hopi reservation land." To make sure she remembered, he stopped and called out to her: "Amá sání. Hear me!"

In 1941, Navajo families were forced to move off their land, friends of hers and relatives, some Grandmothers dragged from their hogans and hauled away in trucks driven by BIA and Hopi rangers. There was no need to remind her of this. She had seen it with her own eyes. What had been Navajo was now Hopi and had a name: Hopi Partitioned Land. Those who remained were considered criminals. They had no rights, no privileges. Visions still came in her dreams of screaming women, crying children, men beaten bloody, of Grandmothers with wire cutters and shovels destroying freshly planted wire fences in the safety of night's shadows.

Amá sání huffed and mumbled under her breath. How could someone give away something that wasn't theirs to give? The earth was a gift, a precious gift given by the Creator. It was her tribe's responsibility to take care of it, watch over it, to bless each new day and to thank the dark of night as well. In the light there was growth; in the dark, there was safety—these things she knew to be true. Not for the first time she cursed the worthlessness of a language that had no meaning. Words were just words unless there was truth behind them.

She looked at the moon in its new moon phase, narrow, yellow, mottled with gray. Soon it would be time to shear her sheep. Some people on the reservation were shearing now, but she would wait for another week or so until the wool was a little warmer. Though he taught her many things, watching the moon cycles and waiting until the chill was gone was not something she learned from her husband. It was something she knew deep in her marrow, knowledge shared by the spirits of her ancestors, those who lived and breathed meaning into the old ways she cherished.

The land is everything.
The sheep are life.

The pitch of the vehicle woke me, but the fleeting images and vastness within the darkness of night were as jarring as the quick left turn. The desert was now dressed in its luminous bedtime colors: mesa-brown, olives, grays, and blacks, star-white, blinking endlessly in the sky above. Fences disturbed the serenity of the reservation land. *Intrusive* was the word that came to mind. Each section of wire, every post jammed into the earth, was a reminder of the unraveling of the relationship between the Hopi and the Navajo. It must have been strange for Navajo and Hopi veterans stationed overseas to leave one country and fight in another, watch the moon rise and the sun set—observe a multitude of stars as they did at home in Arizona. In World Wars I and II, in Korea, Vietnam, Iraq, and Afghanistan, vets erected barbed wire barriers on an unfamiliar land, while Grandmothers on the reservation were cutting fences down.

That next morning, I was slow to leave my sleeping bag and get myself dressed. Yoga stretches soothed my achy back, but I wished I could take a hot shower. The bus was equipped with a kitchen and bathroom, but neither was usable on the reservation. Catherine and I created our own personal hygiene "washing stations," but our water supply was limited. The bottles we brought from home were needed for drinking and cooking. Bathing was not part of the equation. As residents of the Sierra Nevada foothills, we were familiar with dry, rocky ground and a lack of rainfall, water conservation by way of short showers and the "yellow-let-it-mellow" toileting philosophy. But life here at Big Mountain brought the term "water conservation" to another level. Even when making our morning tea, we were conscientious about turning the propane off as soon as the water began to boil.

Gloved hands were the order of the morning. Boxes of food and fifty-pound sacks of dog food were hefted into the back of Jim's Toyota and wood was packed into the bed of Bear's Ford Diesel. Mark, Catherine, and I road with Jim this day, and Lotus and Kimberly rode with Bear. We had piled into the trucks with a jumble of backpacks, water bottles, and jackets and were as prepared as we could be for what the day might bring.

Bear led the way, the wide tires on his Blue Pearl settling into the ruts. Jim gripped the steering wheel and leaned into each turn as we followed the dry wash from Dove Springs to the main road. A tangle of uncombed hair hung below Jim's wool beanie, his priorities well-placed and in sync with the rest of us. Tales told while driving became a historical storyboard, each adding validity to the chronicle of events at Big Mountain.

"The first time I came to the reservation, was like an awakening for me," Mark said, his body scrunched into the narrow back seat. "Here were these people who for hundreds of years have lived a certain way, done things a certain way, and then the government comes in and says, 'You can't do that anymore. You can't raise your sheep the way you want to or herd them the way you are accustomed to doing.' I mean, what sense can be made of this? I don't understand. I've never understood. There were problems between the Hopi and the Navajo, sure. But then the government steps in and makes all these changes, and the trouble escalates."

Mark's short hair blew softly about, and he reacted, pushing it back off of his face as he might have years earlier when his hair was waist-length, most often tied back in a ponytail. But other than the difference in his hair, pictures of past trips showed him as he was now: in blue jeans, wearing a hat or bandana and sunglasses. He once told me he had cut his hair in tribute to his mother. He'd said, "My world radically changed when she died, and it felt like the right thing to do." His voice had fluctuated as he spoke, rising and falling as emotion struck. "Our hair tells our history," he'd explained. "It's a part of our identity. Cutting mine was a spiritual, metaphysical thing that I felt deeply about doing."

Mark pointed to a green road sign mounted on a two-by-two post, similar to most road signs in towns across America. *Big Mountain Blvd,* it read. "Never used to see that," he commented sharply. "Those only came about in the last couple of years. For the better? I guess, but some things like this boggle my mind. I mean, the roads are in disrepair, but here are these signs, marking their existence." He stared as we passed.

"So the first time I came to Big Mountain," he finally said, "I was with this guy named Coyote. We drove way the heck out here and to an old hogan. As we got out of the truck, we saw this Grandmother walking toward us in the pre-dawn light. It was cold, I mean, I was freezing, and *I* had on a thick coat.

"She'd been out herding her sheep all night, dressed only in a long skirt with short socks and recycled tennis shoes, a threadbare pink sweater. Her legs were exposed, and her neck was exposed. It was crazy. So I went to the truck and grabbed this warm coat we'd found at a thrift store, and I said, 'Grandmother, look what we brought you. It's a gift. This coat will keep you warm.'"

Other than Mark's voice, the only noise came from the rattle of the engine. Jim, Catherine and I listened intently to the story. "So she let me slip the coat around her shoulders, and five minutes later, she giggled. Then took it off and handed it to her daughter, who gave it back to me, translating her mother's words: 'It's too heavy,' she said. 'She can't wear it.'"

Mark pulled his jacket tighter around his neck. "Later we were invited into the hogan," he said. "I walked inside, and the light from the open doorway shone directly down onto a large loom fit with a partially finished weaving. The contradiction, the reality of life out here, took my breath away. The poverty, Grandmother's strength, creativity, and resolve. This little woman, out there in the middle of nowhere, herding sheep all by herself in the dark, the absolute quiet inside the hogan, the intricacy of the weaving—the beauty, the power of the moment, was overwhelming. I called Bear right away, and I told him, 'Man, you've got to come out here. You've got to see this.'"

As we neared the turnoff to Dove Springs, a few cows and a couple of horses stood, heads down, near the fenceline—the boundary separating Hopi from Navajo. Where were the vast herds of sheep depicted in history books? Where was the Grandmother Mark met years earlier? Why was she not out herding her sheep? Where were the wild horses, running free as pictured in so many images of reservation land? Where were the animals and why had we seen no more than six sheep, a horse or two, two or three goats at every homestead we visited?

Back in California, in the library where I work, several books occupy the stacks in the section designated for Navajo history. In *The Navaho,* Clyde Kluckhohn and Dorothea Leighton write about the unsuccessful government programs implemented on Navajo land. "To a degree," they state, "these programs failed due to lack of understanding of certain *human factors.*"

In the 1930s, a forester named William Zeh observed erosion problems on the Navajo reservation and suggested to President Franklin D. Roosevelt that by reducing the number of animals, primarily goats, the issue might improve. At this time of the Dust Bowl and Great Depression in the United States, dust and erosion were of great concern. The President agreed with Zeh's assessment and appointed John Collier, a noted sociologist and writer, as the Commissioner of Indian Affairs. With Collier's appointment, the government's focus turned from goats to sheep. Collier's solution to the erosion problem was to launch a reduction program and remove over half of the livestock, telling the Navajo that their sheep would produce better meat, that the animals would be stronger and yield better wool, if there were fewer in the herd. The natural forage the sheep ate would last longer and regrow at a better rate.

"The Navajo saw it differently though," Mark continued. "To them, large herds of sheep were symbols of prestige and honor. They tried to understand what the government was telling them, but it made no sense, and they became angry and suspicious. To them, the government was trying to take away a symbol of who they were and what they valued within their community."

"To change a way of life, you must change a people," Kluckhohn wrote.

To change a way of life, you must change a people. Most of us have ancestors who came to this country from abroad. Our families were not born to this land. Mark and Bear, me, Catherine, Jim, Kimberly, Lotus—none of us had to *change* who we were or deny the teachings of our ancestors. How would that feel? What must it be like to have your culture ripped out from underneath you? The Spanish brought sheep to the Navajo as far back as the 1800s. To the Navajo of the twentieth and twenty-first centuries, the animals had *always been* and were a central part of life.

Back on the bus, the conversation about what happened between the Hopi and the Navajo, and how these tribes became embroiled in such a bitter battle, continued. The reassignment of reservation land, the mining operations, and the livestock reduction program had each, in turn, started a reign of terror that still goes on today. We huddled in our seats with our hands wrapped around hot cups of tea. Bear, Lotus, and Kim had finished their run and joined us for a light meal.

"What you have to understand," Bear said, " is that there are traditional Hopi and progressive Hopi. The traditionals don't think the way the progressives do. Then there's the traditional Navajo—these people are more aligned with each other. They do their ceremonies; the Navajo have adopted a lot of the Hopi cosmology into their way of doing things. The whole Tribal Council system and the Navajo-Hopi land dispute was created to buy and sell the resources. When Navajo people say the Hopi come in and take the sheep, what they are referring to is the Hopi rangers. People hired and trained to do a job. And a lot of the so-called progressive Hopi and Navajo, they're more—they've been raised in the boarding schools, away from tradition, away from their elders and the ways of the earth."

"Our friend John Benally was sent to boarding school, the same but different from the one we just passed along the road," said Mark. "He was one of those kids. Even as late as the Sixties and Seventies, a lot of them were taken from their homes, forced to go despite the wishes of their families.

"Alice Benally, a Grandmother who's passed on, refused to send her sons and daughters. She went to the school and stole John back after the government hauled him away."

"John Benally, though, he came out okay," Bear said, smiling.

"John told this story, and it's one of my favorites," said Mark. "He said, when you get to boarding school, the teachers are always telling you, 'Speak English, speak English!' But in Dineh, to the children, it sounded like the teachers were saying, 'Piss on the dog,' and John was like, 'Why are they telling us to piss on the dog?'

"You have to hear the Navajo language," Mark said. "It has all these guttural sounds, and John, just imagine being a kid and having been taken away from your family and you have all these weird people yelling at you, and they think they're trying to teach you something and the kids are like, 'Why do they want me to piss on a dog?'"

Mark and Bear laughed.

Bear ate a bit of lentil soup and then sipped his tea. "Still," he said, "these are incredibly adaptable and resilient people out here. Despite the odds, their ties to the ancestors and their cultural beliefs keep them strong."

To this day, the people pray to the beings that live on the San Francisco Peaks. The Navajo believe that the beings bring rain. For hundreds of years, medicine men and women have walked or ridden horseback or more recently have traveled by car or truck to these holy sites. Grandmothers climb the ridges and rocky trails with a basket slung over one arm. In their long skirts and colorful blouses, some of them come to pick botanicals for medicines. The plants on the mountain are powerful; some are even deadly. The healers know how to make medicine from the different species and what to prescribe for specific ailments. For the Hopi, the peaks are home for part of the year to the Kachina spirits—ancestors who have passed on and who serve as guides. Visitors from both tribes chant and sing, thanking the beings for life. They pray for the mountainous ecosystem. This igneous range is considered *female* and is endangered now by mineral extraction and more recently, an alpine ski resort called Snowbowl operating by permit from the United States Forest Service. Elders travel to the peaks to feel the mountain's heartbeat and renew a connection. Some wail when they see the scarred faces of the land and sense that the holy ground is suffering, that her *womb* is sick. Looking toward Black Mesa, they might close their eyes and imagine the death of the long silver snake of a pipeline, pumping its slurry of water and coal, away, away from their source.

I've camped a lot in my life. I've often awoken on cold mornings, built a fire and squatted by the flames, my hands curled around that first warm cup of tea. Here though, the cold is a way of life in winter, constant and unrelenting. Both economically and logistically, on-the-grid electrical heat is an unobtainable luxury for some. Power is available on Navajo land, and people living in resettlement houses have solar, but those living on Hopi Partitioned Land (HPL) have no infrastructure, no grid—no rights to obtain power even if those components were available.

Aside from all that, the dry land, the draining of the aquifer by Peabody Coal, and the dead and dying vegetation have all contributed to a change in the topography. The ground has dropped nine feet; there are sinkholes all over the reservation. Flash floods are a common occurrence. The roads become mud-slicks, impassable without a four-wheel drive vehicle, and even with four-wheel drive, the situation is dicey.

It was just after sunrise, our third day of deliveries, and this day I rode with Bear and Lotus. The warmth of the sun through the windshield was comfortable enough that we pulled off our coats, stashing them under the seats as we drove. According to Mark, in past years, the distance between homes and families was problematic in the harsh northern Arizona winters. Between snow and mud, it was difficult to reach many homesteads. During a typical winter, there are months when the elders are alone for extended periods. That's when Facebook alerts on personal or group pages announce the need for help: "Can someone go check on Shìmà Benale? No one has heard from her for two weeks." Or "If anyone is traveling to Coal Mine Canyon, can you get some water to Anna Begay?" Or "Leo Yellowhair is out of firewood. Does anyone have any to spare?"

While we drove along, my cell phone pinged. The fact that there was cell service seemed funny to me, and I couldn't help but laugh. Even on the reservation, where people had so little, where life was a challenge on every level, modern technology had crept into the lives of the Navajo.

Even more gripping was the message that a man living on the edge of Coal Mine Canyon—a resource so massive, so impactful on Navajo lives—now had no fuel to heat his house and was out of wood in the bitter cold. Within miles of him was a ribbon of coal running from three to fifteen feet thick in places, the most significant coal deposit in the United States—estimated at one point to be approximately twenty-one billion tons.

As far back as the fiasco at the Bosque Redondo, government officials recognized the value of the natural resources on Navajo land. "In the 1900s, private corporations approached the tribes about mining resources on tribal lands," Mark said. "Way back then, the government interfered, hand-picking tribal councils, people more in favor of leasing tribal lands."

Black Mesa stands on the northern end of the 1882 Executive Order area. In the mid-1950s, a coalition of twenty-one utility companies from Arizona, California, New Mexico, Colorado, Nevada, Utah, and Texas joined forces as the Western Energy Supply and Transmission Associates. This restructured corporation implemented "the Grand Plan," which involved the construction of coal and nuclear power plants throughout the region.

Miles from Hotevilla, a dirt road forked off on the right, split and then merged back together, narrow in places, dropping off into the

Moenkopi Wash. A single windmill and water tank stood on the flat land next to the remnants of a deserted hogan. Clouds of dust trailed each of three trucks, covering the hoods and windshields of the next in line with a tawny glaze. An hour or so out, tire tracks marked a turnout on top of a broad plateau where gypsum crystals breached the sandy topsoil.

From there it was a short walk to the canyon's lip, where sandstone hoodoos stood erect, the weathered spires constructing a landscape of deep ravines and flat plateaus, colors varying from white to ochre, orange to red, gray to black—the black being that ribbon of coal. The only voice was that of a red-tailed hawk, effortlessly catching an updraft, eyes ever-watchful. Beyond her call, the deep quiet, the eerie solitude rim to horizon, felt like a link to ancient history, back to people pulling travois or riding horseback, speaking by using their voices, communicating through words or song.

Bear stood on the edge of a crumbling escarpment, staring down into the canyon. "Without the water, life is so much harder. The Navajo used to graze their sheep out here," he said, pointing across the mesa behind us. "They raised corn. They would plant four seeds in a little mound, then take eight big steps and plant four seeds in a little mound and take eight steps and plant in another little mound over there. They count on the rain—but when it doesn't come, and when the springs are dry…well…" He shrugged his shoulders.

Mark's face expressed what I was feeling. The beauty of Coal Mine Canyon merged with melancholy, a deep ache for the Navajo and the losses they had suffered—that sense of *place* that is so important. Catherine Lambie walked beside me, both of us quiet and reflective. As a French National, Catherine was familiar with leaving her homeland and settling somewhere new. As she had said at the fundraiser earlier that month in Grass Valley: "I was shocked to discover that a brutal injustice was taking place here in the United States, that the plight of these people was little known and mostly ignored." As we walked, I touched the ribbon of coal, running my finger across its coarse black surface—this prized commodity, drooled over and schemed upon by men as far back as Kit Carson.

Down the road several miles, we visited Leo Yellowhair. Though Leo's brother lived in a small stick-built home, Leo preferred an earthen hogan. Built into the side of the plateau, the mound-shaped hogan was made of mud and clay and supported by posts and beams. It had a dirt floor and a wood stove for heat, the stovepipe reaching up and out of the hut, sending smoke signals skyward in the cold mid-morning air. As with all cone-shaped hogans, the door was facing east to welcome the morning sun. Both Leo and his brother wore blue jeans, flannel shirts, and baseball caps. They were happy to receive the clothing donations, warm coats, more pants, and long-sleeved shirts. Some shoes. The brothers spoke English, sharing a year's worth of news in a few sentences.

Inside Leo's hogan, nails in the crossbeams held baskets and bags of necessities, keeping them off the ground and away from mice and snakes. From one of the baskets, he pulled a hand-carved clay pipe, a gift he made for Bear. Little needed to be said. Bear was nearly tearful.

"That's where Leo used to plant his corn," Bear said, pointing to a spot in the bottom of the canyon, a flat expanse of land where crops had once grown. "He'd walk down there daily and tend his crop."

"Leo's garden was spectacular," said Catherine. "You could stand up here and look down on these green tassel-topped stalks, planted in the cream-colored sandstone. It was beautiful. Now, no water, no rain… no corn."

While at Leo's, Bear asked about Anna Begay, the Grandmother they found squatting in the engine of her pickup truck several years back. He and Mark knew she was ill but hadn't heard recently how she was doing or whether she was home. "Not sure," said Leo's brother. "Last I heard she was doing better."

From Leo's, it was another thirty minutes to Anna's place. When we drove into her yard, there was no one in sight. "She must still be with family," Bear said. "She'll be back though. She's a tough woman."

Anna's dogs ran to greet us, barking their warning. Her penned horses stood in a corral made of weathered cedar one-by-fours and tin siding. These horses were cared for, well fed, donning their thick winter coats. Drawn to them, I walked to the corral and clicked my tongue, wondering if they would respond. The white stallion raised his head and nodded twice, then walked toward me, his eyes watchful but relaxed. He wore a sky-blue halter. A single braid decorated his mane. I raised my hand and gently placed it on his forehead. Again, he nodded, blowing short puffs of air. I felt Anna Begay's presence then, her love for this animal, his trust in Anna. He leaned into my shoulder, pressing for more attention. All around me was Anna's life. Small altars she had made: a weathered juniper limb standing upright, surrounded by rocks; flat stones piled one on top of the other—the only ornaments on her property—her simple hogan standing in the center of it all.

I grew tearful. This land was a part of Anna. It held her life. *Why are you digging holes in my heart? Why are you taking out my liver?* This question was asked by the Navajo Grandmothers who fought against the 1974 Navajo-Hopi Settlement Act, or Public Law 93-531 and the subsequent fencing of their lands and the extraction of coal by Peabody Coal Company. To the Navajo, there is one earth, one homeland. To the Navajo, the coal that ribbons the landscape throughout the Big Mountain region and is so in demand by the outside world is considered *the liver* of the earth—that black, fibrous rock that filters the rainwater as it flows down into the soil, filling the once-plentiful aquifer that fed the Colorado Plateau.

When we left Anna's house, all in the truck were silent. The light washed in the windows, soft, almost glittery. Through slitted eyes, Bear studied the landscape, a bluff here, a boarded-up hogan there. All the while, the Blue Pearl rumbled and growled, the rocks beneath its tires crumbling and shifting, and testing the truck's suspension.

Thinking back to nearby cities, just miles away as the crow flies—to the freeway drivers heading north to Idaho or Utah, I wondered if they knew the history of the San Francisco Peaks? Did they know the peaks were one of the four sacred mountains? Did they know that the Navajo believe their Creator placed their people between these mountains to watch over the land, and to keep them centered and grounded to the earth and their spiritual foundation? Mount Blanca (White Shell Mountain) to the east, Mount Taylor (Blue Bead Mountain) to the south, San Francisco Peaks (Abalone Shell Mountain) to the west, and Mount Hesperus (Big Sheep Mountain) to the north, represent the four sacred directions, an integral part of Navajo religious beliefs. Did these commuters feel a sense of *place,* inquire about the people who live nearby, wonder what they do for a living, or how they survive?

This land that seems so barren, so empty, to passersby is in fact rich in history. It is holy land to many, a place where mothers buried the umbilical cords of their children as assurance that they will always know where home is and will always find their way back should they get lost during their travels. To the Navajo, home is significant—as it is to the Dykens, as it is to me.

Though outsiders will never fully understand the Navajo experience, our personal histories caused us to respond empathetically. At one point in life, I moved off the land where my children were born and raised, and since then, have felt unsettled. The loss of home, stability and the life I had lived for twenty-five years left me emotionally adrift. I've traveled from place to place, landing in one spot and then another, but nowhere feels like home. Nowhere has that umbilical connection like the space I shared with my babies, where they gurgled and cooed and said their first word, where they played with my pots and pans, where they caught bugs and worms in the shade of manzanita and pine.

Perhaps I inherited some of those feelings. Both of my grandmothers experienced separation and a loss of connection with their roots. After suffering the death of her husband, my maternal great-grandmother and her eight children were evicted from their homestead—because she was Choctaw and Indians couldn't own property in the 1920s in America. My paternal grandmother was Jewish, forced by fear to leave her beloved homeland of Austria as war threatened and Hitler came to power. My grandmothers. Both exiles. Both survivors—influencing future generations by making tough choices. Home was the connecting fiber, but discrimination was the unraveling rope.

During the Butte fire of 2015 in California, Bear lost his home, his bus (Sahabi), bicycles, guitars, family photos—all were burned up, as was the land around him. After years of living nomadically, he'd settled at Cedar Creek. He'd found and experienced that connection to place, stronger and different than what he'd experienced as a child because this home rested upon the foundation he'd built from scratch. He had that "umbilical connection." Though his loss of home was a much different experience than what his Dineh friends had suffered, the infliction of pain by an uncontrollable, outside force was devastating.

"We watched the fire come," he said. "It was burning up the canyon in the north fork of the Calaveras River, towering over us, a 200-foot wall of flames. There are no words to describe the force of that thing. You could hear popping and explosions and sizzling. It was tremendous.

Apocalyptic. You think your home is stable, the land at least—your ground—and then something like this happens, and you have to leave it. I mean, we had to make decisions about what to take or not. All I knew for certain is that we had to get out of there. And I kept thinking, what's going to happen tomorrow? What will I do tomorrow, and the next day, and the day after that?"

Scientists have long known that parents pass genetic traits down to their children, but studies suggest that life experiences can also produce chemical effects on a person's DNA—which may directly affect future generations.[14] Why are you digging holes in my heart? Why are you taking out my liver? say the Grandmothers on Big Mountain. The reality of losing a home, all that was familiar to them, was a reality for which they were unprepared. When dealing with the eradication of one's home, one's culture, the soul wanders, never settling, never completely recovering. Such loss is non-negotiable, not in a treaty, not with false promises, never by forced removal from all that holds you to this earth.

All of us on the bus felt the weight of what we'd seen those last few days: poverty, denial of fundamental human rights to clean water and decent shelter, animals neglected because of environmental circumstance. "It hits you in the gut," Mark said. "No student can learn in one paragraph of their history book what it's like out here. It's real, and it's happening today."

---

14 Yehuda, Rachel, Dr. "How Trauma and Resilience Cross Generations." *O Being*, onbeing.org/programs/rachel-yehuda-how-trauma-and-resilience-cross-generations-nov2017

Mark Dyken, loading the Silver Eagle
with donations for Big Mountain (2016)

In Flagstaff, Arizona
Left to right: Catherine Lambie, Mark Dyken,
Jim Lundeen, Lotus Allen, Kimberly Bass

Into the Night 75

Camp at Dove Springs, Big Mountain (2016)

Tim and Belinda Johnson (2016)

Food donation boxes, ready for delivery

Lotus Allen bagging up cedar clippings for the Grandmothers (2016)

Helena and Jaia (2016)

Mark Dyken loading wood for supply deliveries

Bear's truck, the Blue Pearl, out for deliveries (2016)

Reservation dogs

5

THANK YOU FOR THE MUSIC[15]

Music is my medicine, music is my very best friend

Są ná'oogą́ą́' = Lifetimes

On the reservation, the Dykens' bus, named Smokey, was our temporary home. The curtains were open, the sleeping bags stowed, and duffle bags cleared away. A mourning dove cooed, calling for its mate. Sheep bleated in their pen. A dog barked, his chain clinking across the sandstone as he traveled a well-worn path from the fenced sheep enclosure to the top of the rock where he could see the world around him, north, south, east, and west. One by one, we organized for another day, talking and sharing stories in a place where stories were as much a part of the landscape as the sun and the sky and the earth beneath our feet. In the background, music filled the small space, matching our pace with a slow, steady beat. Bruce Cockburn. Leonard Cohen. Clan Dyken.

In the bus lay the instruments we'd brought on the journey: guitars, a djembe, a buffalo hide drum, crystal singing bowls, and flutes, but the pulse of the reservation provided the only constant sound. In the distance, the sudden sweet vibrato of a Native American flute delivered an unspoken *thank you*, lifting spirits, adding smiles and energy to our

---

15 Clan Dyken. Music is my medicine. "Wake Up the Sky." *Revive the Beauty Way.* CD. Track 7.

goals for the day.

When I was in my early twenties, I was hiking a trail alone, heading to Nevada Falls, a waterfall tucked far above Yosemite Valley. As I neared a bridge leading to the Nevada Falls campground, I spotted a black bear. Both the bear and I stopped in our paths, he on one side of the bridge, me on the other, watching one another, waiting, for what, I wasn't sure. The next few minutes were stressful, as I didn't know whether to stand my ground or run. Suddenly, from behind a large pine on the bear's side of the river, came the sound of a Native American flute, harmoniously blending with the thunderous roar of the falls and muted bird calls and the soft rustle of grass at the river's edge. The bear turned his head toward the music, sniffing the air and shifting his weight from one foot to the other. A long-haired young hippie strolled from behind the tree with his flute, a man I recognized immediately and had traveled with before, one of a group of classmates and friends I was supposed to meet at our designated campsite. At that moment, the bear visibly relaxed, his muscles quivering, his mind traveling inward, concentrating on something other than me. As he lumbered back into the forest, I knew this encounter was one I wouldn't forget.

"Corbin said that all living creatures respond to music, that even inanimate beings like rocks create vibrational sound," Mark said, tapping his fingers on a chunk of wood as he hefted it into the truck. "People feel the heartbeat. Animals feel it, trees, plants, all things respond to song and music on a fundamental level. Every *being* has roots grounded in music. Somewhere in our human past was an ancestor sitting around a campfire pounding out a rhythm with rocks and sticks—or blowing through a hollow reed, creating whistling sounds."

Music: the courtship of sound and rhythm and the spoken word has long healed wounds, relieved tensions, and influenced personal decisions. Rock against rock, stick against stick. Flutes made from bird bones and mammoth ivory. The human voice paired with percussion instruments. Thirty-thousand years ago, early man stretched an elephant hide across a log to create a sound that, no doubt, had listeners swaying and stomping around a campfire. Panpipes, bullroarers, rattles, and wooden xylophones added to the prehistoric rhythms. The first stringed instruments included bowl harps made from tortoise shells and a long-necked stringed instrument with a pear-shaped body made of cedar, known as a tanbur. Later in history, minstrels wandered the streets of Europe, singing about the human condition, of love and heartbreak, battles won and lost. Those early troubadours were the rebels of their time, protesting in the streets and alleyways, making their feelings known while strumming and humming and singing along.

There is no denying that musicians and storytellers are called to their craft by personal experiences, desire and loss, hypocrisy and autocracy and political motivation—the need for change—a wanderlust—and the need for home.

On the reservation, every movement had a musicality. As we gathered around the firepit, heating water for coffee and tea, and warming tortillas and beans for breakfast, we spoke of gatherings, arrivals, and departures, building futures out of ashes—common threads, musically and otherwise—strings of random thoughts. The sun rose over the cream-colored bluffs, raining light on our faces and hands as we fed our bodies. We talked as we ate and digested the conversation as we digested our food, tapping out rhythms with a fork, fingertips, and back to guitar strings.

The rhythm of the morning carried us through breakfast and then chores, the dry air leaching out night toxins, sweat stiffening on our faces like a mask of aloe and clay. As on previous days, apples, oranges, and jars of peanut butter were pitched underhanded from person to person, assembly-line style, and then arranged in delivery boxes. Lengths of cut and split firewood traveled from one gloved hand to another, our bodies moving in a syncopated swing and glide motion as we transferred the logs from the ground into the pickup trucks.

The orderly disorder of tossing wood into trucks prompted a song, an old Bob Dylan tune: "Gotta Travel On."

> *Done laid around, done stayed around*
> *This old town too long*
> *Summer's almost gone, winter's coming on*
> *Done laid around, done stayed around*
> *This old town too long.*

Mark's harmony and Bear's vibrato blended with the beauty and tonality of Dylan's song. When they finished the chorus, Mark looked up and smiled. "We've lived that life," he said, "moving on, traveling from place to place."

For Mark and Bear, their love for adventure started in the forested hills of Saukville, Wisconsin, constructing homemade rafts and floating down the Milwaukee River, building tree forts and staying out for days, away from home, away from their parents and siblings. Each morning they would load their bicycles with the newspapers for their paper routes and plug into their headphones, their music, Bear riding his bike to one side of town, Mark to the other. Their musical preferences were as varied as the streets they traveled, ranging from Dylan to the Beatles, Jimmy Hendrix, the Allman Brothers, and Sly and the Family Stone. Both brothers agree as to the influence of these musicians stylistically, but there was the added vibe of *happenings,* environmentally, politically, and musically in other parts of the country, the lure of the road, and the idea that music can be a medium for the voice of activism.

"When we were in high school, there were these brothers, friends who were just like us, totally untrained musically, but they had a sense of musicality, and one of them told me, 'play against the drummer and the bass players,'" Bear said, stacking the last of the wood in the back of his truck. "'You play against them. Whatever they're doing, you respond to it.' And so we used to make a lot of terrible noise."

"Our parents put up with it though," said Mark. "Friends would come over and play music with us. The more serious we became, the louder things got."

The Dyken basement was a literal rumpus room, and Richard and Dorothy allowed the kids the freedom to decorate it, within reason. There were standing closets and two single beds, a couch at one point, and many throw rugs. The boys tore out an old bar counter and flopped bean bag chairs on the floor. Bear painted a cartoon landscape on the walls and murals of wizards. He and Mark bought black lights and strobe lights and strings of colored lights, hanging them randomly, sometimes in patterns. Musically, it was the Dyken kids' playroom, their disco—a semi-chaperoned, parentally-permitted neighborhood hangout.

"What kicked me over the top musically," Bear said, "was one snobby rich kid who had all the nice gear and a good amplifier, and he showed up at one of those jam sessions we had in our basement, and he said, 'Dyken, you suck. You are never going to be good at this. You might as well give up.'

"That was it for me," Bear said, grinning. "Nobody was going to tell me I couldn't play guitar."

Migrations and the adventures of those who wander dominated the discussion as we readied to leave camp for the day. It was a natural connection in this environment where the once nomadic Navajo settled so many years earlier. The survival of a tribe, a restless spirit, financial necessity—all are reasons for leaving the familiarity of home. Whether from one end of the North American continent to the other, Europe to Ellis Island, or Wisconsin to California, when nature demands it or spirit calls, we as humans respond. Historically, hunter-gatherer tribes, like the Navajo, followed the animal herds they hunted, carrying their belongings with them from place to place. Early immigrants to the United States, like the Dykens' great-great-grandparents, traveled to America by boat, hauling their belongings in steamer trunks. During the Depression years, singer-songwriter Woody Guthrie, hopped trains and roamed the countryside with his clothes in a rucksack, took odd jobs in hobo and labor camps, played guitar and wrote music about the devastation of the Dust Bowl and the Depression. Woody Guthrie's lyrics about injustice and inequality, hard times, and living on the road inspired future travelers like those from the Beat Generation including Jack Kerouac—and the Hippies in the Sixties and Seventies, like Mark and Bear Dyken, and myself.

In 1974, I packed my old Ford Falcon station wagon with everything I owned, bound for Colorado. Stuffed in the car were a suitcase, my bicycle, a backpack, a small stereo and a cardboard box filled with 33 rpm records, an autoharp, and my animals: one dog, two cats, and a goldfish in a bowl. "This looks like the Joads' car in *The Grapes of Wrath*," my father teased. He and my mother watched from the curb as I drove away, both of them smiling yet tearful with worry over their oldest daughter's need to discover her way in the world, to find answers to the many questions and concerns that plagued the youth of that time. For me, the Rockies were a place to experience the "back to nature" philosophy I had adopted so vehemently. The University of Colorado in Boulder had founded an eco-center, a student-led environmental center that appeared to be impactful. From Denver to Boulder and into Estes Park, there were retreats and workshops, environmental, spiritual, and musical happenings—just the place for a *seeker* like me to make a pilgrimage of sorts.

In 1978, the Dyken household experienced a similar breaking away. In Wisconsin, Mark took to the road. The West Coast, San Francisco, and the whole hippie scene resonated with him, and he knew he wanted to be part of it somehow.

"I went to junior college for a year, and then to the University of Wisconsin at Stevens Point for a semester," Mark said. "But then I thought, you know what, I've had enough of this for now. It was the right time, things were happening, and I wanted to see and be part of it. So I decided to hitchhike around the country."

In the middle of winter, when the snow had gathered in icy clumps, Mark talked to his parents about leaving. "They were worried," he said, "but the house was so damn crowded by then, what with so many kids. I was a sophomore in college and pretty much on my own, anyway."

The Dyken children, ranging from teenagers to adolescents, had homework each night, and sports activities to attend: the patterns of work and family were well entrenched in school schedules. There was no major crisis; life was steady. Then came the news of Mark's decision. "Mom was disappointed that I was dropping out of school, but she knew there was nothing she could do to stop me," Mark said. "Besides, she was used to both Bear and me disappearing for days on end, taking off on crazy adventures."

It was easy to imagine the Dyken household bulging at the seams with eight kids and two adults. Mark and Bear's descriptions of life as children in a small town filled in the gaps. Though it wasn't an uprising or the migration of animals that urged Mark on, he was ready. "Life is a series of small adjustments," Richard often said. Whether it was something as simple as a rain disrupting Mark's plans to play basketball, frustration with school or music or a girl, perhaps, *adjustments* while growing up were commonplace. Mark's experiences with Freeman Chemical, reading Rachel Carson's *Silent Spring* and Thoreau's *Waldon Pond*, the first Earth Day in 1970—all of these contributed to his decision to leave home. Saukville, with its cornfields and parks, the lapping waters of Lake Michigan, the Milwaukee River where the two brothers played at building rafts like Tom Sawyer and Huck Finn, were a piece of it as well. Mark had a strong foundation. The call of adventure, the lure of the unknown, and the fantasy of the living on the West Coast pulled at him.

"For a long time, I'd been looking at this stuff, the pollution in the river and creek by our house, Freeman Chemical, and I remember thinking, *this is not the way we're supposed to live,*" Mark said. "I knew there was a better way. So when I hit the road, that thought was in my mind."

From a family of ten to traveling alone was *not* a small adjustment. "So I made this decision, and my mom was like, 'Oh my God. Please be careful.'" Mark laughed. "My dad, he just said, 'Goodbye.' Such a typical response for him." Mark laughed again. "Mom made me promise I'd stay in touch, but there were no cell phones at that time. I sent postcards now and then or would call from a pay phone."

No one in the Dyken family had ever owned a backpack. Mark packed his full—seventy pounds including clothes, a military-type sleeping bag, poncho, and tarp. A simple camp stove, mess kit—nothing high-tech. There were no firm plans as far as a route. Thumb raised high, he stood on the interstate, over-packed yet minimally prepared. The first night out, he found himself in Chicago, navigating his way through the subways. "I mean, a few hours and 100 miles from Saukville, and I'm wandering around in the big city all alone," Mark said. "I was ridiculously confident, but it was a little intimidating."

After Chicago, Mark headed west to California, shedding some gear to lighten the load as he traveled. He spent time in the Los Angeles area visiting a friend and then went east again and through the southern states to Florida where his Grandpa and Grandma Dyken now lived. From there, he headed back to Wisconsin, always camping in the woods, or on the side of the road—never in an actual campground.

"I got myself in a few situations while hitchhiking, but I learned more in the eight months that I traveled around the country than I ever could have imagined," he said. "It's surprising how many people pick you up, just because they want to talk. They can tell you their life story because they know they won't see you again. I kept myself clean, so people weren't afraid of me. That was part of it, I think."

Traveling by boat, by train, on foot—hitchhiking—the call of the nomad to the sea, the rails, the road is as timeless as a drummer responding to the beat of his heart. Mark's call led him to travel across the United States by foot, learning the tempo of the road and about life outside Wisconsin.

"I learned a lot about self-reliance," he said. "I was nineteen and turned twenty on the road. When you are out there on your own, you are *really* out there. I had some money in my pocket when I left, but I didn't have much." Mark looked down, brushing some dirt from his jeans and then thrumming his knees. "I took a few odd jobs here and there and made a little bit of money on the way, but you learn to survive. You learn to get yourself out of tight jams. You learn how to battle emotions like loneliness."

He recalled gazing at houses lining city streets, the lights from their windows glowing yellow and warm. In the Dyken home, his family would be sitting at the kitchen table. Perhaps Richard told a joke or said something to make Dorothy laugh. Perhaps they were missing Mark as much as he missed them at that moment; maybe they wished him well in a goodnight prayer.

"I remember thinking how nice it would feel to be with people who loved me," Mark said, "to be home again. When you're on the road for a long time, you start to feel like an outsider. Some people treat you like a transient as if, by your being in the vicinity, crime will increase in their town. But for me, those feelings never lasted long. I liked the idea of waking up in the morning and moving on in ten minutes, of being completely unencumbered."

From lying on the warm beaches at the Florida Keys to thumbing on an onramp in the midst of a snowstorm in Wisconsin, travel varied day-to-day. "That's the thing about traveling," Mark said. "Your life experience expands, and you come to see things in a whole new way."

By now we were well into our delivery run. Bear's Blue Pearl hammered over reservation roads, the bed filled with wood for Navajo families. There were no hitchhikers on this route, only random vehicles carrying passengers, possibly to Flagstaff, or to visit relatives, or maybe to Dinnebito Trading Post. The roads we traveled harbored the histories of the people who drove them.

"I got semi-kidnapped one time," Mark said, speaking as a passenger while Bear's truck rumbled along. "I got some pretty strange rides back then. I got propositioned by men, and that was a first for me. But it gave me some perspective on what it's like for a woman to get hassled or pursued just for the way she looks—like she's a piece of meat."

Mark emphasized the word *meat*, showing that he did *get it*. "One time," he said, "I was so desperate to get away from a bad situation, I climbed in a Cadillac with a drunk guy. It was 2 a.m. and pouring rain. I had my thumb out, and this person stopped. Well, I realized very quickly that he was beyond a couple of drinks. I mean, he was really drunk. I asked him if I could drive, and he said, 'Hell no. Nobody drives my Cadillac but me!'"

The Cadillac's windshield wipers could barely keep up with the deluge. *Swish, swish*, the rain pitching one direction and then another, while behind the wheel, a man much older than Mark struggled to keep the car on the road. Several times, Mark grabbed the wheel, correcting the vehicle, cursing silently as his mind pounded out visions of head-on collisions or careening off the road into some obscure and off-the-grid gully. They were screaming down the road at eighty miles-an-hour, heading to Phoenix, the driver nodding out now and then, literally asleep at the wheel.

Mark laughed, accentuating words with his rising voice. "I got out of this guy's car as the sun was coming up, and I fell to the ground and kissed the earth—seriously! That's the kind of shit that happened, and I'm telling my mom in postcards and when I call her, 'No need to worry. Everything is fine.'"

It was 1978. While Mark traveled the country, Bear attended college in Northern Wisconsin. He absorbed music—voraciously, listening to different styles and genres. He worked odd jobs, insulating buildings, tearing off old roofing, and installing aluminum siding.

"After high school, I went to Nicolet College, a small community college in Rhinelander," Bear said. "I wasn't shooting for a degree. I took some philosophy classes, and all the art classes they had available."

Whether painting with acrylics or watercolors, using watercolor pencils, or drawing black and white etchings, Bear had a style of his own. "A person born with your kind of passion and drive to create must use it," his mother once told him. His art teacher gave him a section of the classroom and let him do his thing, working on canvas frames of all sizes and painting murals. "I liked to work big," Bear said, grinning, and he picked up his guitar again, plucking out chords.

Nicolet College had an active theatre program, but not enough actors to participate in their plays. While in art class, Bear met some of the drama students. They were outgoing and funny—comfortable in their skin—creatives learning to express themselves through art, music, and on-stage drama. These students were not afraid to don colorful costumes or perform in public, and they appealed to Bear's fondness for the performing arts. He took part in several plays and went to their parties with live music. Even then, Bear carried his guitar. "One time I got up," he said, "and they had a band with a bass player and a drummer, and I remember I played 'Sympathy for the Devil,' and people danced, and they clapped, and I went home from that and thought, *You know, I could do this.*"

I liked imagining these early beginnings. Bear finding his way, becoming "comfortable in his skin," learning his craft while Mark was away. Two brothers, nearly inseparable during their childhood, spending time apart while molding a future and a shared dream.

"Around then, Mark came back home, and we rented a house together. That was a crazy house, on Beech Street in Grafton, Wisconsin. We did our thing. There was always something going on, like parties and music and all kinds of other stuff."

"We made a little sign," Bear continued. "We were the Beech Street Band. Our friend's dad was running for state assembly, and this guy was a real scammer. He gave us our first paying gig playing for one of his campaign fundraisers."

"Grafton is just a few miles from Saukville," said Mark. "And again, that was just a wild situation—four or five of us guys, and we were seriously crazy."

Drugs, sex, and rock n' roll—no parents invited. Five guys, ages nineteen to twenty-one. Music, music, and more music. "The place was decorated with bongs and beer cans," Mark said. "That was about it. A couch. Some mattresses."

The guys made music together with acoustic and electric guitars and drum kits—their all-night jam sessions rocking the neighborhood. "We had no electricity half of the time," Mark said, "because we didn't pay the bill. The meter reader would come out and shut it off, we'd pay a little bit, and he'd turn it back on. It was like that all the time. We had this fandango one night to help pay the rent. It was a raucous party. People were smoking and drinking. The cops came. It was nuts, and after all of that, someone stole the cash box, so still, no money to pay the bills.

What was that line from the Kid Rock song?" Mark asked, laughing again. "*My thoughts were short; my hair was long.* That was us."

6

HEAL THESE GLOBAL WOUNDS[16]

Let the air I breathe give me strength to do, the work of the One Great Spirit

Hooghangóó = At Home

Smokey's silver and blue siding shone like a welcome beacon at Dove Springs. The glare on the windows and metal roof reflected an odd image, surreal almost, like an old hippie transport bringing friends with news and supplies from afar. As word of our arrival spread, locals came to visit, riding in two pickup trucks and an older sedan, cruising up the road trailed by a tail of dust.

The drivers of the vehicles slowed down to take a look as they passed the bus and then drove on to the main camp where people gathered for breakfast, cups and utensils clattering, a quesadilla sizzling on a comal. Bear zipped up the door to his shift pod tent, and Jim and Tzaddi readied their trucks for daily deliveries, shifting boxes and night gear. Lotus, who preferred the privacy of the yurt rather than the shared bus space, stowed her belongings as the vehicles approached. She hummed as she worked, her silver-black hair draped across her shoulders.

"Yá'át'ééh, hello," our visitors said, in Navajo and English. They checked out the yurt, and the boxes of food, and the tarp filled with clothing. They, too, had things to share, trade, or sell—beaded earrings,

---

16 Clan Dyken. Let the air I breathe give me strength to do. "Heal These Global Wounds." *Retrospective.* CD. Disc III, Track 11.

necklaces, and woven bracelets. Two women, both weavers, displayed their rugs on the hoods of their truck and car. "Many prayers come with these weavings," said Elsie Benale, who had just introduced herself and her sister, Susie. The sisters—dressed in jackets and jeans—each held up a rug. "Our sheep provide the wool," Elsie explained. "We make yarn from the wool and use native plants to dye the yarn, as our mothers and Grandmothers taught us to do."

Indigo blue, reds, yellows, and shades of brown, black, and gray wove patterns in her work. Diamond shapes, representing the Dinétah homeland with its four sacred corners marked by the four sacred mountains, were prominent in several of the weavings, as were triangles—the building blocks of Navajo design. Symbols representing earth, air, fire, and water, along with those of animals and spirit beings, told a story significant to each weaver.

"Changing Woman taught our ancestors how to live in harmony, but it was Spider Woman who gave them secrets to find their way in this world," one weaver said, "including a special way of weaving."

To the Navajo, Grandmother Spider, or Spider Woman, is a healer, a teacher—and a spiritual guide. In the stories of old, Spider Woman wove the universe and is associated with the emergence of life. Her connect-the-dots pictures still fill the night sky—Ursa Major, Orion, the Hunter, Pleiades, or *Dilyéhé*. Changing Woman is the holy being that created the four original Navajo clans, forming a matrilineal line by which all Navajo people can trace their bloodlines. Legend says that Spider Woman taught Changing Woman how to spin thread and weave cloth, with the stipulation that she in turn would pass the skill to others.

To the Navajo, weaving is not just an art skill or personal practice; it is a prayer in motion. Weaving is a connection. It represents balance in all that *was* and *is* within nature and the universe.

The origin of Navajo weaving is an integral part of their history. According to legend, what began as two identical blankets woven together to create wrap-around dresses became an individualized craft, each weaver incorporating her own stories and dreams by way of symbols and motifs into her creation. Navajo weavers use an upright loom, with one continuous warp, and each strand of yarn is placed into the warp one strand at a time, resulting in a rug that won't unravel. As Elsie said, each weaving carries the love and blessings of its maker, a tradition reflected in the beauty of each piece. As early as the 1700s, Spanish explorers spoke of the intricacy of these weavings in letters sent home and in their journal writings.

"Beautiful," Mark said while admiring Elsie's rugs. "These bring to mind another weaver I knew. Roberta Blackgoat—one of the great resisters. She kept a flock of sheep and continued to make rugs, well into her eighties. Even as an elder, she traveled the world, telling people about the struggle at Big Mountain and painting pictures for them through her art."

Near the fire pit, a Navajo man worked a cat's cradle with his fingers, eager for one of us to join in his game. It was a nostalgic sight, as I had played this finger-dexterity puzzle with my mother many times while growing up. Looping string around our hands and fingers, pinching the patterned crosspoints, passing the loops from her hands to mine and back again, forming new geometrical designs, each more intricate and challenging.

Behind us, to the east, a ribbon of coal marked a definitive line, the coal mine itself, the genesis for years of strife and bad blood between the Navajo and the Hopi tribes. The contrast between the beauty of the weavings and the desecration of the land, people who honor the earth and those who defile it, was hard to ignore. The knowledge that we were breathing air polluted with traces of uranium contaminants and coal dust made it difficult to deny the environmental wreckage. Visiting houses with no running water, knowing people traveled miles to fill up plastic storage bins and buckets from functioning springs and faucets, and seeing the bulging eyes and pitiful cries of thirsty animals thrust the reality of industrial genocide in our faces. How long would the land sustain the sheep that provide the wool for these women's weavings? How long would plants that produce the dye to color the wool exist under these conditions?

"I've long believed that Native people have answers to questions that we haven't even figured out how to ask," Mark said, rubbing his hands together to warm them. The camp was empty now. The weavers were gone. The men who visited had walked down to the Johnson's hogan. "They were at the forefront of this climate change thing before anyone coined a name for it. The Dineh resisted this coal mine because their instinctive and spiritual beliefs told them that we should not be treating the earth in this way. They didn't have the science like we do to back those instincts up—they've just known this all along."

"The coal is the liver of the earth," said Bear, as he stirred the fire. "It cleanses and purifies the rainwater as it percolates into the aquifer. To remove the coal is like removing one of the earth's vital organs. Water is life. Billions of gallons of water pumped out of the aquifer to support Peabody Coal Mine caused groundwater levels to drop and wells and springs to dry up. Vegetation is dying. Native plants have failed to reseed. What the coal company took were coal and water. What they left behind was disease—sickness of heart, minds, and body, by way of pollution."

Bear drew in a deep breath. "This place drew us from the moment we heard about it," he said. "Our music was the medium, but the truth of what was happening out here became the message in many of our songs. Even though the boxes of food, the tools, and the clothes we bring are small, the Grandmothers are always happy to know that we remember and are thinking of their families."

It was day four on the reservation. The next would be Thanksgiving. While Navajo families prepared for gathering with loved ones, we filled our trucks with another load of supply boxes and sacks of dog food. As we traveled the dry, dusty roads from house to house, the isolation that is such a part of reservation life brought clarity to the importance of gatherings and ceremony. Visits from family and friends are an occasion, an opportunity to share stories and adventures—and music, dance, and song.

Throughout history, good storytellers have taken raw material and woven a blanket around those listening, warming hearts for pure entertainment, teaching lessons and survival skills, both comforting and fear-provoking. The Navajo creation stories tell a tale of migration, battles with neighboring tribes, drought, and floods. *Long ago, before this world existed, the First World lay in darkness. Six Beings lived in this place: First Man, First Woman, Salt Woman, Fire God, Coyote, and the Child of the Sun. The Child of the Sun created four mountains. However, in this mountainous land, there was no light. The first beings grew tired of the darkness and decided to leave.* The story continues into the Second World, the Third, and the Fourth. Around campfires and at the ceremony, children listen to the history of their tribe. Stories of old heroes and new ones— the Grandmothers who stood their ground resisting forced relocation, using their will and their bodies to protect their homeland.

As we drove past Rocky Ridge Boarding School (Tsé Dildǫ́'ii), I grew curious about the children inside. Rocky Ridge is a BIA Contract Grant School, located on Dinnibito Road, the official town, Kykotsmovi. Its student population is 100 percent Native American, half male and half female, grades Kindergarten through eighth grade, around 100 kids. The school seems fairly spread out, tall brown cement walls surrounded by typically dry ground and sparse vegetation. There is a water tower. There are power poles. How must it feel to the children as they are dropped off at school at the end of each weekend, living in rooms miles away from their families? Here on the reservation, the rutted red roads, the distance from home to school, and the weather, all play a part in a parent's decision to board their children so that they can attend school. My own children came home every day to a cozy house, a hot meal, fresh water, electricity. I tucked my kids into bed each night and read bedtime stories and snuggled with them as they fell asleep. It was hard to imagine leaving them alone days on end, out of necessity, or otherwise, as parents here on the reservation have to do.

Many American kids go to boarding school, but undeniably, there is a distinction between those schools and the ones here on the reservation. Some of the more expensive schools in America offer a top-notch curriculum, plus gourmet food, horse-back riding, yoga, music, and art to name just a few of the perks. Tuitions are steep. Accommodations match that of a four-star hotel. In contrast, a 1969 Senate report declared "a near-total lack of high-quality education on reservations," calling Indian education "a national tragedy." Since then, there has been some improvement. Each school follows nationally approved and accredited techniques, but challenges remain, such as the ability to attract and keep quality teachers. Many schools are in extreme states of disrepair, with leaking roofs, asbestos and mold issues, and aging or nonexistent bus fleets that must travel roads impossible to negotiate in bad weather. Nearly sixty percent of native schools lack the bandwidth or computers to support online learning.[17] The good news is that thanks to the efforts of teachers, volunteers, and elders, children in the reservation schools learn about their culture and study their native language.

The Rocky Ridge Boarding School appeared comfortable. Lights shone in the windows. No doubt there is healthy food and water, as observed by the water tank. However, this building is not home. It is not the hogan and hearth of people who cherish such tradition, yet education is recognized as necessary, both in the old way and the new. "Here on the reservation, the elders understand how to live on the earth respectfully, and they teach their young ones to do the same," Mark said. "Yeah, it's necessary to teach math and English, but this kind of indigenous culture, the way these people care for their ancestral home, the plants, the animals, is not something that kids learn in a book. Here on the reservation, these things are taught first-hand."

I wondered about little Helena, the young Navajo girl we met the first day we arrived, and what her teachers tell her regarding a history steeped in broken treaties, the forced relocation of her people, the coal mine, tribal government, and longstanding federal interference. A couple of days ago, she ran the trails at Dove Springs with Jaia, laughing with the ease of a child, and accepting us, although hesitantly at first. What will her future bring? Where will this fight take her and what might her opinion of us be in the years to come? Will she find herself fighting to maintain her tribal homeland and the fundamental rights of her people? Will she stand her ground against multi-million dollar corporations and rangers in uniform when they are pounding on her door? Will she be accused of trespassing on her land, the very ground on which she was born and raised?

"To understand the frustration these people feel, their hesitation to accept and trust outsiders, you have to learn their history," Bear said, as we cruised the paved road past the school. "On the reservation, grade school kids live in a gap between two cultures. The traditional land-based one their mothers are fighting so hard to hang on to, and the encroaching

---

17 Brenna, Susan. "Why are Native Students Being Left Behind?" *Teachers for America*, 11 Dec. 2014, www.teachforamerica.org/stories/why-are-native-students-being-left-behind.

contemporary one that wants them to move away from all they know and hold dear."

"It's hard for most of us to imagine what it might be like to face the end of your culture and way of life," Mark added. "To know that the government of this country, formed to protect the rights of all of its citizens, has betrayed you over and over, all for the benefit of profit. To watch the plants, animals, water, and the land itself disappear as the traditional Dineh dwindle in number. It has gotten to the point where the simple act of planting corn has become a major act of resistance against great odds. One of the Grandmothers, a friend of ours, often says, 'The sheep are my children. The horses are our relatives too.' This kind of logic, the simplicity and basic truths—it's hard to deny that we feel a calling, or that there is a connection for us. The land is everything. Water is life. You hear that over and over out here."

Thirty minutes later, our four-wheel drive trucks rattled under the strain of steep rocky inclines and roads abused by years of use and rough weather. The sky was a brilliant blue yet harbored the cold. An hour into the drive, the landscape remained the same: a few small juniper trees, pinyon pines, their dark green foliage a sharp contrast to the cream-colored terrain.

"A while back, we talked about Roberta Blackgoat. She was a political activist and resister for many years," Mark said, as he rummaged in his pack for a protein bar. "Roberta hung a sign on her front door that read: IF YOU WANT ME TO MOVE, SUE THE CREATOR. It was good to know that she stood firm to her commitment to the end of her life."

"The last time we visited her place, there was no one home," said Bear.

"No people, no animals, no wool, no weaving, just an empty house and empty corrals," Mark said. "When people like Roberta leave this earth, some of the indigenous ways go with them. No one knows the things and the life she knew. Each of these elders has a special story, one his or her children can't even tell."

Remembering my dreams, I envisioned Amá sání in the daylight this time, a strong, spirit-filled force of a woman. Even in my imagination, her face remained shrouded in shadow. But I felt as if I would recognize her if I saw her now, trudging toward us in her full Navajo regalia, her boots as familiar with the land as her hands were with the loom she worked daily.

Soon our caravan of three vehicles pulled into the yard of Katherine Smith. It was late afternoon, and the rush to complete the day's deliveries was evident in our fast pace while unloading. The rhythm of the crew, carrying food and stacking firewood, was purposeful. Tim Johnson's prayer message on our first morning at Dove Springs came to mind: "Think, plan, do, reflect," he told us. "Begin your day with intention. That is the Navajo way."

From the shared stories, it was evident that Katherine Smith was a woman unafraid to speak her mind. She had lived her life here, and she had buried the umbilical cords of her children in the pen where she housed her sheep. Katherine was a long-time resister. She shot her rifle in the air to "dissuade" men from fencing the land, capping off wells, raping the earth of its coal, hauling away and slaughtering the sheep and cattle, all of which represented life and survival to her people.

Hers was a comfortable house, the small living room attached to the kitchen, yellow/brown walls decorated with pictures of her family, bright weavings, and other native art. Some photographs of Katherine were prominently displayed—one of her standing with her rifle held across her chest, another sitting in front of a large loom in a chinked log hogan, and yet another of her standing in her once productive vegetable garden with several fresh-picked ears of corn slung across her arm. Surrounded by tall stalks of corn, well-tended bean vines, and squash plants, she looked happy and peaceful.

I studied these pictures of a much younger woman, then gazed at Katherine's weathered face. Though aged, she was still lovely and appeared prideful and focused in her long red skirt and long-sleeved blue blouse, and a light blue sweater. Outside the living room window lay crevassed and barren ground, where once lived her ample gardens. And now people she recognized but barely knew unloaded supplies intended to help her survive the winter on land that had once provided for her and her family with help from no one.

We filtered into the house bearing presents—a frozen chicken, dried beans, and squash, bags of cedar, tobacco, oranges, and apples, recognizing that we had been allowed entry, a gift much more valuable than any we had brought. Katherine now lived with her daughter, Mary Katherine, who was not there when we visited. On this day, Katherine sat in a wooden armchair, and we gathered around her in straight back chairs, on the couch, and at the small kitchen table. She sniffed at the bag of cedar we offered and nodded her head then glanced up, her eyes ravaged by age but still filled with wisdom and life. Her hands trailed a message, winding in circles, her gnarled index finger pointing at the peeled orange on the end table by her side, thanking us without words for bringing it to her. She smiled a little and nodded again, listening to bits of conversation between her daughter's partner, Ned, and others in the room. "She can't hear well or see, but she is glad that you are here," Ned said. "She is grateful." Wearing work boots and a denim work shirt, he then nodded and walked outside to help unload the supply trucks.

Once the wood was stacked, we readied to leave. Standing, we thanked Katherine for her graciousness. "Ahéhee', Shìmà," each person said, addressing her one by one in her native tongue, "Thank you, Mother, or Grandmother."

I approached her after the others left, expecting the same nod, a similar dismissal. Instead, Katherine took my hand in hers and slapped the arm of the couch with her free hand, demanding that I sit. Her lips quivered. Her brows drew together, her cataract-clouded eyes staring directly into mine. There was no doubt about her motive. Katherine had fought the building of the fences. She had opposed the coal extraction and the Relocation Agreement. At ninety years plus, she still had something to say. So I sat. And listened.

"They knew, those old people, the old Hopi, the old Hopi and Navajo, the quiet ones, they knew," she said. "But the others, they came to me, and they needed the land. Because of the coal. They wanted the coal. And those people, they lied," she told me. "They *lied*. They tried to move me off my land, but I wouldn't go. I'll never move. This is my own home. I don't want to move. They put up a fence across the wash. They *lied*."

In my mind, Amá sání's breath swirled around my chest. Her neighbor, the old Hopi man, whooped and pointed, past her across the plateau. It was still dark; morning had not yet come, and Amá sání was stiff from sitting, but there, nearer to her home where he was shaking his finger, was a line of lights, vehicles traveling in her direction. The men carried shovels, the trucks filled with barbed wire. Amá sáni signaled her dogs, instructing them to herd her sheep home to the safety of their pen. She grabbed her rifle, walking, nearly running, at the men in the trucks, one of them already digging holes in the heart of the land she loved.

The unspoken name, *John Boyden*, seemed to echo through mesas, along with the other names[18] and government faces who had such an impact on the living conditions and lifestyle here. As history shows, Boyden's two primary clients were the Hopi Tribal Council and Peabody Coal, which wanted to lease out the coal-rich land, land inhabited by Katherine Smith, Ida Clinton, Roberta Blackgoat, Pauline Whitesinger, Alice Benally, Anna Begay, and the others.

"More than 10,000 Navajo and 100 Hopi found themselves on the wrong side of the fence," Mark said, nestled in the truck as we traveled to our next destination.

"Around the time of the 1882 Executive Order," Bear added, "white settlers were moving into the lands surrounding the Navajo reservation, and the Atlantic and Pacific Railroad was being built in New Mexico. As these things happened, more Navajo moved into the joint use area established in that Executive Order."

As Mark and Bear explained, the history of Black Mesa showed centuries of continuous Navajo settlement around the Hopi reservation. The return of Navajos after the Bosque Redondo and Long Walk led to many changes and eventually to the 1962 declaration of the land established in the 1882 Executive Order as a "Joint Use Area" (JUA),[19] though the Hopi still considered it part of their reservation. William McKinley, Teddy D. Roosevelt, and Woodrow Wilson all extended Navajo lands. In

---

18 In 1974, despite the protests of traditional Hopi and Navajo and in light of an exposé by the *Washington Post* of the conflict as fictional, the Relocation Act (P.L. 93-531) was pushed through Congress. The chief lobbyist, Harrison Loesh, a Department of the Interior employee, became Vice-President of Peabody Coal.

19 The 1882 Executive Order Reservation later became known as the Joint Use Area (JUA), which was divided in half by the 1974 Land Settlement Act. From the time of its inception, both Navajo and Hopi people occupied it.

1934, Franklin D. Roosevelt added another million acres, but this still covered less than a third of traditional Navajo lands. The reservation was divided into six districts, including an exclusive Hopi zone, conforming to what the two tribes had delineated by stone markers surrounding the Hopi Mesas in 1891.

"It's important to say again that these people, the Hopi and the Navajo, lived in harmony on this land for *so* long. They had their minor disputes," Bear said, "but it was Peabody Coal Company's public relations and lobbying firm that created the so-called 'Navajo-Hopi land dispute.' They portrayed these two peoples as being embattled in a bloody 'range war,' which was just not true."

The establishing of a boundary between Navajo and Hopi coincided with the establishment of Tribal Councils—part of the Indian Reorganization Act of 1935. This new system was implemented through an election process held on every reservation. Many Hopi people were offended and refused to vote, knowing that their system of government predated the signing of the Declaration of the Independence by more than 1,000 years. The Indian Reorganization Act, however, was passed by a small percentage of Hopi voters. With the ratification of the Reorganization Act, the Hopi Tribal Council was established. Mining corporations now had official entities with which to sign leases, which further divided the "traditional" people who clung to the old ways, and the "progressives," who were more attuned to capitalistic ideas and modern ways. Oil leases opened on the reservation immediately, with uranium and coal to follow. In 1961 John Boyden secured Fisher Contracting Company to prospect for minerals on the Hopi reservation. By 1964 he had successfully opened up sixty-three percent of the Hopi reservation to mining interests.[20]

These facts were easy to research. Even on my iPhone, when cell reception was available, multiple sites told the story of the so-called land dispute in sordid detail. As a library specialist, I had learned how to research correctly, to check my sources and validate my findings. Though many publications and articles represented the differing opinions surrounding the events that lead to the Relocation Agreement, specific details were clear and precise. One of the oil companies with which the

---

20 "An Historical Overview of The Navajo Relocation | Cultural Survival Quarterly" Web. 26 Sep. 2018 <https://www.culturalsurvival.org/publications/cultural-survival-quarterly/histor>.

Hopi Tribal Council dealt was Aztec Oil and Gas, a client of Boyden's law firm, that also represented WEST, which at that time included Peabody Coal Company. Peabody Coal began strip mining operations on Black Mesa in 1968 and until recently was North America's most massive strip mining operation—the site of the only slurry pipeline in the country, 273 miles long, running from Black Mesa to the Mohave Generating Station, a power plant in Laughlin, Nevada. The process was this: coal was extracted from the mine, crushed, and mixed with water to make a slurry and then pumped through a three-foot diameter pipe to Laughlin. At the Mohave Generating Station, the slurried water drained into blackwater impoundment ponds, a waste byproduct of transporting the coal. Peabody pumped over a billion gallons of water from the Black Mesa aquifer each year through the coal slurry line, resulting in the substantial loss of groundwater. According to the Arizona Department of Environmental Quality and the EPA, the pipeline maintained by Black Mesa Pipeline Inc. leaked more than half a million gallons of coal slurry in fifteen separate spills. In May 2001, Black Mesa Pipeline was fined $128,000 for illegally discharging coal slurry.[21] Together with the Kayenta Mine—which supplied the Navajo Generating Station near Page, Arizona—enough coal was produced to power the southwestern power grid for three decades. Kayenta Mine provided approximately seven and a half million tons of low-sulfur thermal coal annually. In 2013, the mine sold almost eight million tons of coal.

The dying sage and ephedra plants on the reservation, the dry wells and creek beds, and people hauling water from fifty miles away offered further proof of what had happened here. In hearings of the House Subcommittee on Indian Affairs, John Boyden pleaded for a division of the land and a reduction of Navajo livestock. He insisted that Navajo intrusions into the Hopi reservation threatened the Hopis with "systematic elimination as a people." The Hopi Tribal Council, under his guidance, created an ordinance declaring Navajo livestock on Hopi land to be "trespassing" and subject to impoundment. In 1974, Senator John McCain penned the Navajo-Hopi Settlement Act and subsequent Relocation Agreement, which amounted to a division of the jointly-used ancestral

---

21 Ghioto, Gary. "https://azdailysun.com/pipeline-faces-fines-for-spills/article_65bf9770-e3ae-592b-b379-f3ae1f97f12e.html" ["Pipeline faces fines for spills"]. *Daily Sun*, 2 Aug. 2002, azdailysun.com/.

lands—land occupied primarily by Navajo people. By 1975, the mineral prospecting leases had been signed. The first fences went up in 1977. In addition to the environmental impact of the mine itself, the 10,000 to 15,000 Navajos and 100 Hopi taken from their lands due to the mining operation was the largest removal of Native Americans since the 1880s, "removal" in this case meaning relocation to nearby towns. Rather than employ military force to aid in the removal of the Navajo, the federal government implemented a moratorium, which made it illegal for people to build or even repair their homes. The government also established the livestock reduction program, which limited the number of stock animals a family could own. Said Lee Brooke Phillips, staff attorney of the Big Mountain Legal Office, "The reality is that people are really faced with a surrender or starve situation."

My first trip to canyon country in 1970 was with a group of geology and biology students, all of us eager to experience the wilds of the Grand Canyon, learn its flora and fauna, the geological sequence of rock, the significance of time and place—and to raft down the Colorado River.

I traveled through adolescence into adulthood on that trip, experiencing the freedom of pummeling down whitewater rapids, spending nights surrounded by Visnu schist, Zoroaster granite, the primordial smells and majesty of ancient rock. I scrambled up loose tailing piles, tracing skeletal remains of trilobites, brachiopods, and prehistoric coral with my fingers, lightly and reverently. I observed artifacts left by people I had studied about in anthropology classes: pottery shards, an arrowhead, broken beads, and small shells.

On that trip, we walked the South Rim's Grandview Trail. My classmates and I made drums out of rocks and drumsticks out of branches, and in the moonlight, danced our collective spirits into the rock dust on a small plateau marking the halfway point to the bottom of the canyon. Crumbling, broken bits of prehistory crunched beneath our feet as we forged our way down to the Colorado River. I celebrated my nineteenth birthday there, scantily clad bodies plunging into the blue-green water as Havasupai Falls roared above us. "Be respectful," my geology teacher often said. "When you enter Native land, you are entering their home."

My second trip out to Navajo land, in 1972, was with a group of friends, and we traveled by Volkswagen bus from California to Flagstaff, much as we did on this journey with Clan Dyken, stopping in Tuba City, driving north onto the reservation. On this present-day trip, I closed my eyes and tried to reflect on what I saw back then. There were no fences at that time. I remembered herds of sheep wandering free, men on horseback riding like the wind over wide-open spaces, women in brightly colored skirts and blouses selling their jewelry and weavings at small stands along the roadways.

Today the herds of sheep are gone, and contrails mark the bright blue sky. F-16 fighter jet flyovers disrupt religious ceremonies. Means of intimidation include twenty-four-hour surveillance by government agents. Those resisting the government relocation have been subject to enforced livestock reduction actions to prevent overgrazing. Hopi rangers say that there is never violence involved when animals are impounded and that Navajo herders receive ample warning before the trucks roll in to haul off the animals, but the Navajo disagree. For the Navajo, there are also bans on wood gathering, home repair, and new construction. Gathering of wild herbs and medicines without a permit is no longer allowed. Wells have been capped off and springs destroyed, forcing people to haul water on unimproved dirt roads.

"Many of these people are getting their water from Rocky Ridge School," Mark explained. "It's hard enough to get by when you have to travel twenty miles over rough desert sand roads in an old vehicle to haul water for a household. It's nearly impossible if you are trying to grow food or raise livestock. Other people are traveling to the coal mine for water. That's a fifty mile trip for some."

My dream Amá sáni chanted a refrain as familiar on this reservation as the white sandstone and that black string of coal. *Water is life. Sheep are life. The land is everything.* She had her jet-black hair tied back in a chignon and wore a long black skirt and an orange blouse draped with a turquoise necklace; her strong brown hands held a rifle pointed at the sky. I saw her face now: chestnut brown, eyes tired, yet proud and committed. I saw her standing tall, her fists cradling rocks, hurling them at the men building fences.

We were climbing slowly, making our way to Anna Mae Camp.

There were no street signs, no streetlights or neighborhood watch programs, though people looked out for each other on a level that was noticeable. Eyes were open and watchful. Cell phones and text messages passed the news that we were nearby. The people at our next stop knew we were coming before we got there.

Located on the Benally family homestead, Anna Mae Camp is situated in the high desert, surrounded by rising mountains and sandstone bluffs dotted with sage and low brush chaparral, pinyon, and juniper. According to Mark and Bear, the camp has a history of gatherings and celebrations, well known to all who live here. Thirty plus years of resistance stains the earth. This place was home to the Sundance Ceremony, a prayer ceremony for healing and renewal, until August of 2001 when agents from the Bureau of Indian Affairs and the Hopi Tribal rangers bulldozed the sacred Tree of Life and the cedar arbor in the center of the ceremonial grounds.

"The BIA and Hopi Tribe say that this was done to prevent illegal gatherings," Mark said. "The excuse was that the Hopi were asserting their jurisdiction over Hopi land and that by arresting trespassers and destroying the ceremonial grounds they were deterring future use."

As we drove into Anna Mae Camp, the old Sundance grounds came into view. A short wire fence erected by Hopi rangers stood as a reminder of the damage that took place here. A harsh wind blew over the land, removing precious topsoil a little at a time. Stories shared over the last weeks told of Anna Mae Pictou Aquash, a Mi'kmaq Indian from Canada, active in the American Indian Movement back in the 1970s. In 1976, her badly decomposing body was found thirty feet down a ravine in South Dakota, wrapped in a blanket, the back of her head matted with blood, and a single bullet hole at the base of her skull. Much speculation surrounded her death in light of her anger toward governmental interference on tribal lands. Her name became the rallying cry for many Native activists, including those on Navajo land.

To this day, Anna Mae represents a symbol of bravery and resistance. At Big Mountain, at Anna Mae Camp, a vague circular demarcation is all that remains of the Sundance ground named in her honor, erected to support the resistance to the 1974 Navajo-Hopi Land Settlement Act and Relocation Agreement. Dancers and participants came from afar to help the Navajo in their fight to stay in their ancestral homeland. Now at this sacred place, the tattered ceremonial remains cling to the parched land like the furrowed skin of the Grandmothers.

"This camp has seen its share of confrontations and trouble," Mark said, "but it has always been a peaceful, welcoming place when our caravan arrives."

The air itself seemed to be mourning, the land grieving, the contrast between life and death palpable. This homestead was part of a culture—a sacred ceremonial ground, broken, empty, the sagging wire barrier fence strung by the Bureau of Indian Affairs and Hopi rangers, the bones of an old sweat lodge, willow branches bent into a tortoise-shell structure that without life-blood is unable to survive.

"The Sundance is a healing ceremony, both for the land and its people," Mark said. "Navajo elders invited the Lakota Sioux, Joe Chasing Horse, and his family, to bring the ceremony to Big Mountain. Sundance is the most important ceremony practiced by the Sioux and other Plains Indians. The ceremony provides a time for renewal, both for the people and the land. The Lakota had been fighting the effects of resource extraction for a long time, only on their reservation it was about gold instead of coal. Still, they had an acute understanding of what was going on here."

Joe Chasing Horse—an ordained Sundance Chief, and a direct descendant of the Sioux Spiritual Leader, Crazy Horse—once said, "I see a time of seven generations when all the colors of mankind will gather under the sacred Tree of Life, and the whole Earth will become one circle again."

"To set the scene, as we saw it back then, during Sundance, Anna Mae Camp was a hotbed of activists," Mark said, pausing long enough to gaze across the horizon. "There were AIM (American Indian Movement) folks, tribal reps, Sundancers, and lots of families from the reservation and elsewhere. The numbers peaked at the time of the Sundance itself, but spring gatherings and our food runs brought large groups of activists too. There was always an undercurrent of tension—like something could go down at any minute. Anna Mae Camp was under surveillance all the time." Mark swept his arm from left to right, indicating a broad distance. "You would see people up on the hills, watching with binoculars—Hopi and BIA rangers, armed with expensive military grade gear, weapons, and vehicles. There were guards at the entrance of the Sundance grounds too, but they were on our side, checking those who entered for guns, drugs, things like that. You had to know someone or have an invite to get in. Big time Indian activists like Dennis Banks, Winona LaDuke, Thomas Banyacya, John Trudel, and Joe Chasing Horse, and so many others would be there. There were planning meetings, sweat lodges, ceremonies, fire circles—there could be up to one thousand people at Sundance.

"Who knows what kind of surveillance was happening," Mark continued, as he scanned the old Sundance grounds, "because this was in 1994, only fifteen, sixteen years after the whole thing went down at Wounded Knee again, so Leonard Peltier's trial was still going on. All that kind of stuff and AIM was always there in significant numbers, and I wouldn't doubt if the FBI was there watching the Indian activists.

"In November of 1994," Mark said, "I was at Big Mountain when Joe Chasing Horse and some of the members of his family came to help build and prepare the arbor for the Sundance that was to come in the summer of that year. Joe is the pipe holder for his tribe. This medicine pipe, the medicine bundle, goes way back. So they were praying about having the upcoming ceremony, and he got this pipe out and walked to the arbor, and this storm was coming up, and it started to snow. So he walked out to the middle of this Sundance ground beneath the Tree of Life. They leave the tree up throughout the ceremony and until the next year and then they take it down and put another one in its place. So he walked out there and put some tobacco in the pipe. They'd already burned some sage and gotten themselves ready, and he raised that pipe up to start going around to the four directions, and right when he did that, the clouds parted in the snowstorm. Not a storm, but a snowfall. And this light came streaming in from above, and there was no snow in the arbor." Mark shook his head, stood up and took a step toward the spot where this had happened. "I mean, I was blown away. I'm not much for that kind of stuff, but when you're right there, and people tell you that someone can change the weather or get signs or omens, that was just literally, watching the sky shift around this man, was like—it was hard to deny what I saw happen."

Besides Sundance, other ceremonies happened at Anna Mae Camp, including pipe ceremonies and sweat lodges. Sweats were a place of sacrifice and prayer, where participants gave up comfort and had time to pray for their work, their families, and themselves—for their common goals and for other human concerns. It was a church—a Native church. The entire site was sacred, used only for prayers, purification, unity, and education; it was a meeting place for the people who were refusing to leave their ancient lands and sacred sites unprotected. Up to thirty Navajo men used to live on site, there to protect the arbor and keep the military from tearing it down. For the Navajo, religious freedom and human rights were at stake. It seemed to be a divide and conquer crusade—if the military could prevent water deliveries, if they could keep more people from entering the site, then maybe the Navajo would become divided. Still, songs like this one could be heard in the surrounding hills: *Grandmother, don't cry, Grandmother. You will walk this land, four seasons, Forever.*

The day we visited Anna Mae Camp, the arbor was gone, the Sundance ground void of people and drums and ceremony. There was no cottonwood tree in the center of the circle, no dancers, no pipes. The smell of tobacco, sage, and herbal medicine was no more than a memory in the minds of those who had attended these ceremonies. Tension could be felt in the air, however. Pickup trucks driven by armed Hopi rangers cruised the nearby roads, watching for infractions to trespassing rules and the moratorium on building and remodeling, and "illegal gathering" regulations established by the federal government. Reports from other activist camps advised that rangers were asking to see travel permits. *Where are you going? What are you doing here? Where did you get that wood and where are you taking it?* they questioned.

Jim Lundeen, who drove one of the three trucks on our run to Anna Mae Camp, stood staring out at the Sundance grounds. "After hearing the stories about what happened here, I feel hollow. I'm not sure what I expected, but there was a heaviness inside me before we even got here."

From Mark's description, it was easy to visualize an arbor made of pinyon trees and set together in a circular pattern. A shelter, like an awning, ten to fifteen feet front to back. When Sundance happened, it was full-on summer, hot, nonstop sun. The cottonwood tree (the Tree of Life) was carried and planted in the center of the circle, its planting being a ceremony in itself. All around the front of the arbor were sticks on which strips of red cloth and tobacco were tied, and each of these offerings constituted a prayer. Mounds of dirt built as an altar held the ceremonial pipes. The pipes rested against two Y-shaped sticks with a vertical stick between them, bowls down on the ground and the stem up against the rack or holder.

"Everything was precision," Mark said, suggesting a straight line with a movement of his hand. "There was nothing random about this ceremony. There were entrances at all four corners, and at the west end, there were sweat lodges, all facing east. There, the dancers purified and sweated for three days before the ceremony started. They didn't eat. They didn't drink. There was a big drum on the south side and women dancers on the north side. People were sitting and standing all over the arbor, and it filled up and up and up, Thursday, Friday, Saturday, until Sunday—the biggest dance of all."

According to Lakota teachings, the Sundance songs and dances have been passed down through many generations. The keeper of the Sacred White Buffalo Calf Pipe, as mentioned by Mark, opened and led the ceremony. His prayers and those of his people were meant for one purpose—the survival of future generations, offering personal sacrifice for the benefit of family and community. The story goes that the pipe was first presented to the Lakota approximately 900 years ago by a female teacher, White Buffalo Calf Woman.

Dancers prepared for Sundance in many ways, including fasting and entering a sweat lodge. A fire was lit outside the lodge and was tended by an experienced firekeeper who heated the stones to keep the lodge hot. Inside, a pit was filled with the hot stones and as the dancers sat cross-legged around the pit, the lodge leader, a medicine man, poured water on the hot stones, which created searing steam. He sprinkled the stones with sage and other herbs while the dancers meditated and prayed. There were usually four rounds, and during each round, the air inside the lodge got hotter, more humid. The dancers breathed slowly, taking in the steam, purifying their bodies and their minds as they meditated and prayed. The sweat could last many hours in temperatures of over 100 degrees. Each sweat experience was unique, both to the lodge and the participants. After the sweat, a medicine man cleansed each dancer's skin with a combination of herbs, then with his thumb and forefinger, pinched a fold of skin just above the pectoral muscle. He then inserted a wooden skewer and attached a rope to each side of the skewer and also to a hook in the top of the cottonwood tree.

"As a spectator, you're watching this process," Mark said, his voice cracking a bit as he explained, "and you know it's painful, but these men endure, sometimes piercing more than once during a single ceremony. The dancers had eagle bone whistles in their mouths to bite down on and also blow air through, in short, little bursts, and while they breathed, it made this sound that was in time with the drums." Mark put his fingers to his lips and blew, *whew, whew.*

"They danced in rounds," he explained, "sometimes leaning back, staring at the tree and praying. As they leaned back, you could see how the tension stretched their skin. Someone, a medicine man or mentor, was guiding them through this process and helping them focus. While this was going on, the drumming got more intense. There was a line of seven buffalo skulls that were attached to each other with leather, and a dancer would pierce in the back and hook their skewer to the leather cording and then pull the skulls around the circle. When the climax of each round happened, and the dancers got told, 'okay, you can start breaking,' the guys who had done it a long time, they had a way, they could lean back and in one quick motion, *pow,* their skewers were out. You saw the skewers pop toward the sky, and you saw this blood shooting out. Once the dancers are released, you'd think they'd just die from the pain, but there was this moment when they would get a whole new energy, and they would dance around the circle and were ecstatic.

"The dancer who pierced his back pulled the seven buffalo skulls through the dirt, sweating, focused only on his body, mind over body, prayer over pain," Mark said. "Children joined the ceremony, running to help him, and they sat on the buffalo skulls, adding more weight, more pressure against the skewers as the dancer pulled, and pulled, driving forward across the ceremonial grounds, and suddenly, *bam,* the skewers popped out of the dancer's back. During some rounds, they'd throw a rope around the crook of the tree, and on the other side of the tree there was a log, and several people held onto the log and started moving back until they lifted the pierced dancer right up off the ground. All the while, women were dancing on the edges of the circle, praying, and singing. All these things were going on at once, and at each climax, the drum got more intense, and people started trilling. The eagle whistles were going, *whew, whew, pop, pop.* Some guys, especially the young ones who haven't done it before, they couldn't quite get there. There was a point; you could feel that everyone was, you could say praying, you could say wishing, you could say hoping, you could say giving them energy. You want so badly for it to be quick and painless for them, or quick and over.

"I mean, people were offering up their bodies, the one thing that you really possess in this world. So when you watch them make such a sacrifice, it has an impact. Standing close to the drum, it just, man, it filled you up. And when the rounds were over, the pipe carriers picked up their pipes, and to honor the dancers, they lit and passed them around.

"I was raised Catholic," Mark continued, shaking his head. "I've been around all kinds of ceremonies, but I've never seen or experienced anything of the intensity and devotion that happens at Sundance. Just the power of the prayer and the collective mind, the drum, the songs, the piercing, and the dancing. The sense of community all around."

At present day Anna Mae Camp, all eyes were on the Sundance ground. Some stopped to gaze; and some wandered to the circle, while others paused and reflected. With fresh stories as a backdrop, it was easy to imagine the ceremonial festivities. From sunrise to sundown, every day for four days. Each round lasted twenty minutes to half an hour before the dancer broke free of his skewer, and a whole new set of dancers appeared. To the north was a pole-post, where Mark said people could make a flesh offering: cutting off a piece of flesh and leaving it on the post as a tribute to the dancers and the cause of their sacrifice: the land, the water, the ancestors, new life, seven generations out.

All this to cleanse the earth, to heal the land from the ravages of strip coal mining. The wind blew our hair in our faces. The sun beat down, but the air was cold. "The people who danced here were so willing to give deeply of themselves, sacrificing so much for the sake of unity with all things in the universe. The harshness of knowing that in contrast, another culture came in and wiped out this purposeful ceremonial ground, is overwhelming," said Jim Lundeen.

Glancing at the surrounding hills, I wondered if even now, these many years later, there were binoculars aimed in our direction, if BIA and others were watching the comings and goings of the Navajo who lived nearby and the activists who visited them.

"I feel such a dark heaviness," Jim added. "This native culture holds the truth. We have a limited-time-offer here. If people, if the earth, is going to heal, to survive, we must circle back and listen with our hearts and our minds open."

For those who were there during those ceremonies and who had built relationships with the people at Big Mountain, the losses were hard to mask. The thought of the eleven Grandmothers who were arrested on the day when enforcement agencies tried to stop the Sundance by blocking the tree from coming in was hard to stomach. The agencies didn't stop the ceremony, and Sundance went on, but the bulldozers came shortly after. The Dyken brothers' faces showed the strain and the pain. As happy as they were to be here, an aura of sadness pervaded.

"Alice Benally, Elsie Begay, Roberta Blackgoat, and others," Mark explained, gazing across Anna Mae Camp, "they had heard the Hopi Rangers were coming, so they came to stand in the way. Can you imagine if people came in and bulldozed a Christian church because the government didn't like the politics of the people who were practicing their religion? To desecrate the Sundance grounds in that way was not only destroying the arbor and the land, but it was also a level of disrespect that broke some hearts. For these people to realize that money or whatever influence could turn Indian people against other Indian people was devastating.

"You can't hold the Hopi personally responsible," he added. "It was a hard road for everyone involved. It's remarkable that people have held out as long as they have and when you talk about multigenerational trauma and hurts being passed on and epigenetics—pain altering your DNA—this is something that is very present on the reservation."

Bear stood looking at the old Sundance grounds. "These people suffered being lied to, cheated on, and outright theft," he said. "They experienced genocide, have had their children taken from them, and were told that everything, from the language they spoke to the religion they practiced, even the way they looked, was less than human. It speaks volumes that they have survived and continue to hold tight to the culture they cherish."

Louise Benally lives at Anna Mae Camp. This land is her family's homestead. It's where her mother was born, where she was born, and her children. Her grandchildren were playing in the yard when we arrived. Smiling. Laughing. Building hogans out of mud and sticks, small miniatures constructed in a low-sided cardboard box.

The beauty of the moment and the threat of their removal was a paradox. The Navajo way of life, the hogans, traditionally built and revered, were facing an extinction of sorts, the same fate suffered at the Sundance grounds. These children built their history with their hands while facing an uncertain future.

"There is a strange relationship between the Hopi and Dineh people," Mark said. "As individuals, especially among traditional people of both tribes, there is mutual respect, understanding, and solidarity as indigenous neighbors. I have met many Hopi here at Anna Mae Camp, including respected elder Thomas Banyacya. They speak of cooperation and the need to stand together against the forces that created the supposed land dispute between the two nations."

"Many friendships and marriages cross tribal lines," said Bear. "We have seen and heard Hopi people speak out against the forced relocation of the Dineh who live on land that now supposedly belongs to the Hopi Tribe. Many were upset at the destruction of the Sundance grounds. The Hopi tribal government, though, backed by the BIA, is openly hostile to the Dineh, especially those who haven't signed the accommodation agreement, which permits them to remain on the land in exchange for some concessions that make it difficult to stay."

"They are confiscating livestock," Mark said, "and threatening elders."

When the Hopi rangers cruise the dirt roads, they ride in pickup trucks with antennae sticking out, wearing dark blue ball caps and sunglasses. They're always heavily armed, supported with weapons and other gear provided by the BIA. On Black Mesa, cell phones buzz and Facebook alerts sound their chain of alarm. "*Ge'*. Be quiet. Listen. Stay safe," people say.

Inside the hogan, Louise's family gathered. Three generations: Grandmother Louise, her daughter, and grandchildren sat together on the couch and on the floor. Sun seeped through the cracks in the hogan door. We visited and exchanged gifts. I noticed the handprints, left and right, memorialized on the cement living room floor, the single room that housed the family. Navajo artwork decorated the plyboard walls. A few shelves held family treasures and kitchen supplies. Boxed and canned food. Clothing. Children's toys and books. Outside, the wind blew. We could feel it through cracks that needed caulking, and the airspace around the woodstove. Still, this family smiled and welcomed us.

    The visit was too short. We didn't want to leave, and our hostess did not want us to go, but we had our deliveries to make before it got dark. Hugs were given all around, and promises were made to come again next year.

    The home of Louise's brother, John, was our next stop. When we arrived, John Benally was skinning a badger, a skill learned from his father, and grandfather before. A message meant for unwanted visitors, law enforcement, and government officials was scrawled across his front door in red ink. It read: "Corporate World is destroying the World." Several bumper stickers tacked alongside added poignancy to the handwritten note. *Free Big Mountain; Our Government has Sentenced the Navajo to Death; Edison Generating Genocide—stop the relocation, shut down the Navajo Generating Station; We Are the Clean Energy Revolution—Ban Fracking.*

    The men watched John skin the badger, while Tracy, John's companion, ushered the women into the house, happy to have female companionship. Filled with the necessities of reservation life (food, water jugs, clothing, an old box radio, and toiletry supplies), the small living space, with its well-swept dirt floor and modest kitchen, felt comfortable and homey. The land outside showed years of continuous occupation. Typical on the reservation, with no garbage pickup, what people have, they keep, trade, or sell. An old gas stove, tires, vehicle parts, plastic jugs, and containers rested against the walls of the house. Logs stretched vertically and from side to side, acted as an awning. Hardly useful during a rainstorm, but then again, this land wasn't likely to see a good rain soon. The land here was as parched as the rest at Big Mountain. The people, however, were survivors. Their house stood on the home of their ancestors. Survival was in their DNA.

7

The Multicolored Buses[22]

Oh, the buses, oh, the buses, those multicolored buses
Rollin' down life's highway, back in the day

Ayóó'áyó'ní = Love

It was late evening, our second-to-last night on the reservation. The stars shone brightly in the blackened sky, a campfire crackling in the fire pit. Bear strummed his guitar, adding melody to the night sounds—a coyote yip-howling, dogs barking, sheep shuffling in their pen. Mark fed the flames a couple of chunks of pinyon wood and then settled into his camp chair. With the Silver Eagle as a backdrop and the white bluffs of Dove Springs center stage, his stories flowed naturally back to 1979 and the reason he left home for the second time.

"We'd been living in the Beech Street house in Grafton, and I decided I wanted to go back to college. I saw an ad in *Rolling Stone* magazine that read: 'Study in the high Sierra near the beauty of Lake Tahoe.' This was the year after I'd taken my trip across the country, and the idea of living in California still appealed to me. The thought of being in the mountains, this call to enroll in a small college, fit with my mindset."

Sierra College had an excellent Philosophy Department and offered classes in religious and environmental studies, fields Mark was interested in exploring. He'd taken some courses in religious studies at the college he

---

22 Clan Dyken. Oh, the buses, oh the buses. "Hippie Trilogy."

attended in Wisconsin and had done some research on his own, and the opportunity to learn more spoke to him.

"I had dreams of leaving home back then," he said. "All the people I knew had lived in Wisconsin forever. I wanted something different."

Mark's freethinking philosophy meshed with the social and enviro-consciousness that was thriving in alternative communities and on college campuses in the many places he'd visited. Young adults all over the United States were examining the world around them. For Mark and many others, the idea that challenging "the status quo" might bring about change was intoxicating. Living outside of the grid patterned by parents and grandparents became a philosophical journey.

"I was a bit of a spiritual seeker back then," he explained, gesturing a circle with his hand. A bedazzled fabric of stars blanketed the night sky, embellishing the storyline with periodic flickers. "I was questioning the rightness and wrongness of everything," Mark said, "not only the pollution erupting from the factory in my neighborhood but the religion I grew up a part of."

Mark and Bear were once two boys dressed in white surplices and black cassocks, carrying candles, ringing the altar bells, and fetching ceremonial items for the priest. In their small church in Saukville, these tasks were a part of Sunday church services. Whether standing or sitting with their fellow altar boys, it wasn't easy to keep their hands in their laps or at their sides. There were pokes and prods while the priest wasn't looking, mischievous grins and giggles, but mostly, the boys were attentive to the detail of the ritual.

"What I learned and what I *saw* didn't always fit," Mark said. "The way that some parishioners behaved, the things they said and the way they acted inside and outside the walls of the church—I couldn't reconcile the two and that started to bother me."

A chunk of wood popped and sputtered on the fire, casting orange sparks into an asymmetrical spiral. Bear settled deeper into his chair, hugging his guitar. Mark adjusted a log on the fire and added another, then continued his story. "Around the time I was in the eighth grade, I started getting in trouble," he said. "I was staying out late, drinking, and misbehaving. Mind you, I'd been an altar boy for years, and suddenly, people I'd known within the confines of the church would no longer shake my hand. And the handshake I offered was a part of the Catholic Mass. I reached out to these people, as Jesus instructed that we do, and they flat out refused my handshake. They would turn and walk away."

Mark and Bear knew that some of the parishioners disapproved of their family's progressive ideas. Richard and Dorothy practiced the conventions of the Catholic religion, yet certain beliefs set them apart. Politically, they were more liberal than most. Socially, the immediate family came first, and as disciplinarians, they didn't adhere to the conventional "because we told you so" style of parenting. There were rules, but there were also family meetings, and decisions were made as a group. At the time when Mark and Bear began to question what they saw and heard while in service to the church, the disconnect between church teachings and the behavior of some of the congregation became harder to swallow. They began to wonder about holy mysteries and teachings outside of Catholicism and felt like there must be more to the story than what they'd learned in mass and catechism.

"Those particular gaps got wider and wider," Mark said, as he readjusted in his camp chair. "And with what I saw and felt, I just couldn't commit."

Mark's feelings toward the church and his self-assured reasoning drove him to explore life outside the boundaries of family, church, and home. He drifted further and stayed away longer, mostly with Bear, but sometimes by himself or with his friends. A few years after he swayed from the church, his mother asked a question that was difficult for him to answer. Her seventh child needed a godfather, and her choice for that honor was Mark. "I said no," Mark recalled, his voice strained. "I'll never forget the look on my mom's face. My decision crushed her."

Being a godfather was a serious responsibility. It meant standing up for the baby at his baptism, plus taking the vows and accepting the Catholic faith unequivocally. "I was eighteen years old at that point and felt like I couldn't make promises that I no longer believed in," Mark said. "Particularly when those processes involved accepting a faith I questioned for myself, let alone my new baby brother, Greg."

Not only did Dorothy want Mark as the Godfather for her youngest son, she most likely felt his disconnect and saw him pulling away. For her, there must have been sleepless nights, and tears, though never in front of her children. She was, after all, a devout Catholic, yet a mother, beyond all else. When she was younger, before marriage, Dorothy had thought of becoming a nun. But after marrying, she followed the doctrines of the church and bore eight children—plus with the last three, she risked losing her life to give birth. Dorothy was more than a church member. She took part in most every church activity. She and Richard tithed all their lives. They barely had the money to do so but gave ten percent, regardless of whether the kids needed new shoes or a trip to the dentist. They just made it work.

The central principle of tithing is that what we do with our money shows where our heart lies. Matthew 6:21 says, "For where your treasure is, there your heart will be also." As with other Christian denominations, tithing is a choice, but also a responsibility. The Dyken family took that responsibility, and that of their children's education, seriously.

"I remember when we left Catholic school," said Bear, laying aside his guitar and joining the conversation. "The school was closing, and Mom moved us to public school. I was butting heads with my teacher at that point," he recalled. "Also, our priest was speaking about things and making decisions that Mom didn't necessarily believe in, so at one point, she moved us all into public school and got herself elected to the school board. I had one semester in Grand View School in Waubeka, the second half of fourth grade, and then moved on to Thomas Jefferson Middle School."

"There was all of that," Mark said, "and somewhere along the line, Mom realized that women were second-class citizens within the Catholic church. There was a lack of respect for their ability to lead or be responsible for church policy. Only men could be priests and even the nuns of the order lived by their mandates and under their ultimate authority."

Dorothy Dyken was a "reluctant" feminist, according to Mark. She listened and paid attention to what was happening around her socially and politically. In the 1970s, the feminist movement grew. In politics, in the media, in academia, and in private households, women's liberation was a hot topic. Feminists marched, lobbied, and protested. Women spoke up, acted, and reacted to issues of injustice, the most intense fight being for passage of the ERA (Equal Rights Amendment).[23]

---

[23] The text of the Equal Rights Amendment is: "Section 1. Equality of rights under the law shall not be denied or abridged by the United States or by any state on account of sex. Section 2. The Congress shall have the power to enforce, by appropriate legislation, the provisions of this article. Section 3. This amendment shall take effect two years after

Richard was a layperson in the church but didn't *love* it the way Dorothy did. She was a multi-tasker, managing the household, caring for the kids, attending community and church meetings and other functions. Opinionated and feisty, she was not one to hold back. As with the young Mexican girl she helped so long ago, she spoke out when she felt there was an injustice that needed correcting.

"Still, it came as a surprise when Mom announced that she had decided to leave the church," Mark said. "After she made her final decision, Dad was right behind her. It was strange too, because as devout as Mom was, only one person came to her and asked her why she'd made her choice to go, and I remember her being hurt and miffed by that."

"I'm sure there was a lot to her decision," Bear added. "I was a teenager when she kicked the church. Mark and I were just not into it anymore. As Mark said, the whole altar boy thing wasn't cutting it for us. We were surprised by her decision, but proud of her for making it."

At that time, along with the drinking and pot smoking and staying out late, Mark's grades were slipping. He and Bear would disappear for long periods of time. "I remember when we started skipping out on catechism," Mark said, "taking the family car and saying we were going to church, and taking off instead and going to a fast food restaurant or something. There were no *wow* moments, no joy for us there. We just weren't into it anymore, and were questioning everything."

There were parts of being a Catholic that left impressions, however, like the Stations of the Cross, the teachings of Christ, and especially the parables. As a young boy, Mark would sit with his hands in his lap, tapping his fingers to the priest's masterful inflections as he told stories about Christ's life, demonstrating examples of holiness, mercy, and love. He and Bear observed the holy water poured over the priest's hands and learned what the drink offerings meant, and what the blessings meant. "I came to appreciate those kinds of ceremony and tradition," Mark said. "Later in life, I recognized why the ritual of the sweat lodge, like gathering the right rocks, and the proper use of water and steam and herbs was necessary."

Ritual resonated with the brothers. Perhaps the early exposure to ceremony, or being naturally attuned to the importance of it, drew them.

---

the date of ratification."

It *did* something to them. They deeply felt the importance of those types of experiences.

"As I said, at the time I left home," Mark explained, "I was a self-righteous nineteen-year-old. I was doing all these things, and saying to myself, 'Who am I? What do I want to do with my life?'"

As Mark explained it, in another lifetime, he could have been a priest or preacher. "It's a world I seem to understand," he said. "I believe there is more than what we see, but I can't figure out how anyone believes that they know the true nature of the spiritual world. I've had fleeting glimpses, but perhaps greater minds touch this level of spirituality on a regular basis."

Mark practiced meditation on the road while hitchhiking but grew more serious after attending religious studies classes at Sierra College, specifically a Science of Creative Intelligence class, which included an off-campus group focusing on transcendental meditation. The study of transcendental meditation allowed Mark to further his belief in the importance of detaching from anxiety, promoting harmony in one's own life and with others. It fit well with his philosophical viewpoint and has remained a daily practice ever since.

While attending Sierra College, Mark met Laura Hardin, a transfer student from Colorado. Laura and Mark had a creative writing class together, and Mark had seen Laura around campus playing folk music with her sister Judy—Laura on guitar and Judy on mandolin. Mark would set up his drum kit in the quad and Laura, shouldering her guitar, would wander over and listen to him play. "I was smitten," Laura admitted later. "I pretty much stalked him throughout the day. I positioned myself in the upstairs library that overlooked the main campus buildings. As soon as I spotted Mark, I'd corner him in some subtle way. Yeah, there was competition for his attention, and I was like a prowling cat!"

Laura had curly brown hair, brown eyes, and a great smile; she was a talented guitar player and singer. She was smart and funny, and she was also a good conversationalist, all qualities Mark admired. The two struck up a friendship, which then grew into a relationship and the shared dream of pursuing life on the road. The notion of an alternative lifestyle, combining music and travel, and finding enlightenment beyond what college life provided, appealed to them both.

"The idea of getting a bus came about after reading a few books about travel," Mark said. "I was encouraged to drop out of college by reading *On the Road* by Jack Kerouac, and a book called *Vagabonding in America* by Ed Buryn and Stephanie Mines. A book called *Rolling Homes* was also a significant influence, as well as the stories of Stephen Gaskin and The Farm in Tennessee."

Filled with color pictures, the book, *Rolling Homes* provided a cornucopia of ideas for buses converted into living spaces. Featured artisans put their creative minds to work, building small homes on wheels. Stained glass windows, a variety of woods, tile, and antique hardware added character and charm to these homes. As was typical in the 1970s, the colorful cruisers rolled down the highways, limited only by funds and imagination. *Rolling Homes* was the perfect book to propel Mark and Laura into the realm of bus transformation.

Mark's recollection of *Rolling Homes* and Stephen Gaskin brought back pleasant memories of my time spent in San Francisco and my college years just north of the city. Stephen Gaskin was a hippie icon, of sorts, in the 1960s. Though I didn't know him, I knew *of* him. There was often talk about his revolutionary ideas that were in sync with the values of us back-to-the-landers. Stephen and his friends took the notion of developing an alternative community seriously, and in 1971 drove eighty school buses and other vehicles carrying 320 hippies to Tennessee. They went with a positive attitude and mission: to create a place where they could live a nature-centered lifestyle. As they traveled, the banner on their band bus read: "Out to Save the World!" The reasoning was contagious, and their cry to minimize possessions and maximize creative consciousness was a happening.

Bear too, was digging the vibe of the hippie lifestyle. Though still in school, he was ready to try something new. "Yeah, I was up north, freezing my ass off," he said, "slugging it out and working toward an Associate's Degree at Nicolet Community College. I finished three semesters, and then Mark called and said, 'Hey, come on out here. We'll put the band back together in California.' So I hitchhiked out there."

In the Dyken household, one son after the other was leaving Dorothy's nest, not in the traditional way, but hitchhiking across the country. "Keep your vision and your dreams before you all of the time. Remember to take care of yourself along the way," she told them, her motherly concern reaching out.

"Stories of the road. I've got a few," Bear recalled, chuckling. "Like the time I hitchhiked to the Mexican border ingesting peyote as we traveled. Somehow, on that trip, I became a beekeeper and traded the bee pollen for more peyote. On another trip, I hitched to the Rainbow Gathering in Washington, traded the last of the peyote for a ride out of there and ended up as the judge for a cherry pie contest."

In the 1960s and 1970s, it was common to see longhaired, carefree college-age kids along roadsides, thumbs to the wind. Some came with dogs, some with backpacks or knapsacks, and some with nothing more than the clothes on their backs. By trial and error, thumbing rides on the highway was a learned skill. As Mark mentioned when telling his hitchhiking experience, "the way you look, how you handle the conversations, the manner in which you choose your rides, all affect the outcome of the experience." Traveling alone, Mark dealt with issues of loneliness and for the first time in his life, being without family. Bear did it a bit differently. When he hit the road, he had company.

"I had my girlfriend, Jeanne, with me that first trip out," Bear said. "Hitchhiking to California from Wisconsin was a positive experience, all the way around, but as happens when you're hitching, our plans kept shifting. Scenarios constantly change on the road, depending on a multitude of variables, so when we finally got to Lake Tahoe, when I finally saw Mark, he and I were, let's say, pretty happy to see each other. It was an epic reunion, to say the least."

In the firelight, the smiles on the faces of the brothers reinforced the memory of their 1979 reunion's sweet, raucous, joyful noise, as imagined in my mind. It seemed like a rare gift that these men spent the majority of their youth side by side, and that their bond was genuine and not fractionalized by the years they spent together since that long-ago meeting-up. The family atmosphere of Clan Dyken events is real. As Liz Tree said early on in Williams, Oregon: "It's more than the music...their songs are a part of our bones. Mark and Bear are like brothers to all of us."

In 1979, a new version of the Dyken family started to grow, centered on a desire to reestablish the band and the ideals of commitment to one's dreams, plus the freedom to claim and follow one's passion that Richard and Dorothy instilled in their children.

"So, as a group, we bought this big old bus," Mark said. "I had no idea how to drive the thing. I just got in it and drove. It was a new adventure, a little like being a hitchhiker, but now we had expenses. We would work as we traveled. We bought an airless paint sprayer, and we'd get jobs painting houses. We did tree planting. We did all kinds of things. And in between, we'd get jobs playing music. We'd stop wherever, in a coffee shop, on the street, or if we were at tree planting camp, we'd set up and we'd say, 'We'll play music.'"

Mark's explanation summarized the outcome of a six-month creative explosion. The acquisition and renovation of the bus and the revitalization of a garage band. Loose, free-form practice sessions took place in the living room of their condominium with minimal equipment: Mark's drum kit, Bear's guitar, Laura's acoustic guitar, and Phil's bass guitar. The brothers, their girlfriends, and friend Phil were living communally, rolling into parties on weekends and setting up, belting out their songs and showing people a good time.

"We were writing some of our own music," Bear said, "but like most bands, we started with covers, picking music that we liked, and then we progressed into writing more originals."

The bus the Dykens bought was an old fire camp search-and-rescue bus, purchased in significant disrepair from a private party. Along the side, big red letters declared SEARCH AND RESCUE. Mark, Bear, Laura, and their friends dismantled the bench seats to build sleeping platforms and a kitchen area with a stove and countertops. They added a closet with a toilet and a woodstove for heat. They banged some things with hammers and twisted other things with wrenches, so the remodel became a belabored fun-fest. Ideas came with the puff of a joint while music blared via radio and cassettes—these long-haired young hippies, radiant in the glow of their creativity.

As time went on, the desire for travel and music meshed with the Dykens' political and environmental consciousness. Jimmy Carter was President. In January of 1979, the United States established full diplomatic relations with China, and the state of Ohio agreed to pay $675,000 to the families of those killed in the Kent State shootings. It was the Year of the Child, and the Bee Gees hosted a concert held at the United Nations General Assembly with all funds going to UNICEF. Actions related to the environment were erupting across the country. A grassroots movement percolated around Harry Caudill's book *Night Comes to the Cumberlands*. Published in 1963, it described the devastation of eastern Kentucky by the coal industry as a human and an environmental catastrophe. Greenpeace activists defied whalers' harpoons, and clean air and water activists tried to stop pollution through action-based protests and emotional pleas. The contaminated water sample that Mark and Bear deposited in the mail and sent to the Department of Natural Resources many years earlier had sparked a small flame within them. That initial action was a stepping-stone. Their DNA, a history of family activism, their father's perseverance and their mother's empathy stoked the inner light as they expanded their geographic and social experience.

Things were changing, both in the United States and around the world. Visits to National Parks jumped from twelve million in 1946 to 282 million by 1979. The American lifestyle included forays in nature promoted by the burgeoning "back to nature" philosophy, the whole-food/clean eating revolution, and a focus on caring for a planet that was showing the wear and tear of a post-war industrialized society. Early key environmental legislation included the Clean Air Act (1963), the Water Quality Act (1965), the Wild and Scenic Rivers Act (1968), the National Environmental Policy Act (1970), the Resource Conservation and Recovery Act (1970), the Federal Environmental Pesticide Control Act (1972), the Endangered Species Act (1973), and the Toxic Substances Control Act (1976).

At the end of 1979, the group of five left Lake Tahoe on the bus. The experience of living communally and sharing close quarters in their condominium seemed to have worked. The hippie lifestyle still appealed to the Dyken brothers, Laura, and their friends, drawing them into whatever came next. It wasn't always easy, however. The concept of fair distribution, who's doing what, who's not doing enough, and who's doing too much was challenging, but together they worked it out. Making decisions on where they might travel and what route they might take involved a group decision. The whys and where-to-goes of each venture inevitably changed, and the twists and turns were open-ended.

The Multicolored Buses

The acquisition of the bus and the need for fuel, food, and supplies for five people required money. As they traveled the countryside, they'd stop here and there to work, painting, tree planting, picking fruit—whatever odd jobs were available where they landed. They were young and energetic, "just out there making a go of it," Mark said. They had no credentials, no license, but they had acquired the paint sprayer and would bid jobs for painting apartments, houses, whatever. They worked hard and did a good job. People trusted them.

From California, they traveled to Arizona, and then across the United States through Kansas and the farm belt. Their long-term destination was Florida, culminating in a planned visit with Grandma and Grandpa Dyken, who had moved to Naples to retire in the late 1960s. Short-term, they stopped anywhere that caught their eye, usually somewhere with a hot spring.

"Hot springs were our thing," Bear said. "Any excuse to stop and explore a new spring was a reason to change our course of travel."

College campuses were also of interest. By this time, hand drumming was big among the group, and they would park the bus and parade around university malls and classrooms, pounding on their clay-bottom Doumbek drums, inviting curiosity and encouraging others to join in the fun. "We were done with college at that point and so convinced we were doing it right," Laura later explained. "We were like, hey, look at us. We're out here, and you're in there, studying your asses off, for what? I guess you could say we were feeling the freedom of the road. We were a circus," she said, laughing.

Long hair, don't care. Students stared from behind closed windows, curious, some throwing a peace sign, some with mouths agape. Barefoot and laughing, the Dykens and friends then reloaded the bus, floating on a new high, exhilarated by their freedom and more convinced than ever that their lifestyle was the right way to go.

The lyrics from Bear's new trilogy of hippie songs set the scene better than any explanation he could have given:

> *Oh the buses, oh the buses, those multicolored buses*
> *Rollin' down life's highway, back in the day*
> *There was sunlight through the tie-dye curtains*
> *Gypsy bells were jinglin'*
> *On those multicolored buses, back in the day*

As they traveled and practiced their music, the group developed a style of their own. They continued to play cover songs but often played original tunes composed by Bear. "I was always interested in topical songs," Bear recalled. "They have a certain power in their intent to actively involve listeners in current world issues. Even in the early days, I wrote and created songs and art as a way to process and intercede with reality, using the art as a practical force, a way to focus and amplify intent. Later, I was influenced by the book *Singing for Power* about the Tohono O'odham people of the southwest. These indigenous people are one of those tribes that straddle the border between the United States and Mexico. Their wealth is in their song. Each tribal member has a whole repertoire, and the way they do battle with their enemies is to stay up all night singing. Singing for power. They sing of the world as if it exists the way they want it to exist, and by doing that they keep reinforcing their belief and since the world is vibratory, the singers are generating the vibration the way they want it to be."

On the heels of Bear's early compositions came his new generation of trademark songs with thought-provoking lyrics and a danceable beat. Friend, activist, and fellow musician Darryl Cherney once said, "Bear can convey the urgency of the issue while painting with broad strokes the overall injustices of our times. He can pick out the quintessential components of the issue without getting bogged down in the minutiae. My favorite song of his is 'In Search of Enemies'[24] because in that title alone Bear sums up one of the key problems of the entire world in just four words. 'Heal These Global Wounds' is another great one, where rather than bemoan the awful problems of the world he offers a sing-a-long prayer for action. He manages to capture the spirit of the Native Americans' struggle without any cultural appropriation. Part of his authenticity comes from him being a homesteader and a family man. He doesn't live in his head. He lives in his heart."

In those early days, they were the Search and Rescue Band, naming themselves after the Search and Rescue bus. With their limited equipment, they played some bars, and as they traveled, they would set up at any place that would allow them the space to play. As with all musicians

---

24 Clan Dyken. Where do the weapon makers go? "Search of Enemies." *Shundahai*. CD. Track 6.

starting out, the road became their home and provisional agenda, including stops at Gaskin's Farm in Tennessee and at Rainbow Gatherings.

While Stephen Gaskin's *family* settled on their farm in Tennessee, the Rainbow Gathering was an annual event. The Farm family's philosophies were founded on their belief in nonviolence and pacifism, the importance of truth and compassion, and their respect for all religious practices. They developed specialized techniques in natural childbirth and midwifery, alternative technology, and organic farming to name a few. Alternatively, the Rainbow *family* met each year during the week of July fourth. These organized gatherings drew a community of people to remote forests around the world, where people met and shared their like-minded philosophy: peace, harmony, freedom, and respect for one another and the planet. Anyone could attend, and participants called themselves the *Rainbow Family*. The family also held regional gatherings with the same intent.

"By this time, our bass player, Phil, couldn't hang," Mark said. "He told us, 'you guys are just too optimistic. You think everything can work out.'"

After visiting Florida, the Dyken group headed to Wisconsin with the idea of becoming a serious band. Brother Gary was developing as a bass player by then and was interested in playing professionally, so again they had all the elements: lead guitar, bass player, rhythm guitar, drummer, and singers. Bear continued to write, so they had original material. The idea was to go back to California and play the festival circuit. It was the 1980s by now, and they figured they could head there and find a piece of land.

"Why were we drawn to the hippie movement and others were not?" Bear questioned. "It's hard to say. My family, the way we lived, the things we learned, all had a part in it, I think. My conservative Lutheran grandmother, Grandma Dyken, was so supportive of our passions. By the time my grandfather died, she was branching out spiritually, questioning everything. She had these expansive spiritual yearnings and wanted to join Yogananda's ashram. She was open to exploring and displayed that in so many ways. She was a little *hippie* herself, I suppose."

In the 1960s, Ken Kesey ushered in the era of psychedelic drugs, mind-expanding experiences shared by a generation of young people through stories about the hippie subculture. In 1964, Kesey's followers, a group calling themselves the Merry Pranksters, set out on a cross-country trip in an old bus they dubbed Further. The bus, painted with a kaleidoscope of graffiti, took the LSD-worshiping Pranksters to the World's Fair in New York City before returning to Kesey's ranch in La Honda, California. There, the Pranksters conducted "Acid Tests," wherein attendees would receive a cup of "electric" LSD-laced Kool-Aid. A band called the Warlocks provided the music at many of these events—a group that would later become known as the Grateful Dead. Tom Wolfe's book, *The Electric Kool-Aid Acid Test,* became a literary event, changing the way the world looked at the nonfiction writing style, and opening another door to other books that spoke of psychotropic plants like peyote. *The Teaching of Don Juan: a Yaqui Way of Knowledge* by Carlos Castaneda[25] not only incorporated the use of psychotropic plants, but it also brought to the surface the internal/external search for knowledge so many youths of that time desired, and the teachings of the Native American way of thinking.

In the 1970s, psychotropic plants continued to play a role in the lives and decisions of "seekers of truth" and adventurous spirits around the world. Peyote, mescaline, and psilocybin mushrooms were drugs of choice, with users intent on mind-expansion and understanding the natural ways of living as stated by Castaneda and others.

"Back when we were fruit tramps," Mark said, "living in the desert, traveling around, we got ahold of little bits of peyote. Not enough to experience the plant as in a peyote ceremony, but enough to feel it, feel what it was about."

"Yeah, high times," Bear added, his eyes shining and full of mischief.

"There *was* one time, we were playing music, and Bear was riding

---

[25] The book is divided into two sections. The first section, *The Teachings,* is a first person narrative that documents Castaneda's initial interactions with don Juan. He speaks of his encounters with Mescalito, a teaching spirit inhabiting all peyote plants, divination with lizards and flying using the *yerba del diablo* or Jimson weed, and turning into a blackbird using humito a smoked powder containing psilocybin mushrooms. The second, *A Structural Analysis,* is an attempt, Castaneda says, at "disclosing the internal cohesion and the cogency of Don Juan's teachings.

this wave," Mark said. "This happened much later in our careers, but still…"

"I felt the music sucking me off the stage. It was as if there were this huge wave pushing me along, and I had no choice but to go where it took me. I figured since I was doomed to follow, I might as well jump, and so I did—clear off the stage to the ground."

Mark laughed. "Yeah, that was classic Bear style. He was into it, going for it."

After leaving Wisconsin, Laura realized that she was pregnant. Though welcomed, the news altered the group's plans a bit. Back in California, the band split up for a while, and she and Mark moved into a house in Watsonville. With the Search and Rescue bus parked in the driveway, however, the conduit to the dream was never far away.

While Mark and Laura settled in Watsonville, Bear and Jeanne went on a bicycle adventure. For six months, they traveled throughout the Southwest from Moab, Utah, to Tucson, Arizona.

"Down at Healing Waters Hot Springs outside of Tucson, we met a Vietnam vet named Harry Free," Bear said. "He would take a few steps and then look up and then take a few more steps, all hunched over. We were going in and he was coming out, and he looked at me and introduced himself and said, 'When you get to Tucson, look me up.' He wrote his name and phone number on a piece of paper and gave it to me. 'I've got something for you,' he said.

"Jeanne and I were both really skinny," Bear continued, "and she was pretty tired of bike touring. A month later, we bike into Tucson and were in a laundromat, and I was going through my pockets and found the piece of paper. So we called him up."

As Bear found out later, Harry Free left Vietnam, as many vets did, with emotional and physical disabilities, but he also came home with the *Chinese Oracle: I Ching, the Book of Changes,* the oldest of the Chinese classics. "You throw these yarrow sticks," Bear explained, "or you can also throw coins in a certain way, and you count, and they have a system of sixty-four hexagrams made by combining trigrams."

In I Ching, the way the sticks or coins land creates a picture of how energy is flowing throughout a certain situation. The hexagrams are not so much static pictures as ways to move, to create, receive, and sustain.

So when Bear met up with Harry, he gave Bear this book. "He showed me how to do it," Bear explained. "He showed me how the book worked, gave me three pennies and said, 'you're on your own.'"

This exchange with Harry and the I Ching shaped Bear's life, as he recalled. While walking around Tucson, he found rocks with the word *FREE* written on them. "All of these rocks came from Harry Free. Harry gave the book out to many, many people. He was working on such a warrior level, indirectly affecting a lot of people's consciousness. He was an unsung hero, a trippy looking guy with long hair and a Fu Manchu mustache, super skinny and with that bent-over stance."

In Tucson, Jeanne and Bear split up, and she left with a man she'd met at the Rainbow Festival. "So here I was, in Tucson, deeply in love with a woman who walked away from me. I should have been 'closed for business,' because when you're vulnerable and broken-hearted, danger and chaos enter your life," Bear teased, speaking of another woman he met at that time.

"I'm at my house in Watsonville," said Mark, "It's sometime in June, and the doorbell rings. I go to the door and there stand Bear and this girl I don't know."

"She was beautiful. Stunningly beautiful," Bear said, smiling.

"So I open the door, and there were Bear and this girl, their eyes fricking lit. What hallucinogen were you on again?" Mark asked Bear. "You were freaking lit!"

"Peyote, which brings me back to the hitchhiking stories," Bear said, chuckling. "I hitchhiked down to this little town called Arivaca to meet a friend, my street urchin, orphaned, super talented guitar player friend, and we were going to do peyote. We did that, and then wandered into the little town and a town festival, and the first thing I saw was this woman selling bags of bee pollen, all different colors." Bear took off his hat and adjusted his bandana. "As we talked with this woman, we found out that her husband had just died, and her son had gone off to university. Her daughter was allergic to bees and couldn't help her harvest the honey, so she needed help. We offered to help her with her bees, and in exchange, she traded us bee pollen. We then took the honey to health food stores back in Phoenix, Tempe, and Tucson. Meanwhile, another buddy had all this spirulina, so he rented a to-code kitchen at the Tempe Co-op, and we made the very first spirulina bee bars. I drew a little logo of Aunt Bee with tennis shoes. He ended up selling that recipe to Knudsen. Those were seriously some of the best spirulina bars I've ever tasted."

"Yeah," Mark agreed. "To this day, I'd say those were the best energy bars I've ever tasted."

"So we were connected with that co-op in Tempe," Bear said, "and there was a guy who was the produce manager who knew these Indians down in Gila, New Mexico, and so we would go down there and trade the bee pollen for peyote. I swapped my bicycle for an old guitar, and this new girlfriend and I decided to hitchhike to a Rainbow Gathering in Washington, with a huge sack of peyote and a bunch of grapefruits."

Bear laughed again. "We built a sweat lodge in your backyard on that trip," he said to Mark, "and stayed in it until the fire department showed up to hassle us."

"This was 1981. You were twenty-two at that time, and I was twenty-three," said Mark. "In Watsonville, on July fifteenth of that year, Peta, our son was born. We decided on a homebirth, so with the help of a midwife, Laura delivered at home."

"Yeah," Bear agreed. "That's right. We left just before the baby was born."

As Mark and Laura settled into becoming first-time parents, Bear and his new friend hitchhiked to the Rainbow Gathering in Washington state. "This girl was trouble, trouble with big capital letters," Bear said. "She got sick with giardia at the festival and needed to get out of there, so I traded peyote to a guy for a ride for the two of us. We made it to this little town where some folks were having a cherry pie contest. While my friend slept, I judged the pie contest and had a blast tasting all the cherry pies." As Bear recalled, he left the festival alone and hitchhiked to Lake Tahoe. By this point, Phil, the bass guitarist/friend, had bought a second bus, a 1949 Dodge with a Hemi engine (no back brakes, only front brakes) and had parked it in a trailer park in Tahoe City with no real thought of living there. At Phil's invitation, Bear moved into the bus, bought a Centurion bicycle to get him back and forth to work, and got a job as a framer building a house.

"I was the guy who would nail the top plates," Bear said. "At first, the building crew made fun of me and what they called my 'bird seed' food, but after a while, they'd say, 'What's that stuff you're eating?' because they saw that I had all this energy. Also, at the Rainbow Gathering, I'd met these people who were doing a breathing technique called Rebirthing,[26] and there was this guy named Leonard Orr who was having seminars and teaching this technique. When I made enough money, I quit that job and drove that bus out to one of Leonard's seminars at the Sierraville Hot Springs."

The pools at Sierraville Hot Springs were open twenty-four hours a day. There were indoor pools and outdoor pools and all were clothing optional. For centuries, Native Americans regarded the area as sacred and healing. In the time Bear was there, hippies gathered, attending classes and workshops. The vibe was liberating—walking barefoot in little or no clothing, sliding into soothing pools of warm spring water, and cleansing afterward in cold refreshing plunges.

"I stayed there for two weeks," Bear said, his honeyed voice reflecting the serenity of the experience. "It was one of those times in my life when I was carefree and unencumbered by a relationship—ready to absorb everything about health and consciousness."

When Bear left the hot springs, he got as far as Colfax when the bus, aptly named Behemoth, threw a rod. He called Mark, who came with their brother Gary to help. "After two weeks spent rebuilding the engine in a parking lot, we left Colfax. I was driving behind Bear at this point," Mark said. "Remember, this bus had bad brakes. Flames were shooting out of the exhaust pipe, and I kept thinking, man this thing is going to blow up. I kept flashing my lights, but Bear didn't see me. Once we got to Auburn, it died completely. We pulled out the stove and anything worth saving to put in Gary's bus, a school bus he'd purchased in Wisconsin that'd he'd named Betty Lou."

On August 15, 1981, Mark and Laura married. They said their vows on Manresa Beach in Watsonville, California, standing barefoot and dressed in white robes sewn by Laura. Family, including Laura's father, Larry Hardin, Richard and Dorothy, and Mark's brothers and sisters circled them, each reading an offering meaningful to Mark and Laura. Bear performed a song he had written for the wedding, called "Help You Bear Your Load." People wandering on the beach walked closer as Bear

---

26 Rebirthing is a breathing technique. It brings awareness not only our unconsciously held beliefs and emotions but also the bonds we have with our bodies, our relationships, and our world.

played, and the family opened the circle, welcoming them in.

"At that point, Peta started crying," Laura later shared, "and I had to get real. I was a mom. I had to get out of that gown and feed my baby."

A few months after the wedding, the group talked about reforming the band. While at Sierraville Hot Springs, Bear had met Bill Rogers, a showman and a keyboard player with scheduled gigs but no musicians to play them. "He had this concept," said Bear, "for what he called the Allright Family Band, so I thought, *great, we have a family band with no gigs to play. Bill's idea is going to work out.*"

Bill had recorded an album. He had experience with a working band, and his concept fit the mold for a "family" traveling and playing music, so in the fall of 1981, he and the Search and Rescue Band meshed their sounds into what became the Allright Family Band.

Though they continued to play together for a while, Mark, Bear, Laura, and Gary eventually split off, preferring musical independence. The last gig they played with Bill was a benefit for the owner of the Village Sauna in Fair Oaks, California. At that venue, in December 1981, Gary met Linda, a massage therapist, and Bear met and fell in love with a folk-song singer named Harmony.

With the addition of Harmony, there were now five players in the band. Along with Mark and Laura's baby, Peta, and Harmony's four-year-old daughter, Suneca, the group, including Linda, traveled in two buses—the Search and Rescue bus and Gary's bus, Betty Lou. From Fair Oaks, they drove to California's Coachella Valley, where Harmony had connections for fruit picking work. While there, Bear bought a converted school bus, the third in their caravan. He painted the body Navajo white, turquoise, and yellow and painted a camel on the marquis above the windshield.

Mark, Laura, and Peta were in the Search and Rescue bus; Bear, Harmony, and Suneca, in the bus they named Sahabi; and Gary and Linda, in their bus, Betty Lou. Recognizing a need for alternate transportation, the family then bought three Volkswagens, towing them behind the buses as they traveled. From the West Coast to the East Coast and back again, they continued to work odd jobs and played music anywhere they could manage. Following an I Ching reading, "Return of the Light," they changed their band name to Searchlight.

After a tree planting job in 1982, the band drove to Durango,

Colorado to get paid. The Dykens had been there before and liked the area. It seemed an ideal spot to nest for a bit—mountainous and serene, with an old west history but contemporary vibe. The buses were in need of repair, and with their growing families to support, money for living expenses had run low. Three children were traveling with the group now: Peta, Sunny, and Gary and Linda's new baby, Adom. After spending some time in a small campsite on some abandoned land, Laura's sister Judy, who had joined them while traveling, found a job caretaking a piece of property that was large enough for all three buses to park comfortably for an extended period.

The group found more tree planting jobs, and Mark and Laura opened a restaurant and juice bar, introducing their health food diet to the citizens of Durango. The front page of the hand-written menu partially read: "We at Nathy's firmly believe in the adage, 'you are what you eat.' Good food is essential to health. Happy, healthy people enjoy a fuller life and help create a beautiful planet." The introduction was signed, "The Dyken Family and Friends."

Everyone worked at the restaurant, but Mark and Laura ran it, Mark managing the front of the house and Laura working as the head chef. Bear and Harmony traveled back and forth from Coachella Valley bringing fresh citrus and dates to Nathy's. When in Coachella, they worked on organic farms, and in the spring Bear worked as a palmero, hand pollinating date trees. Spanish-speaking farm workers taught him some Spanish, and with that, how to climb the male trees, collect the pollen and then climb the female trees, dusting the flowers with powder-puff like applicators. When the dates were ready to pick, Bear and other palmeros hung suspended from chain harnesses, swinging from one side of the tree to the other, hacking off stalks laden with sweet, ripe, wrinkly dates.

In Durango, after the restaurant closed each evening and when Bear and Harmony were home, the Searchlight Band played music at the Southwest Coffee Shop. The owner of the coffee shop hired the band because he was tired of paying ASCAP (the American Society of Composers, Authors, and Publishers) and BMI (Broadcast Music, Inc.) for royalties: Searchlight played original music. It was a paid gig, and the patrons dug the band's vibe. Here, in a regularly scheduled venue, Searchlight focused on growing their sound. "This is where I learned that I could play electric guitar rather than acoustic," said Laura. "I was inspired and excited, but I was also pregnant with our second baby, caring for our son Peta, and running the restaurant. There wasn't an extra hour in the day to practice and play with the group, so I decided to step back for a while."

"We'd been playing at open mics," Bear said. "We kept getting better and better, and composing and arranging different music, but didn't have the venue for it, until the coffee house. At that point, we opened up to some different ideas. We did this Halloween event in and around the coffee shop, where we had a wicked drum parade, and we got all dressed up crazy."

"People went bananas," said Mark. "We got pinned up against a wall at one point, fearing for our safety. People were going wild with these drums, and we weren't smart enough to stop playing, you know, but it got hairy. We literally had to escape that place."

"While in Durango, we met an outstanding guitar player named Jon Baumgartner," Bear said. "There were people along the way who showed me things, but this guy took me under his wing and boosted me along. He was the best I'd ever met."

"Gary's wife, Linda, told us about the Whole Earth Festival in Davis, California," said Mark, "so I sent the organizers a recording of us playing live music, and they hired us. We had the idea that we could not only play music at the festival but earn extra cash by operating a food booth with some of the same menu items and nutritious food we served at Nathy's."

In the mall near Nathy's Resturant, they met a saxophonist named Ken Nahan. With Ken, the band packed up their buses and drove across the country again. "We'd broken away from Bill Rogers," Bear said, "and were trying to 'mismanage' our careers. Landing at the Whole Earth Festival put us in exactly the right spot."

After nearly two years of living in Durango, the group headed west to Southern California. They worked picking fruit and then headed east again, to Saukville, Wisconsin. All three buses made the journey in the summer of 1984 for sister Julie's wedding. Afterward, Mark and Laura stayed behind when the others returned to the road. Their daughter, Kiri, was born in the family home in Mark and Bear's old bedroom in November 1984.

"I was picking apples in an apple orchard, driving a tractor, and working as an activist for the nuclear freeze movement," Mark said, "and it was right then when Ronald Reagan was elected. I was pounding on doors, raising money for the nuclear weapons freeze and campaigning for Walter Mondale, but really against Ronald Reagan. I quit the campaign thing after the election and worked in a steel mill. The Search and Rescue bus was at the end of its road, so after Kiri was born and winter had passed, we bought an International Harvest bus, did a significant conversion, and drove back out west. I didn't name that bus but called it the Corn Binder."

Bear and Harmony had their first baby, Silas, on May 17, 1984. "Yeah, we thought he would be born at the Whole Earth Festival," Bear said, smiling. "But he refused to come out. So we went to stay at Linda's sister's house, and he wouldn't come out there either. We headed for a cabin in the national forest, thinking that would be calmer, more personal, but we couldn't get to it in the snow, so we found a place in the national forest, and we had Si. He didn't want to come out in the city, you see. He was waiting for just the right spot."

A year later, Bear and Harmony were back in Coachella Valley, awaiting the birth of another child. Bear worked picking dates while Harmony cared for Suneca and Silas. Their bus, Sahabi, was undergoing major renovations, including the addition of a second story. In the meantime, they rented an Airstream trailer, a comfortable place in the midst of a "sweet oasis," according to Harmony. "There was an artisan well with a pond for swimming and a rose garden," she said. "I chose Pachelbel Canon in D as birth music. It was very soothing, and as my labor progressed, I began to chant with the music. On July 20 of 1985, about 10:30 a.m., I was pushing this baby out of me, and Bear was there ready to catch. I had planned to call the baby Sage, but when I first held her, saw her thick dark hair and her sweet little mouth, I decided that she was a Rosebud—Rosebud Darshana Dyken."

While traveling, birthing babies, and playing the festival circuit, the Dykens' band began to mesh again, and a buzz developed around their music. After playing a gig at the Whole Earth Festival in Davis in 1986, they changed their name once more. Still feeling the rightness of the concept of a family band, they played with words, different iterations for *family*, finally settling on *clan*. They were the Dyken family. Clan Dyken. It fit and stuck.

Soon after, a friend named Madeline said, "'Hey, if you're looking for a place, I'm living on this land trust, and you guys can come and stay there too,'" Bear recollected. "So we drove our buses to this land trust in the foothills of the Sierra Nevada, just outside San Andreas."

On the land trust, blackberries grew wild in gullies and near creeks, and the hills were covered by lush underbrush, manzanita, cedar, oak, and Bull Pine forest. Bear, Harmony, Gary, and Linda decided to stay, settle, and build homes there. Mark and Laura chose to move closer to town. After so long on the road, according to Laura, she was ready for hot water and a washing machine and felt strongly about placing her children in public school.

For every hairy gnome with a rolling home / Hippie mamas with their kids in tow / Hair braided, barefooted, beads bouncing on their breasts. These words, written by Bear years later, reflect a portrait of those times. Since they'd left home, Mark and Bear went from being leather tramps to rubber tramps, following the highways and byways first on foot and then by bus. There were bumps in the road, happy and sad times, but the buses rolled and the family grew. Somewhere along the line, the Native American phrase "to live and work for the benefit of the seventh generation" resonated for them on a deeper level, and became the tie-in between their growing children, the human condition, and issues relating to environmental protection. As Clan Dyken transitioned along the journey, the buses became the vehicle, and activism became the cause.

Big Mountain waited, just out of view.

Search and Rescue Bus, Sierra Nevada College (1979)
Paul Johnston, Marguerite Conti, Jeanne Klose, Mark Dyken,
Laura Hardin, Phil Fellenz, Bear Dyken

Loading the Search and Rescue Bus, Saukville Wisconsin (1980)
Paul Donahoe, Mark Dyken, Bear Dyken

Weiler's Ballroom, Port Washington, Wisconsin (1980)

Old Gulch Road, San Andreas (1987)
Mark, Harmony, Gary, Laura, Bear

Laura and Peta, Grafton, Wisconsin (1981)

Nathy's Restaurant, Durango, Colorado (1982)
Front: Harmony, Suneca, Judy Back: Bear, Peta, Laura, Mark

Mark Dyken, Sonora CA. (1988)

Red Rock Nevada (1992)
Front: Laura, Corbin, Harmony
Back: Mark, Bear, Jeff Jones, Leon
Photo by Lisa Law

Leon, Mark, Harmony, Bear, Gary, Laura:
near Me-Wuk Village, CA (1987)
Photo session for Techno Voodoo

Bear: Portland Oregon Community Market (1989)

Bear: Davis CA (1989) Whole Earth Festival

Laura, Hundredth Monkey Concert: Red Rocks, Nevada (1992)

Harmony, Hundredth Monkey Concert: Red Rocks, Nevada (1992)

Mark, Hundredth Monkey Concert: Red Rocks, Nevada (1992)

Leon Dyken, Hundredth Monkey Concert: Redrocks, Nevada (1992)

Mark and Laura, backstage, Hundredth Monkey Concert; Redrocks, Nevada (1992)

Laura: Arnold, CA (1992)

The family painting Gary's bus, "Betty Lou": Cedar Creek, CA (1989)
Front: SilasDyken, Isiah Dyken, Bear Dyken, Rose Dyken,
Adom Dyken, Peta Dyken
Back: Kristi Charrion, Linda Dyken, Hopi Dyken, Kiri Dyken,
Laura Dyken, Harmony Dyken,
Gary Dyken, Leon Dyken, Mark Dyken, Jeff Jones

Bear painting Gary's bus, "Betty Lou": Cedar Creek CA (1989)

Bear and Harmony: Cedar Creek (1996)

Photoshoot for Family Values CD cover: Cedar Creek, CA
Dyken children: Adom, Peta, Silas, Suneca, Hopi, Rose, Kiri, Isiah

Bear's bus, Sahabi: Cedar Creek, CA (2000)
Mark, Bear, Leon, Gary

Mark, Murphys Creek Theatre: Murphys, CA (2004)

Bear, Murphys Creek Theatre: Murphys CA (2004)

Kris Osward and Mark Dyken: Arcata, CA (2010)

Mark: Nevada City, CA

Clan Dyken, Riverrock Campground: Tuolumne, CA (2017)
Silas, Mark, Bella (Bear's granddaughter), Bear

Mark, Pride in the Park: Murphys, CA (2018)

Bear, Pride in the Park: Murphys, CA (2018)

Bear in Smokey, the Silver Eagle, on the road to Alaska (2018)

Clan Dyken at Cooper's Corral, Sheep Ranch, CA (2017)
Mark, Silas, Bear

8

SEVEN GENERATIONS[27]

Look ahead seven generations
Where will you be?

Dineh Bikéyah = Navajoland

A herd of horses saw us coming and took off at a run. The leader, a large black stallion, flared his nostrils and bucked, veering around the others, marking a clear path between the herd and the road. When we first saw them, they stood heads down near a reservation water tank, an image worthy of a photograph. I couldn't help but think of other animals we'd seen, many of them water deprived, thirstily gulping when offered even the smallest reserves from our canteens.

The spring-fed tanks themselves were a history lesson. These sparsely situated holding tanks depicted the reservation's long-standing water issue. Most were painted with graffiti, and the artist's use of traditional symbolism and hues, a palette of reds, blues, yellows, and blacks expressed both their pride and concern: *I Love Rez; Water is Life; Do Not Drink; Poison.* As the wording suggests, some of the water in these spring-fed tanks is safe for human consumption; some is not. Jonathan Yazzi is the Production Supervisor/Youth Coordinator at Tó Łání Lake Enterprises. When asked how people know whether the water is good to drink or not, he said: "They just know."

---

27 Clan Dyken. Look ahead seven generations. "Seven Generations." *Family Values.* CD.

Nearly forty percent of Navajo families have no running water in their homes.[28] The families that do have running water are uncertain of its purity, even though EPA (Environmental Protection Agency) inspectors have assured them of its safety. "These people were lied to; their land was stolen, their heritage defiled," Bear reminded us repeatedly. "Why they would trust anything any white man tells them is truly a mystery, particularly someone from a government agency. Water is life. Life is water. The excuses vary but amount to crap as far as what happened out here."

On my bookshelf at home sits a geology field guide filled with handwritten lecture notes. Highlighted on one page is the word: *Water*. My geology professor had explained the noticeable "depressions" or "caving in" of specific areas outside of Flagstaff and Tuba City caused by overuse and "diminished recharge" or refilling, of local aquifers. Rainwater seeps through open spaces and fractures in the layers of sandstone and limestone, he taught us, thus refilling the groundwater supply. "Along the Colorado Plateau, over an average year, the amount of water available for people, animals, and plant life," I wrote, "is dependent on rainfall and usage."

Bear put it this way: "Removal of groundwater from wells, such as those used by Peabody Coal Company, put a strain on the ecosystem. A tremendous amount of water was used to transport coal to the power plants and to convert that coal into electricity. The mining process polluted the air, so when it does rain, all that stuff leaches down into the soil and pollutes the water as well. Low water, no water—contaminated water."

On any given day, residents of the reservation line up to fill gallon jugs and large plastic barrels at one of these tanks, or at a watering hole that is known to be a safe water source. "When we first started coming here, we didn't see this kind of thing," Mark said. "There was enough water at that time to sustain the people and their animals. The Dineh resisters, like the Yazzis, used spring water to grow food, not only for their families but for others as well. They had excess corn, squash, and beans to sell at roadside stands and stores in town to earn extra cash. The sheep they raised provided not only food but a source of barter. They would

---

28 Millman, Ethan. "Water Hole: No Running Water on Navajo Nation Reservation." *Indian Country Today*, 6 June 2017, indiancountrymedianetwork.com.

trade wool or meat for other needed items, things that were necessary for daily living or valued in some other way. Now their source of water, the springs, are mostly dried up, or no longer viable. When the water situation worsened, so did their means of livelihood."

Bear's truck slowed to a creep as we crossed a metal grate, a cattle guard marking a boundary between Navajo Partitioned Land (NPL) and Hopi Partitioned Land (HPL). One of many on reservation land. "We're on HPL now," said friend and respected Navajo elder Louise Benally, who was riding with us. "These people up here, the Grandma who lives here in this hogan, is one of the resisters. She's old now, but she continues to fight. The people living on Hopi Partitioned Land are, according to the law, living here illegally. They are considered illegal aliens, yet they are living on their ancestral land."

Straining to see a difference, to notice something about the landscape that would distinguish NPL from HPL, was impossible to all but the Navajo and the Hopi. The land was the same. The vegetation was the same. The trees, the topography, the sky, all the same. In the outer reaches of the reservation, only the fences and the cattle guards showed evidence of the BIA demarkations separating the two tribes. To the naked eye and in all detectable ways, the land was one, the history of two peoples combined, if not genetically, culturally. The obvious was this: where piles of harvested blue, red, and yellow corn once lay, there now was barren ground.

As Mark and Bear told stories of what had happened here, those miles of green stakes and barbed wire took on a more precise meaning. This metal barrier shattered the lives of the Navajo. It separated families and cut people off from their grazing lands, watering holes and sacred sites. Also, sheep, cattle, and horses, birthed by or purchased by Navajo families, were now regulated, confiscated, and taxed by BIA representatives, sometimes slaughtered, sometimes sold. Pinyon trees, which provided nuts for the Navajo people, had been, in some cases, torn out by the roots. Holy places, once thriving and revered, were now dust under our feet. Life-sustaining water had, over a generation, disappeared. The Navajo were considered squatters on the land of their ancestors.

Images of past and present blurred in the afternoon light. In the distance was Alice Benally's old place, and Anna Begay and her horses, and Roberta Blackgoat's wooden hogan. Shadowed by clouds, Big Mountain appeared as the remnant of a time when fists pumped the air and guns fired a warning, all to keep those fences from being built and the barbed wire from being strung. In the 1970s, women took up arms in the middle of the night, sneaking across their ancestral land to destroy what outsiders had built. Elders placed their bodies in front of the bulldozers invading their homesteads. What must it have been like for these Grandmothers to see tractors tear up the mountain? To hear explosions caused by blasting dynamite at Coal Mine Mesa? To feel the devastation and disruption of their lifestyle and the land they loved?

The geography of this area is a study in sociology. In years past, life in this part of Arizona was synergetic. The Navajo provided seeds and mutton, which they traded to the Hopi for corn, beans, and melon. The two tribes were dependent on each other for their livelihoods.

The Hopi that are living on First, Second and Third Mesas—located on the southern arm of Black Mesa—are descendants of the Ancestral Puebloan, a historically settled people who farmed and never traveled far from home. The heart of Black Mesa is Big Mountain, an area of land occupied by the Navajo, a nomadic people who lived in vast areas surrounding the Hopi and herded their sheep from camp to camp. Over time, Big Mountain became a sacred site and ceremonial ground to the Navajo, a place they collected herbs and where they prayed and danced. Some of the Navajo people living there are the most committed to resisting, and to dying before signing a lease agreement or relocating.

As different as are their cultures, there are distinct similarities. Both tribes see the world in balance. They synchronize their energies to the rhythms of the universe and believe they were placed here as caretakers and stewards to protect the earth. To the Navajo, a matriarchal society, Black Mesa is considered female. She is "alive" and a part of them. The land is *everything*. Water is *life*. Members of the Navajo tribe like Elsie, Louise, Jonathan, Tim, and Belinda, pray in the places their Grandmothers were buried: *Grandmother, I come to you for strength; I come to you for guidance. You have seen it all and are wise. From you, I seek an answer.*

"Sometimes we forget to slow down and to appreciate the world around us," Bear said, "let alone give thanks to the earth, the four directions, the animals, the plants, the water, the way native custom teaches us to do. You see this reverence for the old ways here on the reservation more than other places, but with their youth working outside the reservation and living a faster-paced lifestyle, it's hard. Corbin Harney used to tell us, 'The main reason humans are here is to say thank you. If we don't do that, the plants, the animals, the water, and the earth as we know it, will go away.'"

Bear rolled down his window, resting his elbow on the window frame. "Look at what's happening all around us, in regards to our planet. It's easy to see the connection these people speak about and recognize as truth. We sing about this in our song, "Seven Generations."

> *Look ahead, seven generations*
> *Where will you be?*
> *You gotta live in the world you create, don't ya?*

Like all Navajo women, the Amá sáni in my dreams learned about life and survival from her mother and grandmother, and her grandmother learned from her grandmother, and on and on back as far as memory took them. To remember a family history and preserve the culture, instinctively knowing how it was and should be, and understanding the continuance of the cycle of life through the elders' eyes, is battle-worthy to them. "I raised my gun and shot a bullet into the air to chase away the government men. I pulled out their fence posts. I will never leave my land," said Navajo elder, Katherine Smith.

"To the Dineh, relocation," Mark said, "the *act* of relocation, means to disappear and never return. The elders have seen friends move away, and then they never see them again. The fact that the people who relocated are in a city somewhere, far removed from their land, does not compute in a Grandmother's mind. To her, these people are gone. They have died emotionally if not physically. It must feel symbolic to them in a negative way, that people have vanished, as has their water and way of life." Mark pointed to a dry wash, a pocket where a spring once flowed. "As their land suffers, so does their culture and means of subsistence."

From the moment the BIA set the first fence post and established the Hopi rangers as a law enforcement entity, the Navajo elders resisted.

Each treaty signed into action over the years had blurred reservation boundaries a little more, and by the 1970s, cultural differences, expanding populations, and government interference had set up the Navajo and Hopi for more infighting and tribal disputes. The members of the Navajo tribe who accepted and signed the relocation agreement were at odds with those who stood their ground, and Traditional Hopi (mostly the elders) argued policy and purpose with the younger, more progressive members of the tribe who believed in and followed the precedents set by the new laws.

In the 1970s, activists throughout the United States were demonstrating for causes related to equality and freedom, but the Navajo at Big Mountain rallied for tribal survival. Grandmothers and Grandfathers took to the streets, carrying signs, and singing prayer songs in the nearby towns of Flagstaff and Tuba City. Elsie Benale remembered her mother going to Tuba City to protest Relocation and the Bennett Freeze,[29] a ban on building and repairs enacted on Navajo land. "She used to tell us that we were marching to protect our religion and the culture that ties to our family. When I was a teenager, we would sit for hours and talk about this stuff. She told me we did this to protect our sheep. A sheep is like a mother because it takes care of you that way."

As Rangers came with guns to enforce the new laws, members of the Navajo tribe traveled to Washington D.C. They addressed Congress to try to get the Relocation Agreement repealed, but Congress refused and allowed relocation to continue. Katherine Smith once told Mark and Bear, "The building of this country happened by stealing indigenous land. To us, the United States flag is a symbol of their greed. The red part of the flag stands for the Native blood that was shed. The white part of the flag stands for who spilled that blood. The stars on the flag represent all the land bases that were stolen and lost."

"The act of relocating the Navajo," said Mark, "made Peabody Coal's job easier. Even though they initially had mining lease agreements with both tribes, the Navajo were in their way. Many of them lived on

---

29 The Bennett Freeze was a development ban on 1.5 million acres of Navajo lands by the US Federal Government. The law was enacted in 1966 and lasted until 2009. Named after Robert L Bennett, Commissioner of Indian Affairs, it meant that in the "frozen" area, no development at all could occur. This included fixing roofs, building houses, constructing gas and water lines, and repairing roads.

land near the mine, and the coal company wanted to expand. If the government passed a bill into law that forcibly removed the Navajo, well, they didn't have to do a thing. Just sit back and wait for it to happen."

Cirrostratus clouds drifted across the bright blue sky, teasing those below with an impression of rain—the possibility of rejuvenation. Lunch that day consisted of apples, hummus, and tortilla chips. We ate picnic-style amid pinyon trees and sage, with our boots in the sand and the sun on our faces. The apples were juicy, California grown, and our drinking water was fresh and straight from the source—Bear's well at Cedar Springs. Still, the water was hard to swallow at times, knowing how many people on the reservation were going without. *Be still, and the earth will speak to you*, reads a Navajo proverb. At that moment, standing in the high desert, it felt as if the earth might *shout*.

For the Dineh and traditional Hopi, the loss of land and food and water sustainability was tragic, but their spiritual connection foretold a broader concern. Elders from both the Navajo and Hopi tribes warned of the consequences of strip mining Big Mountain. "Back in the 1970s," Bear said, "a Hopi elder named Thomas Banyacya warned the government about what would happen if we carried out the kind of devastation that was occurring on Big Mountain. He said, 'We are facing a dangerous period ahead. If we do not stop and correct some of these wrongdoings now, we are all going to suffer. Either things that we make will overtake us, or nature will take over.'"

When Katherine Smith raised her .22 rifle and fired that single shot, scattering federal agents who were building the first fences on Big Mountain, her spiritual bedrock, as she saw it, was in jeopardy. Congress had revoked her right to live on her land and to pray in the holy spots of her ancestors. While some members of the tribe left their homes and moved to nearby cities, Katherine and many others stood their ground, watching while the relocatees—their friends and relatives—struggled to cope in the world outside the reservation. The Hopi were as confused as the Navajo at first. They didn't understand the boundary changes or the forced relocation imposed by the government. When sixteenth-century Spanish explorers originally encountered the Hopi, they were desert farmers who lived in pueblos. Four hundred years later, as documented by the 1900 census, they lived in much the same way. The Hopi people are an agrarian culture, non-nomadic, living in and around the area settled by their ancestors, but they too experienced the trauma of forced familial separation. In the 1800s, nineteen Hopi "hostiles" were jailed by federal agents and sent to Alcatraz. Their crime? These men resisted the removal of their children (some as young as five years old) and refused to succumb to the government's new rules and regulations regarding English-centered, government-run boarding schools. In the later 1900s, the relocation of people of any age, at any time, was a source of renewed friction to both the Hopi and the Navajo (who had experienced the Long Walk to the Bosque Redondo).

While the core dispute rested in the hands of Congress and the courts, the Dineh resisters continued to believe that the truth lay in the hands of the Creator. To quote Roberta Blackgoat in an interview with *Mother Jones News*: "How can it be that this is not my land when my great-great-great-ancestors were born here and were buried here, and they are over here where I live? Our great-ancestors' dust is right here. Their prayer is still here; their holy song is still here. It's been carried on, on, on, and it's still here. So this is what is holding us tight here."[30]

As the Navajo resisters planned their first protests, Mark and Bear were in Wisconsin, going to school and learning their craft as emerging musicians. It was during this time in the early 1970s that their predecessors, the first activists to come to the aid of the Navajo, rolled their multicolored buses over the unpaved roads at Big Mountain. This happy band of hippies had no idea where they were going, but toting their stash of marijuana, guitars, and harmonicas, they were travel-ready.

"These guys, the early hippies," Bear said, "were the first to come out here like this and stay with the folks they met. Many of the people on the reservation at that time didn't speak English. They didn't have television sets, nothing like that—so funny thing—some of them learned English from Wavy Gravy and the Hog Farmers."

"In many ways, we're following their inspiration," said Mark.

"Wavy Gravy is a hippie icon, an artist, a clown, and an activist

---

30 *Wrong Side of the Fence*. Mother Jones, Jan. 2000, www.motherjones.com/politics/2000/01/wrong-side-fence/.

for peace. He and the Hog Farmers were beacons of creativity," Bear said, "courageously moving forward with color and humor and music. They were generating hope at a time when people didn't have hope, especially out here on Big Mountain."

In the mid-1960s, Wavy Gravy and his wife, Jahanara, and other peace and political activists bought an old hog farm located in the hills above Sunland in Southern California and co-founded the Hog Farm Commune. Their extended family bused across the country in much the same way as the Dykens, taking gigs as they traveled, clowning, announcing and hosting different musical events, and playing some themselves.

"Wavy was responsible for so many things that happened back in the day," Bear said, as we stood on the roadside, taking a break from the bumpy drive. "He was the MC at Woodstock. The Hog Farm was security for the event. They were the *Please* Force. Wavy and the others used what they had on hand—oatmeal, and raisins—to make the first granola and feed all those people. It was genius."

After Woodstock, the Hog Farmers moved to land they had purchased in Llano, New Mexico. These members of the Hog Farm Commune, now based in New Mexico, drove from the Hog Farm toward Tuba City, Arizona, drawn north by the joy of traveling together by bus and the beauty of the landscape they encountered. The stretch of the Southwestern United States these activists visited was a psychedelic paradise, where wind, water, and time had weathered the land into a three-dimensional visual delight: vast canyons, tabletop mesas, and valley floors consisting of multicolored layers of rock and vegetation unique to the area. Kaibab limestone, Coconino Sandstone, and Hermit Shale, Vishnu and Brahma Schist, were among the geologic formations that stunned the rubber-tramp wanderers, painting a picture of an environment dating back 1.84 billion years. Geologically speaking, the centuries of Navajo and Hopi habitation was relatively recent, but their footprint was an indelible one, etched deep in the canyons and the trappings of small towns and villages for the hippies to ponder.

Known historically as a trade center for the local tribes, Tuba City boasted dinosaur tracks and petroglyphs and the legacy of the Navajo Code Talkers. However, an hour away, members of the Hog

Farm Commune stumbled across something unexpected: sporadically spaced Navajo hogans, their condition deteriorating, the people who lived there welcoming but confused and angered by the recent changes imposed on them by the federal government. In this land set apart from modern society, where barter was currency, and simplicity a lifestyle, the dispute was brewing between the Navajo and the Hopi, with Peabody Coal Company at the center of it all. Plus, in sordid contradiction, the water that formed the landscape through which the hippies traveled was seriously threatened as a life-giving source.

Deep on the reservation, the hippies drove up to a weather-beaten hogan, climbed out of their multicolored buses and knocked on the door, according to Bear. After introducing themselves, they stayed, and they listened, spawning a campaign of compassionate activism that remains today.

Years later, after moving the commune to Laytonville, in Northern California, Wavy and the others established Camp Winnarainbow, a circus and performing arts camp for both kids and adults. "The Hog Farmers brought many kids from the reservation there on scholarships," Bear said, "including Louise Benally. So many kids out there benefited from their kindness, including Mark's kids, and Si and Rose. They all attended Camp Winnarainbow."

As the sun set, we stopped at the Rocky Ridge Trading Post, a small roadside grocery and supply store on Dinnebito Wash Road, otherwise known as Big Mountain Boulevard. Here we found the standard grocery fare plus some local favorites: mutton in various iterations, and Blue Bird Flour—grab-and-go supplies like hats, gloves, rope, twine, knives, flashlights and batteries. Souvenirs included small weavings with designs representative of generations of families: the Gap-in-the-Rock Clan, the Deer Watering Clan, the Towering House Clan, and others. T-shirts displayed the great seal of the Navajo Nation, a small map of the Big Mountain region, pictures of sheep, insignias—*Proud to be Navajo; Speak Dineh; Straight Outta Dineh Bikéyah* (Bikéyah meaning land)— the towering white monuments and sandstone buttes, pictures of the land— always the land—and symbols for water—always the water.

What the activists saw back in the 1970s, and what we see now, boils down to the same thing: land and water are the centers of life on the reservation. Everything the Navajo do revolves around their relationship with the earth and their animals. They make their living with their sheep. Their sheep depend on natural forage and the water. A culture of a people is fading.

"The Veterans for Peace[31] followed the hippies, as far as early activists on the reservation," Mark said. "Their whole thing was in response to unethical military interventions. They brought food and clothing to the resisters at Big Mountain, establishing the first official food runs and routes. The Veterans for Peace stepped it up, as far as service, and set the path for future activists."

This early activism happened during the peak of Indian resistance. There were demonstrations at the Peabody Coal Mine. For a time, Navajo occupied the mine, as other activists occupied Alcatraz Island[32] in California, and Wounded Knee[33] in South Dakota. Said AIM activist, Dennis Banks: "The Trail of Broken Treaties cross-country protest [of 1972] is a reflection that Native people are no longer going to tolerate the kinds of conditions that they've been subjected to for the past 200 years."

By the late 1980s, it was no longer possible to separate environmental issues from concerns about cultural genocide. AIM, environmental activists, peace activists, political and anti-nuclear activists came to the aid of the Navajo, knowing that the land defined the Navajo as people. The shrines, the petroglyphs and pictographs, the animals, and the water, were a part of their soul. Blood, clan, or marriage related all people—they and the land they lived on were their own societal ecosystem, in a way. People were connecting the dots.

---

31 Veterans for Peace was founded in 1985 by ten U.S. veterans in response to the global nuclear arms race and U.S. military interventions in Central America.

32 The Alcatraz Occupation lasted for nineteen months, from November 20, 1969 to June 11, 1971. The Occupation of Alcatraz had a direct effect on federal Indian policy and, with its visible results, established a precedent for Indian activism.

33 The Wounded Knee incident began on February 27, 1973 when approximately 200 Oglala Lakota and followers of the American Indian Movement (AIM) seized and occupied the town of Wounded Knee, South Dakota, on the Pine Ridge Indian Reservation.

9

THIS IS MY SOUL JOURNEY[34]

Up ahead I see somethin' new, it's just now comin' into view

T'áá k'ad t'éiyá = Now is the only time, now is the only chance

One day in the spring of 1980 in Tuscon, Arizona, Mark and Bear Dyken attended a showing of one of Helen Caldecott's video-recorded presentations. "We went to the campus to shower and play a little basketball," Mark said. "And while there, we heard that a local activist group planned to show her pre-recorded talk, so we wandered in to take a listen."

Thirty or so students gathered in a small air-conditioned classroom connected to the library. A projector screen hung in the front of the room, and a VCR sat on a cart near the back. The students were focused on their event and paid little attention to Mark and Bear as nonresident observers. The video started, participants took their seats, and as Helen spoke, gasps, sighs, and an occasional *fuck* or *oh shit* slipped from the lips of listeners.

"To quote Albert Einstein, " Helen Caldecott said, "The splitting of the atom changed everything, all reality, save man's mode of thinking. Thus, we drift toward unparalleled catastrophe."

Hearing the anti-nuclear activist talk about the possibilities of nuclear destruction took the Dyken brothers' commitment to the no-nuke

---

34 Clan Dyken. Up ahead I see somethin' new. "This is My Soul Journey." *The Last Ride at the End of the Old World.* CD. Track 1.

philosophy to another level. She "knocked us over the edge," said Bear. "We were already open to hearing what she had to say, but her honesty, the way she presented the information, flipped us over the top."

"She synthesized information about the aspects of a thermonuclear war from a health perspective and spoke about the consequences of nuclear fallout, and what the political and geopolitical scope of such a conflict might be," Mark said. "She went through the ugly details. How easily a thermonuclear event might occur. How it might happen—the aftereffects, including death rates and radiation poisoning and how this would affect our water, our food supply, and our planet, well into the future."

While Bear and Mark recounted the impact of Helen's speech, I thought of images of dried-up springs, uranium tailings, and spoiled gardens. Hopi elder Thomas Baynaca's words looped through the issues like the cat's cradle in Native hands: "We are facing a dangerous period ahead. If we do not stop and correct some of these wrongdoings now, we are all going to suffer."

""Hearing Helen speak brought on a profound period of growth for us," said Bear. "She talked about personal responsibility, and her organization the Physicians for Social Responsibility,[35] and how this group of physicians became known as an entity by documenting the presence of Strontium-90 in children's teeth. I mean, Strontium-90 is a highly radioactive byproduct of the atmospheric testing of nuclear weapons, and they were finding this stuff in the mouths of our kids!

"The whole experience was life-changing," he said. "We got involved on many new levels after this. There was a progression to our activism, from Wisconsin to Colorado, to Arizona, and then to California. It happened in an order that pulled us along."

One earth; one air; one water, rally for the people, rally for the land

---

[35] Physicians for Social Responsibility advocate on issues that threaten communities, using their medical and public health expertise to prevent nuclear war and proliferation, to combat climate change and to reduce exposure to toxic chemicals.

Scientific arguments both for and against nuclear proliferation escalated after WWII and the dropping of the bomb on Hiroshìmà and Nagasaki. In the 1950s, the nuclear arms race had American families building bomb shelters in their yards and children in elementary schools hiding under desks during required "duck and cover" bomb drills. On November 1, 1961, 50,000 women marched in different cities in the United States to demonstrate their concern over nuclear weapons and atmospheric testing of atomic weapons, a program vigorously maintained by the United States beginning in 1945.[36] In the 1970s, a contentious debate over the performance of emergency core cooling systems in nuclear plants received coverage on television and in magazines. Spills associated with uranium mining operations occurred far too regularly. The meltdown at Three Mile Island in Pennsylvania that occurred on March 28, 1979 was rated a five on the seven-point International Nuclear Event Scale.[37] The Church Rock uranium spill in New Mexico, which occurred on July 16, 1979, sent over 1,000 tons of solid radioactive mill waste and ninety-three million gallons of acidic, radioactive tailings into the Puerco River. Contaminants traveled eighty miles downstream to Navajo country in Arizona.

The birth of the anti-nuclear movement in California was the result of public outcry over a proposed power plant in Bodega Bay. The conflict began in 1958 and ended in 1964, with the forced abandonment of Pacific Gas and Electric's plans to construct the facility. Rancho Seco Nuclear Generating Station was located in southeast Sacramento County. On March 20, 1978, a failure of power supply for the plant's non-nuclear instrumentation system led to steam generator dry-out—a possible precursor to a nuclear disaster.

From a Bureau of Land Management mining claim in Sonora, California, where I lived in the late 1970s, friends and I could see the two massive nuclear cooling towers at Rancho Seco. The view from our

---

36 DeBenedetti, Charles. *An American Ordeal: the Antiwar Movement of the Vietnam Era.* Syracuse, Syracuse University Press, 1990. *Google Books,* onlinelibrary.wiley.com/doi/10.1111/ j.1468-0130.2009.00628.x/full.

37 The International Nuclear and Radiological Event Scale (INES) is a tool for communicating the safety significance of nuclear and radiological events to the public.

mountaintop home was unobstructed, a clear shot to the Central Valley and points north to Sacramento. Back then, white-grey smoke billowed skyward, the wind carrying it east toward the foothills of the Sierra Nevada. Concern for the vapor that spewed into the sky was on the minds of assembled hippies as we watched from afar. "Fuck," someone said. "They're killing us off."

On November 28, 1979, a group of activists staged a protest at Rancho Seco while another group of approximately fifty people marched to the governor's office at the state capitol. At the plant, protesters scaled the main gate and climbed fences, carrying signs that read, Shut it Down. They held die-ins, lying on the ground, body to body, and formed blockade lines, linking arms, hundreds of people strong. "Shut it down now! No meltdown later!" they shouted, waving signs, pounding on hand drums, and shaking rattles. At the state capitol, protesters marched past the floor-to-ceiling murals depicting mythical griffins, huge urns, and intricate floral swags. The focus of the room, however, was a massive centerpiece statue titled "Columbus' Last Appeal to Queen Isabella." Activists stared at the likeness as they circled the rotunda, making their way from there to the governor's office. There, protestors sat cross-legged on marbled tiles, some of them barefoot, some wearing moccasins or sandals, chanting, and some threatening a hunger strike if their concerns weren't addressed.

During the next thirty-eight days, representatives from the Physicians for Social Responsibility joined the effort. AIM activist Dennis Banks made appearances, agreeing with the action but worried that such a massive sit-in might affect Jerry Brown's chance for reelection. Although the governor stressed that he was sympathetic to the anti-nuclear campaigners' concerns, he maintained that federal law prevented his immediate action. Still, he offered the following: a $2,000 donation to the anti-nuclear activist efforts; accessibility for public testimony at the U.S. Nuclear Regulatory Commission hearings in Sacramento; an anti-nuclear information kiosk in his office; and sponsorship for three screenings of Caldecott's film on nuclear waste. The protesters accepted the governor's terms, ending the official occupation, and anti-nuclear activists continued to represent their issue at the statehouse by staffing the nuclear information kiosk in the governor's outer office.

In the early 1980s, while activists made their treks to Big Mountian, the Dykens were traveling the festival circuit, armed with a new conviction to become more involved politically. Along the way, they began experimenting with genres other than rock and roll, like world music and reggae. Bear was still writing songs, and the band was creating their rebel-rock sound. "The whole anti-nuclear movement and having heard Helen Caldecott, created the mood we were in when we came out west," he said. "On our way to Davis, we passed the Rancho Seco Nuclear Generating Station, and those huge hourglass-shaped cooling towers were staring us in the face, and we're thinking, this is where we need to be."

"Rancho Seco was a municipal facility, so people had a say in what was going on there," Mark said. "It was a big deal, and one of the first activist actions we did here."

"It all fell into place in and around the festival scene," Bear said. "The movement was growing, and we were ripe to add our groove. Rancho Seco was a working power plant, and stuff was going wrong all the time. Some of what happened wasn't made public. Jessie Jackson spoke there about shutting down the plant, and the plant workers gave him crap. They fought back hard. It was working people against working people, like in Woody Guthrie's song, "Massacre." Woody's lyrics influenced our music and the songs I wrote during that period. Rancho Seco was the catalyst; the songs were the instrument, the festival, the vessel."

The time and the place were right for Clan Dyken's kind of music, and the people attending the Whole Earth Festival in Davis, California, were ready as well. Liz Tree, one of the supporters from Williams, Oregon, was among the people present at the festival when the band landed there. The family thing, the Clan's message of peace and protecting the earth, became a rallying cry. "So we'd show up at these places, like the U.C. Davis campus," Mark said, "and by then Gary had kids, and so we had multiple children, and husbands and wives, and we were all wearing colorful clothes and living in buses. Plus we were fired up politically and ready to put it out there for the no-nuke campaign."

Like others before them, members of Clan Dyken marched along the asphalt road leading to the power plant, singing and shouting, carrying signs, drumming, and chanting—locking arms with fellow activists to stop supply trucks from flowing in and out of the facility.

Ten years after the initial protests began, the City of Sacramento shut down the Rancho Seco Nuclear Generating Station, citing economic failing rather than environmental or societal safety. Time magazine called the activists' efforts "the most potent demonstration ever against nuclear power."

"The end-all at Rancho Seco proved to be one of the first times in history that the public voted to close down a nuclear power plant," said Bear. "Those were heavy times."

As Clan Dyken traveled the festival scene, they met a man named David Katz, a pioneer in the field of solar energy. "David had the idea of bringing solar panels to Northern California," Bear recalled. "Because all the hippies were living in the woods. These people were back-to-the-landers, and they were hooking up their lights to their car batteries so David said, 'We can do better than that.'"

For Clan Dyken, David's ideas and his philosophy behind solar power and solar energy were a natural fit. Since the late 1970s, David had been bringing power to the people of Northern California by generating electricity using innovative technologies, beginning with lighting homes by using car batteries and then moving on to using solar panels for home and business energy needs. Intrigued by the idea that they could potentially run their shows and play music using alternative energy sources, the band bought into the theory and put it into practice.

"So we were anti-nuclear activists, but we became pro-alternative energy activists, and it all came together around Rancho Seco," Bear said. "Gary built a bus that had a stage that rolled out of the side. It had big doors that opened up and had solar panels on the roof. At that time, we could drive our bus on to the state Capital lawn in the middle of Sacramento, no permit, no nothing, and open up and start playing music, protesting against nuclear power."

At this point, the band's members fluctuated, but their core base remained consistent: Mark, Bear, Laura, Harmony, and Gary, and now little brother Leon playing percussion on and off. Others joined the caravan of multicolored buses as well, friends they met while traveling. The idea of living in rolling homes, spreading their message and a strong family vibe, appealed to fellow activists and musicians, including folks prominent at the Woodstock scene, like Wavy Gravy and Fantuzzi.

"Because we didn't need to plug into electricity," Bear said, "we could go for it, and no one stopped us. So we did the no-nuke thing, another thing called the Twenty-First Century Road Show and another tour that we called Ecotopia by Bus. By then, we were a whole caravan of buses and hippies, including some of these other folks. We traveled all the way up the west coast into Humboldt County and Southern Oregon. We played the Trinity Tribal Stomp, the Oregon Country Fair, and many other festivals. That established our crowd. Williams, the place we do our fundraiser—a lot of those people are kids who grew up with parents who were watching us back then."

"And just a few years after that, we started going to the Nevada Nuclear Test Site," said Mark. "We first heard about it during the 1986 Great Peace March.[38] Those guys walked across the country, and the test site was part if it. Ray Jennings, known as Raybo the clown, who eventually married Laura's sister, Judy, was traveling with us at that time. His sister, Suzie, put on a little festival around Nevada City, and she had this newspaper called the Community Endeavour. She went out to the test site to cover the story, so pretty soon, we were going out there doing solar-powered concerts. That's where we met Corbin."

Shoshone, Navajo, Sioux, Paiute, Hopi, Apache, Me-Wuk—people representing their Native cultures presented strong at the Nevada Nuclear Test Site: singing, dancing, and praying for peace and the future of the planet. They spoke in their native tongue and in English, their connection always grounded, every marched step breathing life into the cause and adding purpose to the activists' reasons for being there. "Our circle expanded and our experience grew," Bear said, describing Native influence and Corbin's outreach beyond the activist community.

"We are one people. We cannot separate ourselves now," Corbin Harney once said, his deep, gravelly voice adding urgency to his message. "There are many good things to be done for our people and the world. It is important to let things be good. And it is important to teach the

---

38   The Great Peace March was a cross-country event in 1986 aimed at raising awareness to the growing danger of nuclear proliferation and to advocate for elimination of nuclear weapons from the earth.

younger generation so that things are not lost."³⁹

The United States government conducted 928 atomic bomb tests at the Nevada Nuclear Test Site. The most significant test happened on March 7, 1955, and it illuminated Los Angeles (240 miles away) for twenty seconds according to reporters who observed the event. Similar tests occurred in the years following, as documented by various media. "At first, the images seem rather mundane for looking so much like a sunrise—the difference, of course, is that this fission-born light comes straight from man's handiwork, and heralds the beginning of an arms race that in the 1960s tilted perilously close to Armageddon," reported *Wired* Magazine.

Old videos and images, accessible online, paint a picture of what it was like on test site grounds: a moonscape of craters, one after the other in random patterns, were the remnants of every test conducted. At Old Frontier Village in Las Vegas, swimmers stand transfixed beside a swimming pool, watching the nuclear spectacle, a human-made cyclone rising from the earth. Pictures show citizens standing on observation decks mere miles from where the bombs were set off, wearing no protective gear, armed only with cameras and notebooks to record the history of these nuclear explosions. Tours onto test site property were booked a year in advance and were free of charge.

Also depicted are soldiers squatting in the distance as the bombs explode. Nearby signs post the warning: *No Trespassing, Contamination—no pocketing soil or picking up rocks.* Other pictures show a line of 1960-circa cars, people with cameras, a mother with her child, observing a mushroom cloud alongside her small son from the window of their Los Angeles home. There is a photo of horses with radiation burns all over their bodies, and a dead, charred pig, the animal of choice used by the Atomic Energy Commission to test the results of radiation poisoning. Because these animals were determined to have skin most like humans, they were on site as bombs exploded and examined afterward, dead or alive, to study the symptoms of up-close exposure.

At some point in the history of the site, a strategically placed

---

39 Circle Of Stories. *Storytellers.* Corbin Harney | PBS. Web. 26 Sep. 2018 <http://www.pbs.org/circleofstories/storytellers/corbin_harney.html>

plaque read: *Nevada Test Site. Testing of devices for defense and for peaceful uses of nuclear explosives is conducted here.*

Archaeological studies of the NTS area have revealed continuous occupation by prehistoric man from about 9,500 years ago. Several prehistoric cultures are represented. The last aboriginal group to occupy the site was the Southern Paiute who foraged plant foods in season and occupied the area until the coming of the pioneers.

"The government said that no one lived out there," Bear said, "but this was and always had been Shoshone land. Interestingly, by signing the Treaty of Ruby Valley[40] in 1863, the Shoshone gave their mineral rights away. They told the government, 'sure, you can mine, sure, you can cut down trees, yes, you can cross over and transport things, but this is our land.' The entire real estate thing is snake oil when you think about it. The king's property. What's yours is not yours when it comes down to it."

"In the early days, at the test site, the Western Shoshone Nation would set up this table and issue permits to go onto their land," said Mark. "As Bear mentioned, they had signed the Treaty of Peace and Freedom, otherwise known as the Ruby Valley Treaty in 1863, which gave settlers the right to travel through the Shoshone territory, but they never gave the United States government permission to fence off this land and turn it into a test site. So granting this permit was a kind of a ritual, a statement. The Shoshone people would issue the permits, signed by Chief Raymond Yowell, and activists would organize collectively and walk across a cattle guard and peacefully, promptly get arrested by security hired by the federal government."

The gathering place for activists at the Nevada Nuclear Test Site was Peace Camp, a unique cultural phenomenon, according to Bear. It was international. It was indigenous-led and has been foundational for much activism since. Peace Camp was committed to nonviolence, and participants had nonviolence training. "There was a diverse coalition of people," he said. "It was a community. Everyone took care of everyone else."

---

40 The Treaty of Ruby Valley was a treaty signed with the Western Shoshone in 1863, giving certain rights to the United States. The Western Shoshone did not cede land under this treaty but agreed to allow the government the "right to traverse the area, maintain existing telegraph and stage lines, construct one railroad and engage in specified economic activities."

Activist groups such as the American Peace Test and Greenpeace had a presence at the test site. "There were a group of Franciscan friars there as well," Bear said. "They do a thing called Nuclear Stations of the Cross every Easter out there still. The way people did food was beautiful, sharing, cooking together, and we did morning circles and consensus decision making. Wavy Gravy and the Hog Farmers came out there. It was like an explosion of art and music. Nothing was for sale. There was no entry fee or cover charge to get in. It was an annual event, but some people stayed on site and did actions year-round as well.

"There's never really been anything like it, before or after," Bear continued. "We did a thing called Peace Spokes Bike ride that we started, actually at my house. We rode bikes through Central California and stopped at every newspaper and radio and television station we came upon, and we wore shirts that read *Stop Nuclear Weapons Testing*. We rode all the way to the Nevada Nuclear Test Site. All to shut that test site down."

At Peace Camp, there were all-night vigils. There were running vigils. Prayer runs. Drummers drummed twenty-four hours a day, taking shifts in between helping the workers, running, and drumming. "Representatives from so many different tribes were there, including delegates from Big Mountain, like Louise Benally," Bear said.

The spiritual force behind the test site movement was the Western Shoshone, with Corbin Harney as their spiritual leader. When Corbin was a boy, he ran away from missionary school. At the school, as was the case back then, teachers forced him to sit and listen to a language he did not speak or understand. They would not let him speak in his native tongue. Having lost his parents when he was a baby, he turned to his uncle who gave him a choice: stay in school or go into the mountains and learn to survive on his own. So Corbin took two horses and went to Idaho to live in the backcountry homeland of his people.

Corbin learned about medicine and spirituality and trained with his elder aunties at Battle Mountain, Nevada. He ran sunrise ceremonies and sweat lodges, and he understood that all life is sacred. "Everything is alive and has a spirit to it. The rocks, the mountains, streams, animals, plants, birds, oceans, and so forth. We have to get back to the Native way of life. The Native way is to pray for everything. Our Mother Earth is very important. Everything survives on our Mother, the only Mother we've got." [41]

"The first time we met Corbin Harney, we'd just been arrested," said Mark. "When there was an action or demonstration planned at the test site, there was always security, two levels of law enforcement, sometimes three. The department of energy had security guards, but mostly they hired the Wackenhut,[42] and there was also a presence from the Nevada Highway Patrol. We'd driven down to Peace Camp, just opposite the town of Mercury, on Hwy 395, way out in the Nevada desert. Once we received our permit from the Shoshone, we crossed the cattle guards onto test site grounds. Security put their plastic handcuffs on us, hands behind our backs, and we sat in a holding pen until they shipped us by bus to Beatty. People would sometimes give their real names, sometimes not. They would issue tickets, but never take us to court. The whole idea was to move us out of there so the buses filled with workers could get to the site without our interference."

On his computer, Mark showed me pictures of demonstrations at the test site. We looked at some photographs of Corbin with his eagle wing fan, and of activists on their knees, hands behind their backs, secured by plastic cuffs. "We were right here," Mark explained, pointing to a spot near the cattle guards on test site property.

The Dyken brothers' first arrest on test site grounds was typical. On any given day, a dozen to a hundred or more people who *crossed the line* waited in holding pens for transport by bus to Beatty, Nevada. Once seated on the bus, the cuffed activists were transported along Highway 95, past knee-high creosote bushes and sage and a few cacti while their rumble of voices competed with the metallic drone of the engine, the vibratory buzz of rubber tires on the asphalt. On this particular day, from two rows behind the Dykens, the combined voices of Corbin Harney and Chief Yowell rose above the clamor, their spiritual overtones, raspy

---

41   "My Hero Project, Inc." *My Hero,* 12 June 2004, myhero.com/c harney.

42   Wackenhut Corporation provides security services to commercial and government organizations. In 2002 the company was purchased for $570 million by Danish corporation Group 4 Falck. In 2004, Group 4 Falck merged with Securicor to create Group 4 Securicor, one of the largest security corporations in the world.

tonality, the healing and earth songs they sang in their native Shoshone language drawing listeners into the import of the moment. The word *naraborochi* (water) wove a seductive web, *clean water, clean air*, both apocalyptic reminders of the reason for the activists' presence. "*Banoso*," our mother, the earth, our mother. "*Wanososhy,*" they sang. Translated later, the message meant: *we are all rotating with our mother, working together, appreciating each other—living on this mother earth together.*

"So we're listening to this," Mark said, "and Bear and I said to each other, 'we've got to meet these guys.' I often say that I met some of the most wonderful people I've ever met in my life, including Corbin, right across the road from the most destructive force on the planet." Mark paused again, considering, and adjusted the brim of his hat. "Darkness attracts the light," he said. "On one side of the road, people were employed to figure out how to kill the most people possible. On the other side of the road were people who were in resistance to this, but also who were dedicated to living in peace in all aspects of their lives."

The Department of Energy and the Federal Government knew of Corbin Harney. Sometimes called the "hardest working man in shamanism," Corbin traveled the world speaking to teachers, students, and even government officials about the dangers of nuclear energy and the problems facing Mother Earth. As a medicine man, he shared his knowledge with a representative of the United States government, who had phoned him and asked what Native people do about radiation sickness. Using voice inflections, Bear relayed the conversation as told to him by Corbin. "'You grind up rabbit bones,' Corbin told the rep. 'You make a broth out of ground up rabbit bones, and you make a tea out of creosote bush, or just chew on it.'"

At Peace Camp, each day started with prayer. Every morning Corbin performed a sunrise ceremony, drumming, singing, and praying. Before the first morning light, he prepared an altar, a mound of dirt facing east, just to the west of the fire built by his assistant, Willy. On the mound, Corbin placed water, his abalone shell filled with sage and coals, and his eagle wing fans. The camp slept while he made his preparations, the air smelling of creosote and sage and surrounded by night noises:

coyote yip-howling, the shuffling of campers in their tents.

"That drum would wake me out of a sound sleep, *ba bum, ba bum*," Mark said. "I'd lay there for a while but never long because that drumbeat called me, *he* called me, and I couldn't ignore his invitation to rise and join him at the fire. Corbin had two eagle feather fans that he would use to fan the activists. You could hear them, *whoosh, whoosh,* and he would touch you with the feathers—you could feel them on your skin. He would start singing, and it didn't matter if anyone was with him or not, and he drew people to him. Eventually, there were enough people in a circle around him to began a two-step shuffle dance, moving to the left. Corbin would sing a whole range of songs, and he would tell you, 'I'm singing about the horny toad, I'm signing about the crow, I'm singing for our mommy.' He called our earth our mommy. When enough people came, and it started getting light, he would stop. He would say his prayers in his native tongue. He had a coffee can full of tobacco, and sage, maybe some kinnikinnick, juniper, and he would pass the can, and every person would take a pinch of this mixture and hold it in their hand. We would put our intentions for the day into that mix, our prayers, and at some point, during the ceremony, he would tell people to come and throw their tobacco on the fire. He told us that the fire would turn that mix to smoke and that smoke would circle up and carry our prayers around the world."

Gesturing a circle with his hand, Mark continued. "Corbin would always tell us, 'Pray in your way. You do what you do, not what you see me doing here.' He would let people speak until everyone finished. He would say a special prayer thanking the sun for coming up, and then he would say, 'Who's got the coffee, or who's got the ice cream?' Corbin loved ice cream. The beauty of this is that this ceremony went on and on, and when it ended, it ended. It could take one hour; it could take three hours, it didn't matter to Corbin. It was what it was. I would stand there and listen to him sing, and then at the end, he would take sage and his eagle feather and smudge every person in the circle before they left and went about their day."

When all of this was done and the ceremony over, Corbin encouraged participants to take some of the ashes from the fire and mix them with their soup or coffee. One by one, people walked to the fire and did as instructed, taking a pinch of ash and sprinkling it in their coffee mug, or saving it in the pocket of their shirt to add to their morning oatmeal or soup.

"Ash is a powerful alkaline," Bear said, "good for the gut, and Corbin knew this stuff."

With each encounter, Corbin's relationship with Mark and Bear became more personal. "He taught us so much," Bear said, speaking of their friendship and shared activist causes. Corbin invited Mark and Bear to his annual spring gathering to meet the two Shoshone aunties under whom he apprenticed. The women lived deep on the reservation near a little-known creek tucked into the open desert and bordered by yucca, sage and other native medicinal plants.

"Corbin often said that this sacred creek is where his songs came from," Bear said. "There was a spring there, and he listened to the water, and that's where the melodies for his songs grew. He was always singing. That was his way of saying thank you."

With furrowed brows, Bear went on. "As time passes, so much of what Corbin said and did makes more sense to me. Everything that happened at the test site continues to affect me. Growing up as a kid in Wisconsin, I remember the drills in school and pictures of the bombs going off and thinking how those drills were just silly. We were all going to be incinerated under our desks as much as if we were on the playground. I think I was around eight years old when it finally sunk in, and all this other stuff was happening around that time. I remember when Bobby Kennedy got shot. The nuns shut down the school, and we all went into one room and watched the news on television. John Kennedy, Bobby, Martin Luther King, Malcolm X.

"All of this disillusionment and discord happened, and then came Corbin. He believed in unity. He would say, 'We can't afford these divisions between people anymore. We have to come together and realize that we're all red on the inside.' He got a lot of flak for that, but he believed it."

During the years the Dykens went to the test site, there grew an established sense of community. People cared about one another. Took care of each other, and much of this seemed to be a result of Corbin's influence. Each morning after the sunrise service at the Peace Camp, there was a communal breakfast. Tents were set up, and there were workshops on non-violent response, nuclear issues, how to deal with the press, and on where the movement was going.

Native people would talk about their perspective. Hibakusha[43] survivors spoke there as well. Actions planned in the camp happened later at test site. People chose which action interested them each day and how they would participate. "There was a coordinating committee," Mark said. "We tried to do everything by consensus, but there were a couple of thousand people there, so different camps would have different actions planned. Some people were backcountry activists, and they would sneak into the test site, and then radio out their position, telling other activists and the Nevada test site staff that there were activists on test site property. This way, they would delay the tests, because guards would have to remove them before a bomb could go off.

"We had friends who contracted cancer years later and thought it was related to their backcountry activism," Mark added. "This is something you never forget."

Though Mark and Bear were never at the test site when a bomb went off, they were in Las Vegas once when it happened. Mark still recalls the feeling, the reactions of the activists and band members present at the time. "Whenever a bomb went off, everyone was pretty bummed out," he said. "Every bomb test felt like a major defeat."

When protesters were on site, security opened collapsible signs stating, *Demonstrators on the Roadway*. Activists carried their signs, *Stop Nuclear War Now, Respect Life: Remember Chernobyl*. People of all ages marched and stood in lines across the road facing armed guards, as Mark had described. Before the Nuclear Test-Ban Treaty of 1963, mushroom clouds rose high above the Nevada desert. Beyond the cattle guards and open desert, stood the replica of a small town, designed for training purposes to depict the site of a nuclear disaster. Here, casualty response teams practiced and prepared for the worst scenario humans could imagine. Instructors simulated dirty bombs and radiological contamination, city blocks of chaos, children with radiation burns, death and destruc-

---

43 *Hibakusha* is the Japanese word for the surviving victims of the 1945 atomic bombings of Hiroshima and Nagasaki.

tion beyond the limits of the imagination.

Almost daily, demonstrators set up barriers to prevent test site workers from getting to the site itself. Activists erected tripods and climbed on top, the idea being that the guards couldn't dismantle the structure without hurting someone. Demonstrators parked cars across Hwy 95 and chained themselves to the vehicle. Some crawled inside large PVC pipes with the pipes strung together so that security guards couldn't see where one body stopped and the next started, and therefore, couldn't cut the pipes to remove them.

"You had to be careful," Mark said. "Security would hurt you, particularly the Wackenhut. They were not very nice."

Clan Dyken started playing music at the test site in 1989. They came equipped with solar panels and set up their buses and a stage for live performances. Altogether, the group went to the test site twenty times or more, some years, two or three times, from the late 1980s through 2000. Mark and Bear ran in Spirit Runs. "On Spirit Runs," Mark said, "a group of twenty people participated, and each person would run as far as they could, maybe a mile, maybe five miles and then pass a staff to someone else. Participants would then get in a car and drive to the next destination, where they could choose to run again or not. Each footstep was a prayer. Twice we ran all the way from Big Mountain to the test site. People helping us would drive vans and cook food. It was like a bike tour only on foot."

The Clan Dyken family was also present at the test site in 1992, when an incident between a man named Rick Springer and President Ronald Reagan brought the activists' cause some national attention. On April fourteenth of that year, President Reagan was in Las Vegas to accept a Lifetime Achievement award from the National Association of Broadcasters. The action wasn't planned or preorganized by Springer or anyone else; it just happened. "The statue Reagan was to receive was a crystal glass golden eagle," Bear said. "We did these benefits for what we called the Wake up the Nations Tour that ended at the Hundredth Monkey Project to shut down nuclear testing. It was a solar-powered concert at Red Rocks, Nevada. The Band X, Michelle Shocked, Richie Havens, Sha Na Na. I played bass for Sha Na Na. I was coming out of the Porta-Potty, and someone said, 'Can you play bass?' and I said, 'yes.' I didn't have the outfit for the gig, but I did it," Bear recalled, smiling. "Three days of rock and roll and poetry. There was a die-in at the Department of Energy in Las Vegas going on. We had just done a tour with Corbin. It was this huge coming together of anti-nuclear activists. The concert was epic. The die-in was to be the beginning of a three-day walk, starting sixty miles north and ending at the test site. So Rick Springer, the guy who organized the whole thing, learned that the Department of Energy was going to test a nuclear bomb while we were all there. He somehow obtained a press pass, and across the street, the National Press Association was giving President Ronald Reagan a two-foot tall crystal eagle for his contribution to media. When Rick saw the eagle, he just snapped. He did not intend to hurt Reagan; he just wanted to say, 'Hey, this isn't appropriate. A nuclear bomb is about to go off. This eagle is a symbol for Native Americans, and look what's happening out here on their land.'"

Dressed in the casual attire of a stagehand, Springer ambled onto the stage, grabbed the crystal statue and threw it down, shattering it. "Excuse me, Mr. President, there's going to be a nuclear bomb exploded outside of town," he said, just as the secret service grabbed and tackled him to the ground. Bear and his family were in a nearby hotel when Wavy Gravy ran in and told them what had happened. "We were all shocked and concerned," said Bear. "But that one act put this whole thing in the national spotlight."

"I was running on the Vegas Test Site March with my kids," Mark said. "These cars pulled up, and a reporter came up to me and told me what happened. I couldn't believe it."

At this point, Clan Dyken was traveling back and forth from the test site to Lawrence Livermore Lab and Ward Valley in California to play music at activist actions. Their involvement at all three places intensified their commitment to the anti-nuclear campaign: Lawrence Livermore Lab was the site of many nuclear weapons projects, and Ward Valley, a proposed nuclear waste dump site, was a sacred site for many Indian tribes and the home of the desert tortoise, a threatened species.

"The cool thing about Ward Valley was that it was almost entirely Native American people who were doing this action," Bear said. "There wasn't a lot of our usual wild-eyed Earth First![44] people or anti-nuclear people. We went in to provide a solar-powered energy sound system for their gathering."

"We did more than one event there," said Mark. "But one particular night, we went to support and provide solar power. It was just Bear and me. When we got there, there was a large circle all prepared with a fire in the middle. We heard a different kind of Native American music there, different from anything we'd ever heard before. The women were on one side of the circle, and the men on the other. We stayed up all night watching them. It was an amazing experience. These people had traveled from Southern Arizona to be at Ward Valley."

"Cahuilla bird singers," Bear said. "The men sat on one side of the circle, and the women would move toward them, and then at one point, the men stood up with their rattles, and the women and the men would approach each other. When one group of dancers finished, the next group would dance, and it just kept getting better and better, deeper and deeper. Their music was their ceremony, and when they finished, they were gone. Not a word, no meal, nothing; they cleaned up everything, got into their rented charter bus, and *whoosh,* they were gone."

"The morning following these dances, a desert tortoise walked right through our camp," said Mark.

"The dancers said that when the wind came up, it carried their prayers to Washington," Bear said. "A couple of weeks later, the government scrapped the whole plan to put a nuclear dump site at Ward Valley. We were bewildered by the entire experience. That kind of singing."

"Those people there were not messing around," said Mark. "This was not a social occasion. There was an absolute purpose to everything they did."

Though Clan Dyken did several events at Ward Valley and Lawrence Livermore Lab, the Nevada Nuclear Test Site, the Peace Camp, remained their priority. "The test site was such a huge deal, and some people didn't realize what was happening out there," Mark said. "Holes were drilled a mile down into the earth. A nuclear warhead was put

---

44 Earth First! is an international environmental advocacy group composed of small, bio-regionally-based groups. Earth First!ers familiarize themselves with the ecology of their area and act according to any hazardous threats to it.

down into that hole, and then the workers filled the rest of the hole with concrete. Contractors got rich doing this. After a while it occurred to me that most of the people we were dealing with were doing their jobs. The people we *really* needed to talk to were the decision makers and the scientists."

It was also at the Nevada Nuclear Test Site that Mark experienced his first Native-led Peyote Ceremony. For the band, the peyote experience came sequentially. It was, in a way, a continuum of the ceremonies they'd participated in all their lives. There were altars and sage offerings, drums and songs, and the taking of a sacrament. In both ceremonies, sacred objects and the training and dedication of spiritual leaders contributed to the overall experience. "However," Bear said, "the humility, sincerity, and intensity that are present in Native ceremonies distinguish themselves from the Catholic experience in prominent ways."

"People are hardwired and crave a process for things," said Mark, "especially processes that will bring us closer to the spiritual, closer to God, closer to nature and an understanding of one's self. We see it across all cultures. My first introduction to sweat lodges was through books. I read a lot about them and found the idea intriguing. We started building sweat lodges and participated in sweats on our own, but it wasn't until we started getting into sweats with Native people, like at the Rainbow Gathering and later on with Corbin Harney, and in our early years of going to Big Mountain, that it became more than a gathering of people. The entire process resonated with me and I began to understand the depth of meaning behind the ceremony. It was as if I had been there before and as if some part of me had lived in that continuum. Lengthy historical rituals that I participated in when going to the Catholic Church were a piece of me, yet the sweat lodge experiences felt like a better-attuned instrument of practice for me. Frankincense and myrrh, for instance, are not far off from smudging with sage and the rituals and the prayers that I experienced around fires led by shamans and medicine men of various tribal affiliations, creating a similar ambiance. The practice of using different elementals, whether it's frankincense or sage, the herbs perform similar functions, and all have some level of attunement."

Native activists came to the Nevada Nuclear Test Site from all over the country to perform and participate in the peyote ceremonies. Ceremonies included a vast blending of people, Native and non-Native, Japanese, people from South America, people from all over Peace Camp. These people were at this site in Nevada for a common goal; each had issues happening in his or her own country but came there to end nuclear weapons testing and nuclear waste dumping around the globe. The peyote ceremonies were done in large tipis and were a healing time, a bonding time. "These ceremonies were heavy duty," Mark said. "Big-time medicine. Peyote is a Great Spirit-gifted plant. When distributed by a healer or peyote roadman during a ceremony, every minute is monitored and guided with the objective of treating a person or persons."

"My first peyote ceremony was out at Big Mountain during the funeral of a dear friend," said Bear. "It was a healing ceremony for a family in grief. Peyote ceremony is a beautiful, simple, and profound event that helps to bring human beings into balance," he explained. "It puts us in touch with the four directions and the ancestors by honoring the water and focusing intently on the fire, singing songs and saying prayers, burning sage, cedar, and copal. The fireplace, or fire circle, are the oldest altars there are, and great healing and deep insight can happen there.

"With the help of plant medicines, such as peyote," Bear continued, "human beings can be aided in living a better life. These ceremonies are helpful in dealing with grief, anger, and other negative emotional conditions. The purgative aspects also help with physiological problems. There is healing power in reconnecting with joy and euphoria. A strong sense of well being and clear-mindedness from the strict orderliness of the ceremony, in which everything is placed just so, and all actions are done with reverence. From the time the sun goes down, through the darkness, until the sun comes back up, reverence for the earth, the water, the fire, the air, and all of our relatives and ancestors of all life on the planet."

Mark's first Native-led sweat lodge ceremony was at a Rainbow Gathering, his first peyote ceremony at the Nevada Nuclear Test Site. The Dykens had been going to the test site for years by this point and along with other activists, had tried a great number of things to stop nuclear testing—so Mark figured, why not do it in prayer form? There was a group that traveled around the country with a roadman named King Fisher, and he had a following, as good roadmen do. This man was well known, and his ceremonies were open to non-Indian people. Some of the activists who worked with him before invited him to come to the test site, first in 1991 and then in subsequent years.

On the flat desert playa near Mercury, King Fisher's large tour bus appeared like a floating mirage, providing hope and encouragement to belabored activists. Setting up for the ceremony was a well-practiced process, from constructing the large tipi they brought for ceremonial purposes, to carrying and caring for the medicine (peyote) they would distribute, a large enough quantity to service the people in Peace Camp—100 or more at times, depending on participants.

"I'm not qualified to speak about what it took to set that ceremony up and running," Mark said, fist-bumping his chest above his heart, "but it was impactful, precisely laid-out and practiced from start to finish. Every part of setting up the lodge, what goes on inside, arranging the seating, were all perfectly planned out. There were many jobs, like the fire tender and the person responsible for the drum. There was a core group of practitioners who knew the songs and procedures. I've done these ceremonies with a few different roadmen, and each one does it differently. These guys work with an individual, or they work to make something happen within the environment that will affect everybody. They are like maestros conducting an orchestra."

Under the influence of peyote, the usual physical limitations of the human body no longer exist. A person experiencing the altered state might feel carried by the drum and the drummer. At different times during the ceremony, you might feel like the practitioners are doctoring to you individually, or as if a particular song is meant for you alone. The combination of the medicine and the mastery of the person conducting the ceremony, the power of the songs and the ritual, and the impact of the elements brought into it, pull participants into a different plain. The fire is built in a certain way and tended to in a certain way all through the night. The altar is laid out in a specific way, and the grandfather button (peyote) holds its seat of honor on that altar.

King Fisher's crew, like all peyote road crews, carried toolkits outfitted to manage any scenario and sacred tools meant to help people along their journey if necessary: something as soft and sensual as a feather or as audibly stimulating as a gourd rattle and drumsticks. A fan, perhaps, to soothe and cool sweaty brows. Botanicals used for purposes only the roadmen understand.

At the test site ceremonies, there was an order to everything: the way people entered the tent; where they sat; how the roadman and his crew moved about the tent. Activists sat cross-legged, waiting for a peyote practitioner to offer the peyote in several forms: warm, bitter tea in a jar, a mash of cut up peyote buttons, the buttons themselves, and buttons cubed into pieces. This part of the ceremony involved individual preference, how much to take, what form to take—participants were guided but instructed to follow their instincts. "You will know how much to take," the roadman said. He murmured prayers and sang and sprinkled sage on the fire glowing in the center of the tipi. Participants breathed deeply and centered themselves. Sparks spiraled upwards from the bed of coals, orange, flickering in the darkened space. The drum pounded out seven beats per second, *bum, bum, bum, bum, bum, bum bum.*

The medicine is bitter, earthy in taste, like eating the heart of the earth, some say, and not long after ingestion, the purging begins. Helpers come in and clean up the vomit, take it outside and bury it and say prayers over it. Every part of the ceremony, including this, is carefully planned out and done with purpose.

The roadmen somehow know what a person might need and will especially tend to him or her. Though your experience is unique, you are never alone. Through the medicine, you connect to the roadman, the crew, the other participants—and to the earth and ancient ancestral rhythms. Perceptions of time vanish. Connections with music and song intensify and can feel infinite and orgasmic. While on peyote, a person might experience color-laced fluidity of animate and inanimate objects, movement, rainbow bridges. Solid rocks become molten. Life moves or stands still. The experience is an individual one, and the roadman will often say, should be presided over by a professional who can help if necessary.

"The second year we did the peyote ceremony, we did a sacred run, all the way from Big Mountain, all the way around the test site," Mark said. "Immediately following that run, we did a sweat lodge, and then, went into an all-night peyote ceremony. On the day I went into that ceremony, I had run thirteen miles. I went right from the spirit run into the sweat lodge, and it was one of the hottest sweat lodges I had ever been to. I was like a puddle when I came out of there, and not more than fifteen minutes later, I was in the peyote ceremony.

"Through all of these types of experiences," Mark continued, "we come to understand the concept that we are all one, that any of the separations we experience, from family disagreements to war, are a part of an illusion that we accept as real. By using DNA testing, science now shows that redwood trees that are growing around the rivers where salmon spawn show evidence of the salmon's DNA in the trees. The symbiosis of that relationship is real, and we, as people, have that same kind of relationship with everyone around us. Science has gotten to the point where we can see what we have intuited or believed or been led to believe is true, and that's inspiring to me, personally. If you're open that way, if you're tuning in and paying attention you can take spirituality to a deeper level, whether in a sweat lodge, or a peyote ceremony, or meditating in a hot spring somewhere. There is some commonality between all of those, the heat, the darkness, the awakening of the senses, the awakening of the spiritual. The natural world brings the spiritual world into the same place."

In the spring of 1982, activists held a six-week peace vigil at the entrance to the Nevada Nuclear Test Site. In 1983, they repeated the vigil, and from 1986 through 1994, two years after the United States put a hold on full-scale nuclear weapons testing, there were 536 demonstrations involving 37,488 activists, with 15,740 arrests.[45]

According to the National Cancer Benefits Center, workers exposed to radiation at the Nevada Nuclear Test Site may qualify for benefits if diagnosed with cancer. Covered cancers may include cancer of the liver, pancreas, bile ducts, bladder, brain, breast, colorectal, esophagus, gallbladder, kidney, bone (such as leukemia) and a host of others. "Our

---

45 Butigan, Ken. *Pilgrimage Through a Burning World.* Albany, State University of New York Press.

services are always tailored to your unique needs," the site boasts.[46]

"At the test site," Mark said, "there was so much expenditure in the form of nuclear weapons, power, human effort, resources, and expenses, I often wondered what might have happened if that kind of effort was spent to make people's lives better, building schools, developing solar energy. These were super smart people. What if they worked on making peace, and spent their time developing algorithms so that people understand each other better? Sadly, we have nuclear waste buried all over the place as you see on Navajo land with the uranium tailings. People are going to suffer from this for a long, long time."

"Shundahai"[47]

Old man in his native tongue, leaning into his prayer.
Eyes closed, hands raised, asking for a lift for everyone there.

In ancient Shoshone, the word *shundahai* means peace and harmony with all creation. "You can shundahai a person, you can shundahai a place to bring it energy," Mark explained.

In conjunction with his involvement at the Nevada Nuclear Test Site, Corbin Harney inspired the development of the Shundahai Network, which works toward environmental justice and nuclear disarmament. Since its inception in 1994, the Shundahai Network has evolved into an international network of activists and organizations bridging the gap between the environmental justice, peace, and indigenous land rights communities. Corbin was also the founder and director of Poo-Ha-Bah, a traditional healing center in Tecopa, California. He said, "I have established Poo-Ha-Bah for all the people." Poo-Ha-Bah, in Shoshone, means *doctor water*. "It's really important to have healing water here, not only as a human—a lot of animal life has used healing water, a lot of different ways. We are all connected through water."

---

46 *Nevada Test Site Workers Exposed to Radiation National Cancer Benefits Center.* www.nevadatestsite.info/.

47 Clan Dyken. Old man in his native tongue. "Shundahai." *Shundahai.* CD. Track 2.

10

CAN'T BREATHE[48]

Winning and losing is the same if you can't breathe

T'áá shǫǫdi esat-tsanh = Please listen

The sky was clear but for a few meandering clouds, one of which appeared in the shape of an alien spacecraft. Nearby, in a small canyon, petroglyphs had been chiseled by Navajo and Hopi ancestors, images of people, horses, and deer, symbols of the four directions, and the picture of an object similar in shape to the spacecraft cloud. Long ago, an artist carved images of his sheep into this stone, scallop-fluffed bodies with stick legs—a healthy flock, and a sign of wealth and status—a very different experience from what now represented the tribal norm.

This day, our host's six sheep huddled together in the far corner of their rocky pen, motionless, wooly in their winter coats. There was something so intrinsic, so intimate about the way the sheep were standing. They seemed curious yet wary of us as strangers. The dogs on their chains came around but didn't get too close. Though they looked like sweet mixed-breed family dogs, an Australian shepherd, some Queensland heeler, or terrier-cross maybe, they were not pets. They knew their place

---

48 Clan Dyken. Winning and losing is the same if you can't breathe. "Can't Breathe." *The Last Ride at the End of the Old World*. CD. Track 3.

and were there for a purpose—to protect the sheep and bark a warning should unwanted visitors approach. Still, they accepted treats from afar as we threw dog biscuits their way. The sheep, huddled in silence, never flinched.

On this and every day, part of our morning routine was to do a minimal body clean-up, make tea or coffee, and pick up camp before departing. It was a task to wash dishes, to conserve water in the way the Navajo have managed. "There is a responsibility to stay on this land, this place, our Mother," Dineh elder, Katherine Smith, had once said. Her words made an impression. Despite the water issues, despite the elemental struggles, family struggles, the dispute with Hopi or BIA or the United States government, the responsibility the Navajo felt to stay on their land, and to resist to the end remained. Each year, more of the elder resisters die, but their relatives believe that their souls rest in their umbilical homeland.

The desert is always giving gifts. The sameness, the stillness, are an illusion. Even the sandstone mesas are in a constant state of flux, a breakdown of the elements by human-made and natural causes. The buttes remain, but rocky escarpments surround their base: boulders, smaller rocks, pebbles, and sand swaddling each spire in a stony blanket. To the Navajo, these areas are holy and remain as steadfast as always. "On the top of those buttes, there are places where the older people have been praying," Katherine Smith said in an interview with *Cultural Survival Quarterly Magazine*. "You can find rocks that are built there as an altar, and you can see what the Navajos have been doing there. You see pieces of turquoise or jet or abalone or seashell, white seashells you will find there. That shows that the Navajos have been using this land for generations."[49]

The incidence of abalone and sea shells, turquoise, and the black rock the Navajo called "jet" coincide with their fondness for bartering, visitations by traveling peddlers, and traders who carried goods to and from the reservation from distant places over the years. Some of the seashells Katherine spoke of could have come from local sites, fossils, remnants of Precambrian time, 1,200 million to 740 million years ago,

---

49 Parlow, Anita. "Navajo Forced to Relocate." *Cultural Survival Quarterly Magazine*, www.Culrualsurvival.org/ publications/cultural-survival-quarterly/navajo-forced-relocate. Accessed June 1986.

when trilobites, crinoids, brachiopods, and sponges thrived in a once water-filled environment.

"There's something spiritual about the land," friend and fellow activist Daniel Harrison had said. "I've sat down on the edge of a mesa to meditate, and the tears just come. There is an energy there that fills you."

I carried with me a small medicine bag presented by Me-Wuk elders to my son when he fell ill with leukemia in my hometown of Sonora, California. The pouch is made of leather, hand-stitched and decorated with a few colorful beads. Inside are a small turquoise stone, a lock of my son's hair, unknown tribal medicine, and many, many prayers. A man named Brown Tadd, a respected elder, tribal leader, and an acquaintance of my family made it. Its power and relevance have always stayed with me, just as I felt the power of the stones, the animals, and the plants near our encampment.

Days earlier, Hopi rangers had stopped the Hispanic woodcutters from Flagstaff who brought the firewood we'd purchased. The rangers were checking for permits. "Why are you here? Where are you going? Did you get this wood here on the reservation?" the rangers asked. The woodcutters provided the necessary paperwork, answering the questions in a mix of English, and Spanish. The woodcutters knew that on the mountain, Grandmothers waited, counting on the extra bit of cordwood to help them heat their homes during the upcoming winter. As the rangers drove away, the woodcutters phoned via cell to advise Mark and Bear of the incident. All was well, they said. Though the inquiry was uncomfortable, they drove on to Dove Springs and left their load of wood.

"It was worse in the 1990s," Bear said, as we stacked the last of the firewood in his truck. "Vehicles carrying armed rangers and BIA were everywhere, stopping people, questioning everyone. There were human rights violations left and right. When we first heard about this stuff, we felt drawn by the stories—the Grandmothers, the families affected by policy and political blunder. When Ronald Reagan was President, he called this a 'national sacrifice zone.' He did this so the mining industry could come in—it was all about dollars and cents, but the wrong kind of sense."

Bear brushed off his gloves and jumped down off the truck. "The elders who still live here continue to resist because the land is alive to them," he said. "The Black Mesa region is sacred in the sense that she is female, the mother, and the wife."

The colors of the desert grew bright as the sun rose higher in the sky. The winey-blue so loved by the Grandmothers, turquoise, and red, ochre, and black. These colors of earth, plants, water, and even the coal were represented in the women's weavings, their clothing, and the jewelry they wore. In the elders' eyes, you could almost see their perception of beauty, not as a singular image or a store-bought commodity, but as the entirety of their spirit, and all things in the natural world. There was wisdom behind cataracts and depth of vision one could only hope to understand.

It was Thanksgiving. A day celebrated in history books as a day of sharing and giving between the colonists in Plymouth, Massachusetts, and the Wampanoag Indians who lived there. Ironically, this sunny portrait was deceptive, a case in point being the history of the Navajo, the Long Walk, and more recently, the current relocation efforts. For this and other reasons, the holiday felt bittersweet. We finished loading wood and boxes of food in the trucks for the last time, thinking of our families back home, relishing these final moments with our family here in Dinéh Bikéyah (Navajoland). As in most of America, families on the reservation gathered to share food. At the Navajo table, one might find turkey, but also mutton, and menudo (tripe soup). Dressing, corn, squash, and salads. Fry bread. As we delivered our boxes, we were offered a meal in exchange. "Please, come in, eat," the Grandmothers would say.

In their small kitchens, these women cooked for their husbands, children, and grandchildren, offering what they had prepared to the activists who wandered into their world. At Sand Springs, the Yazzi home, Mark, Bear, and I shot hoops with the teenagers, a quick game of H.O.R.S.E. The portable outdoor basketball hoop stood in their yard beside the house, next to a trampoline on which the younger children jumped and wrestled. Mark went for a jump shot, blocked by one of the Yazzi boys. "Ei-ee," Mark grunted, laughing, going for a second shot. Elder Woody and his nephew Jonathan stood near Woody's stick-built house, nodding their approval. A tawny quarterhorse mare and a younger brown gelding took long gulps of water from a large blue half-barrel, swishing their tails, shaking their heads as if offering their opinion on the status of the game. Several dogs circled the yard, keeping their distance but remaining watchful. Jonathan's youngest boy, around three years old, climbed in and out of Bear's pickup truck, turning the wheel, peeking under seats, poking the tires with his finger. His shirt had long sleeves, but he had ditched his jacket near the trampoline. "He's a little warrior," Woody said, smiling.

The connection between the Yazzi family and Mark and Bear went back to their early days on the reservation and their time spent with the elder, John Yazzi. Throughout the Beauty Way Tour, they had shared stories about John and his place at Sand Springs. "The first time we showed up," Bear said, "John's oldest daughter, Alta, came out to greet us. She was the spokeswoman, the one who communicated with visitors, and I found that fascinating. All the men hung back and shuffled around and looked at their feet, like *what are these strange hippies doing out here?* Since then, we've come to Sand Springs many times to help plant crops and work on irrigation." When speaking of John, Bear would often pause. "Even though John Yazzi never spoke a word of English," Bear said, "we somehow bridged that gap and were great friends. We traded seeds. He gave me blue corn, and I gave him pumpkin and squash. He showed me old pictures of the vast rows of peppers and tomatoes and squash, corn, and melons that once filled their gardens. Now Hopi rangers tell his family that they can't grow food. Can't even put in a garden. Can't replant trees, can't do any of that."

"John Yazzi was another good friend who spent time in a boarding school," said Mark. "And he was a peyote roadman." Mark too, often paused, when speaking of John. "John was a medicine man. He knew what he was doing. People trusted him."

"John had this whole farm thing down," Bear said. "He and his family would grow food, corn, beans, squash, and sell their crops to markets in Flagstaff. They had a pretty good thing going and could take care of their own. But that's changed now, unfortunately."

"John Yazzi and many others went to Washington D.C. and traveled all over the country and different parts of the world, in some cases, speaking about what's happened at Big Mountain," Mark said.

"The elder John Yazzi had an amazing presence," said Catherine. "He was a gentle man with a sweet sense of humor. He was very respected."

In the early years, Mark and Bear and other activists would stay at Louise Benally's at Anna Mae Camp during the Thanksgiving runs, but on spring trips they would camp at the Yazzis'. During planting season, there would be gatherings and feasts, and people from all over would come to celebrate the planting. "We got Grandmother Drum out," Bear said, "and would sit around and drum, and they would play songs, and we would play songs, and the little kids all had a good time. Once, before John passed, he invited us to a Beauty Way ceremony. As with peyote ceremonies, Beauty Way ceremonies would start when the sun went down and ended when the sun came up and was a call for healing—it was beautiful, and there was so much singing. Alta could sing in such a way that she had at least two or three voices going at once, kind of like the Tuvan Throat Singers.[50] She had all these tones and undertones."

"John set up this particular Beauty Way ceremony—every item in its special spot. The way he seated people was well thought out. He knew where everyone was, what they were doing, and how they were feeling," Mark shared, his voice subdued, still impressed by his longtime friend. "John took care of everyone who was in that circle. He was aware of everything, down to the tiniest detail."

Many years had passed since those visits with John, yet the homestead remained. The family had grown. There were a few animals, not like before—but a few. The large cottonwood tree beside the spring house grew thicker and taller, despite the odds. The tree stood in sharp contrast to the small and scattered junipers, the nubby scrub brush and sparse grasses growing out of the dry sand. After greetings and basketball, we walked there to talk with elder Woody Yazzi. John Yazzi's grandchildren, Ceejay and Emiah, wandered about, hunting rocks and showing off their finds of small bits of chert and red and yellow sandstone. Woody got tearful as he spoke of the changes he had seen in his lifetime of living at Sand Springs. Today, spring gatherings for planting season are rare. He and his family must carefully plan what to plant. Now, the Yazzis and others who live on Hopi Partitioned Land must obtain per-

---

50 In Tuva, a Russian republic between Siberia and Mongolia, the Tuvan throat singers are able to produce two distinct notes at one time when singing.

mits to grow crops, to live in their homes and on their land, and to keep their animals.

"I worry about how my family will make it out here in the future," Woody said. "We don't have the money for the permit to live here. We don't have the money for the permit to grow food."

If a Big Mountain family has not obtained a permit to grow food, their crops are torn up or burned. Wells are capped. People are fearful of raids by Hopi rangers, who show up unannounced with livestock trucks and haul away and impound sheep, horses, cows, and goats if a family has exceeded their livestock allotment. Just as residents' cell phone texts act as a hotline to announce visitors, they also serve as a warning: "The livestock trucks are coming. Be ready."

On the HPL-BIA War Against Navajo Grandmothers Facebook page,[51] cattle transport trucks accompanied by multiple ranger vehicles are pictured driving onto Navajo family homesteads, and posters to the site voice their concerns about their impounded animals not being fed or watered once transported to the impound stockyards. "Over this past week," one poster said, "law enforcement and Hopi land management officers entered Sovereign Dineh (Navajo) Nation territories at Big Mountain/Black Mesa, Arizona with orders to count Dineh livestock. They issued five-day notices to Dineh families, threatening to impound so-called 'trespassing' sheep, goats, and cattle." On a blog entry uploaded on the same Facebook page, elder matriarch Glenna Begay said to the writer, "In times like these it's hard for me to eat or sleep. I lay up at night worried about my animals. The sheep are my children. The horses too are relatives. They have been with us since the beginning."

Broken promises weigh on the homestead at Sand Springs. The subsidy checks sent by Peabody Coal Company amount to a pittance; there is no evidence here or anywhere else on the reservation of the vast wealth earned by mining concerns. The outhouse sits at the end of a short trail amidst desert nightshade, creosote, and sage. Implements and tools used by the elders are propped against the house and stored in small

---

51 *Emergency on HPL - BIA war against Navajo Grandmothers.* 25 June 2017, www.facebook.com/ Emergency-on-HPL-BIA-war-against-Navajo-Grandmothers-862442917108374/.

sheds—buckets used to gather juniper berries and pinyon nuts, some hand tools. Once inside, Angelita Yazzi showed us her looms. She has two, and the one passed down from her mother is a prized possession. Her fingers gently move across the upper bar and heddle.[52] Each rug she weaves takes many days to create and when sold, brings in money to the family. Fleece from her sheep is carded and spun on a spindle to make her yarn, then pulled and adjusted until the yard is a consistent size from one end to the other. Her yarn is dyed using natural dyes: sunflowers for yellow, walnuts for brown, cactus bugs for red, and other herbs for blue, grey, white, and black. As with Elsie Benale and other weavers on the reservation, items passed down by mothers and Grandmothers include wooden weaving combs, spindles, and the skilled fingers that guide their work.

Angelita's home was warm and cozy. Her electricity comes via wind and solar. The family's spring still holds water; they are fortunate this way. She has a stove to cook on, a refrigerator, and a wood stove for heat. In his bouncy chair, her youngest grandson played with his fingers while *Spirit*, a Disney movie, showed on the television. The women were busy with their children, while the men remained outside, visiting with Mark and Bear.

Angelita's looms and her kitchenware are her tools, given to her, the Navajo believe, by Mother Earth and by the Creator. Grinding stones, stirring sticks bound with leather, a brush used as a strainer for corn pollen, all are considered a woman's *weapons* and are meant to keep her family healthy and strong. "We shake the pollen from the corn plant and offer it to the sun," said Grandmother Alice Benally, in a video recorded history lesson.[53] She sang as she gently shook the plant, and as the pollen fell onto a platter. Her song was an offering, a prayer.

One of Mark's earliest memories of coming to the reservation involved Katherine Smith and her loom, walking into her hogan as the sun filtered across the rug she was weaving. As with Bear's first visit to the Yazzi place, it was women who greeted Mark at Katherine's home,

---

52 Heddle: one of the sets of vertical cords or wires in a loom, forming the principal part of the harness that guides the warp threads.

53 "Navajo Women of Big Mountain." *YouTube,* edited by www.huntleyfilmarchives.com Film 98189, www.youtube.com/watch?v=ANCbF7WkvA8.

and women who welcomed the activists at Anna Mae Camp. Today, many of the younger women, like Angelita and Elsie, work outside of the home to help provide for their families. The elders, however, follow the traditional path. A Grandmother's morning might start with prayer, facing east and greeting the sun, or by lighting a fire using wood she chopped herself. Her day could include cooking, weaving, cleaning, sheep herding, and hauling water, but most likely would end with telling stories to her children and grandchildren. Amá sání (Grandmother), Shìmà (Mom), as the matriarch, her words matter. When she speaks, her family listens.

In the early morning light, Anna Begay herded her sheep. Roberta Blackgoat spun her wool. Alice Benally taught her daughter, Louise, how to grind corn into cornmeal, and which native plants were good for food and for medicine. Elsie Benale and Angelita Yazzi's mothers taught them how to make dyes to color the wool shorn from their family's sheep, as did the other mothers, and each one of them spoke to her children about the importance of protecting their heritage.

After the passing of the Navajo Hopi Resettlement Act in 1974, the women became the face and voice of advocacy for their people. They stood on the front line with the Navajo men and spoke up for themselves and their families. Said Lakota Medicine Man Leonard Crow Dog to a group of gathered weavers at a Sundance Ceremony in the late 1980s: "Grandmothers, you will walk this land forever. This work will help you walk this land. And you will take care of this land forever. It is yours to take care of, forever. For four seasons, forever."

For the women, the weavers, becoming human rights workers was not a choice; it was a necessity. They used their bodies as shields, defending their homes against officials in uniform who were threatening to remove them and their families by force. They marched. They carried signs: *Stand your ground, it's sacred; Coal is dead; This is stolen land; The creator is the only one who's going to relocate me; Listen to the elders; Save our water.*

Around this same time, the Navajo weavers grew tired of the scant money offered them by the proprietors of local trading posts, sometimes as little as eighty dollars a rug, knowing that the trader then turned around and sold their work for up to $800 a piece. The weavers began to work with trusted activists—women who would sell their rugs to private buyers and return all profits to each weaver personally. With the help of activist groups, the weavers banded together and did benefits in Los Angeles and other places. They spoke about their culture, their problems with the mine and relocation, *and* they sold their work—women of the loom, dream-weavers living upon the master loom which was to them Big Mountain.

One such speaker was the elder matriarch Glenna Begay. On behalf of the Dineh Grandmothers and her fellow weavers, she met with diverse crowds, traveling from the reservation to faraway places. At a benefit fundraiser in Los Angeles, Glenna addressed a group of people who were there to purchase rugs and hear her story. Her interpreter, Louise Benally, wheeled her in a wheelchair to the center of the room. Glenna wore a light blue bandana tied at the chin, a long pink skirt, a magenta sweater, and tennis shoes. Her full brows, brown skin, and down-turned lips carried the legacy of her mother and Grandmothers, the clans of her family. In her native tongue, she relayed the truth of her unintended activism while Louise listened, and then translated:

"At this time, we are very oppressed. We have our animals, the sheep, the horses, the cows, the goats, these are the only resources we have to feed ourselves and to clothe ourselves and to shelter ourselves. Those animals are being forced to be impounded, to be taken away from us without our consent. When the Hopi Rangers and BIA come out, they have no mercy. Even old people like myself are treated brutally, harshly by these ranger's agencies. They beat up and throw around old women that are over ninety years at gunpoint. They take the sheep from the corral, and this is the treatment that we are getting."

The audience was completely silent. Vendors stood in front of their booths to get a better look. Musicians left their instruments on the stage and were now seated on the floor in front of Glenna. Children sat on their parents' laps. A black and red paper-mache snake, mocking big oil, lay motionless, its puppeteers neglecting now to slither it around the room. All attention was on Glenna.

"This oppression is what we have to live with," Glenna continued, "and this is why I need to share my story with you so that you will be aware. We don't have any recourse as far as the legal system goes. We don't have anyone to turn to except communities from other parts of the country such as the support networks that come out to Big Mountain, and I often wonder, how can this be addressed? How can this be stopped? Do we need to confront the government and the rangers at their level? These are some of the things that go through my head. I have always lived at Big Mountain. I was born and raised there; I have no place to go. I don't have any plans to go anywhere.

"There are not many elders left now, and I often wonder if they have left to the next world because of being heartbroken and not knowing which way to turn anymore. Recently I traveled to Washington D.C. to talk to the federal government, and it was a woman I spoke to, and when I told her my concerns, she told me that we were on land that belongs to the Hopi and there was nothing she could do."

Louise stood with her head down and her hands clasped in front of her, listening as Glenna spoke. "We are part of that land," she translated. "We have no formal education other than our upbringing. That is what we know, and this is what I want you to know. We are dealing with political oppression. On the other hand, Peabody Coal Company is continuously mining the land, causing environmental devastation. A lot of the animals are affected by this—the pollution from it including ourselves—we all have respiratory issues.

"People who have worked there from the time the mines opened in the 1960s are all gone now due to respiratory illnesses. We watch the land dying. They are blasting it, extracting the coal, exposing everything nearby to methane gas that comes from the earth. We have a lot of environmental impacts. Our groundwater has dropped, and there are no more natural springs, and that impacts the vegetation and all of the trees that are there that we once knew as medicine, as food, they are all disappearing, and this is all due to the excessive extraction of the resources."

In the 1980s, Peabody Coal Company ran their coal slurry, confident that there was enough coal under Black Mesa to mine for the next 100 years. The Department of the Interior set a deadline of July 7, 1986 to have the Hopi Partitioned Land cleared of Navajos. As the July seventh deadline approached, President Ronald Reagan mandated that all Navajo families on HPL must be relocated or face forced removal by the National Guard. The deadline passed with 700 families relocated, mostly to Flagstaff.

Also in the 1980s, the United States government purchased a uranium-contaminated site near Chambers, Arizona, and coined it the "Newlands" for relocated Navajo. This land was part of the Church Rock radioactive spill area—the same area that a year earlier had been contaminated by uranium tailings when the earthen dam owned by the United Nuclear Corporation broke and released contaminated water into the Puerco River. This was one of the incidents that drove the anti-nuclear movement and led the Dykens to Rancho Seco.

At Big Mountain, relocation continued. Families were forced from their land by Hopi tribal rangers and the Bureau of Indian Affairs. Four-wheel drive vehicles filled with armed men drove into yards, broke down doors, brutalized animals, and as Glenna referred to, dragged elders from their homes. Children cried, not understanding why armed men were fighting with their relatives, or why their parents, Grandmothers, and Grandfathers fought back.

The Navajo who moved away struggled with their new accommodations, many unable to adapt to life away from their homeland. They had no concept of property taxes, utility bills, or even fraud by realtors. Alcoholism, illnesses, and broken families grew more prevalent, both on and off the reservation, as families tried to cope with separation from loved ones and the discord caused by whether to sign or not sign the relocation agreement. BIA planes circled the land. BIA agents stopped visitors and ordered people where to park, and where to collect and not collect firewood. They prevented anyone who didn't have a permit from proceeding to their destination. Armed guards shut off water sources. Food supplies dwindled. At night, people gathered for protection. Children were told to stay quiet while parents remained on alert for any unusual sound or outdoor commotion.

As word spread of the conditions at Big Mountain, hundreds of activists from all over the world came to the aid of the elders. They helped plant crops and shear sheep; they brought food and firewood, as Mark and Bear continue to do. Many of the activists felt they were called to assist, to work, and to bear witness to what was happening. Classes were offered on Witness Education Peace Camp at college and university campuses in California and Washington state. Students became activists, and some Navajo like Pauline Whitesinger and Willie Lonewolf acted as their interpreters. Hopi rangers posted notices such as this one on reservation land: *Let it be clear: This resistance is an act of civil disobedience against the United States and Hopi Nation Policy. Those who support these families in resistance are subject to legal actions if they are seen as disobeying legal policies.*

During these difficult years, some activists stayed on the reservation for extended periods, helping to herd sheep and plant corn, using deep irrigation planting to conserve water that was already scarce and made more limited by the coal slurry transport used by Peabody Coal. "Remember," a Grandmother once taught Bear, "Keep the holes about two feet apart, or the rain will grow tired crops. Keep the rows straight. Clear away all the dry dirt on top until you have a clear plate of wet dirt. Keep the dry dirt away from the wet, or it will absorb all the water. Put in about ten corn seeds. Cover that with wet dirt. Then cover the wet dirt with dry dirt."

Always open to the calling of the earth and her people, the Grandmothers reached out, and in the 1990s fought not only the coal and uranium mining operations on their land, but acted as stewards for other issues, such as that on Shoshone land at the test site in Nevada. Though their lives were in turmoil over the terms outlined in the Relocation Agreement, Navajo understood the problems associated with uranium and coalmine contamination. Whether on Navajo land or Shoshone land, radiation contamination was a global problem. They traveled to Nevada to walk beside their brothers and sisters and protect what was most sacred to them: our earth, our water, our air, the safety of our people, seven generations out.

Most ironic is that the majority of uranium that went into the testing of the nuclear bombs at the Nevada Nuclear Test site came from the Navajo reservation around Big Mountain. In 1967 an article in the *Washington Post* warned about the dangers of working with uranium, but even by the 1990s, very little was being done on the reservation.

Yet the Navajo persisted. They protested and they endured, not only for themselves but for all people. The bridge between people that Corbin Harney spoke of and Mark referred to when talking about science and DNA evidence, and the common ground that binds us as humans, was case in point at the Nevada Nuclear Test Site.

"The prayers have been living inside the Dineh Nation since creation," said Roberta Blackgoat. "But our songs cover all the universe. The song goes on and on, ocean to ocean…that is how the song and the prayer is."

> *Clocks are ticking*
> *And the grains of sand*
> *Are slipping through the human hands*
> *What good are all your plans*
> *If you can't breathe.*[54]

---

54 Clan Dyken. Clocks are ticking. "Can't Breathe." *The Last Ride at the End of the Old World*. CD. Track 3.

11

Not A Tree Farm[55]

The trees are our caretakers. Don't bite the hand that feeds,
stop cutting the trees, please.

Ałhaa dasti' = Respect

A ramshackle, boarded-up hogan appeared on the horizon, flanked by a solitary ghost tree. The juniper's trunk was bent over, the branches akimbo, naked but for a metal pail hung over one gnarly twig. In the 1980s and 1990s, trees were sometimes torn out by the roots or burned, but the unburned trees remain, like this one, a hallowed reminder of what once thrived. This tree's death could also have been a side-effect of draught or the diminished water supply. No way to tell at a quick glance, only that its bones held tight, marking it as a statistic. Was the hogan abandoned? Maybe not. Perhaps it stands out of reverence to the elder who lived and died there, as is the tradition of the Navajo. On the reservation, when a person dies while in his or her hogan, they are buried there. The hogan is left, and the door is sealed. People who were living in that hogan move to another place not far off.

As we drove past the hogan, my dream Amá sání came to mind once again. In my journal, I wrote what she might have said if she saw this place. *Yes. A Grandfather lived here, and here he remains; he lies in peace,* she said. *This tree, he once loved. He ate of its fruit. He rested in its shade.*

---

55 Clan Dyken. The trees are our caretakers. "Not A Tree Farm." *Love is.* CD. Track 10.

The tree's roots grounded him and let him know he was home; its heartwood was a part of him.

A song on the radio, sung in Navajo, quieted her imaginary chatter, the motor in Bear's truck, and the occasional static transmitted from the station, competing for attention. Thoughts and feelings rumbled and swirled, as unpredictable as a desert storm. Tribal elders often spoke of the healing power of trees. Through the process of photosynthesis, trees convert carbon dioxide into oxygen; the air we breathe is a byproduct of their unique synergy with the sun and the water and the soil in which they grow. Without the trees, the earth would be uninhabitable. Without the trees, there would be no life.

The bucket hanging on the branch of this dead juniper was not unusual. Similar buckets hung in small stands of trees throughout the reservation, put there for gathering pinyon nuts and juniper berries, both sources of food for the Navajo. Roberta Blackgoat's words played forward, as poignant this time, as they were the first: *The prayers have been living inside the Dineh Nation since creation. But our songs cover all the universe. The song goes on and on, ocean to ocean…that is how the song and the prayer is.* The Navajo prayers and songs were not for them alone. They traveled from ocean to ocean, for all people, for all animals, and for all plant life, including the trees.

The sun rested low in the sky by the time we left Sand Springs. Brilliant oranges and reds marked another sunset, a time for reflection. A jackrabbit ran along the culvert beside us, scampering up the dirt bank, disappearing behind a mesquite bush. Bear took the rabbit's lead, pulling his truck off the washboard road and into the smoother-riding side ditch. The ease of the ride and the unexpected rabbit sighting led to renewed conversations about timelines, the transitions in attitude and activist encounters that prompted the Dykens to come here.

"From the test site to Big Mountain, nothing was random," Bear said, turning down the volume on both the radio and my daydreams. "It all tied together. From that first trip, when Mark borrowed my truck and called and said to me, 'Hey, you gotta come out here. You gotta see this.' He came in January, and I came in November 1991 with our friend Coyote. First time out, we didn't know where we were going. It was getting dark like it is now." Bear grinned. "We ended up lost and drove around on these reservation roads most of the night," he said. "Eventually, we found our way to John Benally's place—the same guy Mark had met when he came to the reservation. John invited us to stay at his house, and so we slept on his floor. That's when I first met both him and his sister, Louise."

During the late 1980s and early 1990s, activists on college campuses, like Mark and Bear and many other concerned citizens, pushed to address a series of contemporary problems, most of them sociologically and environmentally based. Public face-offs between opposing groups were commonplace. The need to protect what was *real*—the earth, air, water, civil rights was the impetus for most campaigns. Memberships soared in organizations like Greenpeace, the National Audubon Society, the Sierra Club, the Friends of the Earth, and Seeds of Change—some of the same groups that participated in actions at Big Mountain.

"In the 1980s, activists were dropping food by helicopter at Sand Springs and other locations," said Mark, "because that's how serious the Big Mountain blockades were—the efforts to keep supporters from getting to the resisters. BIA was trying to flush the Navajo out."

"Those were wild times," Bear said.

"Things were popping out here," said Mark, "and in Nevada and California. Everything was happening at once, including Ward Valley, the Nevada Nuclear Test Site, and the forest actions in Northern California."

"The forest actions, Redwood Summer, were an effort to protect the giant redwoods. People got pepper sprayed and were chaining to things," Bear recalled. "Car bombs went off, and everyone was called an ecoterrorist."

The remnants of the juniper tree and the conversation between Mark and Bear led us in the transition between the desert and coastal forests. It brought to mind the many camping trips I took to the California redwoods around Arcata in Humboldt County. Thinking of the redwoods, I could almost feel the soft give of the damp and spongy trails beneath my hiking boots, the roughness of the red bark as I ran my hands across trees I knew had been there much longer than I had been alive. Unlike the juniper, these giants had survived fires and lightning strikes. They had resisted pest infestation, but they could not withstand the teeth of the chainsaws powered by outside interests. In the case of the redwoods, old-growth trees harvested for homes, picnic tables, firewood, even toothpicks, prompted a series of demonstrations and marches to protest the Northern California timber industry, beginning in the summer of 1990.

California ballot Proposition 130, known as the Forest Forever Initiative, was up for a vote that year. Passage of this proposition would have put an end to the logging of old growth redwoods and unsustainable logging such as clear-cutting. "The goal of Redwood Summer," Bear said, "was to engage in nonviolent action in hopes of raising public awareness. On a whole other level this was happening at Big Mountain, but for completely different reasons and with a different level of response."

"As at Big Mountain, it was a grassroots people-powered resistance against destructive corporate resource extraction," said Mark. "One impressive thing about Redwood Summer, it had all the elements that you see at activist actions today, but we didn't have internet or Facebook, so communication was about people talking to each other by newsletters and telephone, getting a radio interview or a television spot. There was a lot of effort by the people on the ground. This was a fantastic show of unity by different activist groups who got together and were able to organize their message, to show up in the right places at the right times."

Redwood Summer organizer and activist Darryl Cherney said the same via cell phone, months later. "As far as communication goes, all technology is like an arms race. They get a fax, and then you get a fax; they get an email, you get an email, they get a Twitter tweet, you get a Twitter tweet. When we don't have those things, we use the phones, and the phones are as fast as emails and far more effective. I'd rather call twenty people and get all of them to show up to a rally than email 1,000 and get five people to show up."

In this grassroots manner, Earth First! activists Darryl Cherney and Judi Bari contacted other activists in various parts of the country, asking them to show up for a series of pre-planned events to protect the old growth redwoods. Several organizations, including Food Not Bombs[56] and Seeds of Peace,[57] joined in and helped organize participants, set up

---

56 Food Not Bombs provides free food to the homeless and hungry and has branches in every country on every habitable continent. *Food Not Bombs,* www.foodnotbombs.net.

57 Seeds of Peace is a leadership development organization committed to transforming

base camps all over the Pacific Northwest, and handled demonstration logistics. To help publicize California Ballot Proposition 130, Judi and Darryl planned the series of demonstrations they termed "Redwood Summer," hoping to recruit large numbers of college students to help in their effort.

"Redwood Summer was named after Mississippi Summer," said Mark, "the voting act and civil rights action that happened in the 1960s." He turned on his cell phone, fact-checking. "That alone caused people to think the forest action was inflammatory," he said, "but what the organizers were calling for was the kind of *movement* and *support* that Mississippi Summer got in the way of attracting activists."

Newscasters, as well as activists, responded to the call. The events at Redwood Summer became a public outcry, both pro and con. The police response was immediate and constant. In Humboldt County alone, cars lined roadways and demonstrators blocked roads, carrying signs that read: *Earth First!* and *Earth Before Profit.* Those in opposition carried signs that read: *This is not Mississippi. Go home.* Logging trucks piled with felled redwood trees slowed to pass the diverse group of activists, adults, students, and children.

"If you look at the big picture," said Mark, "the amount of destruction, these ancient trees being cut down, clear-cut over these enormous swaths of land—it was like some form of genocide when you consider the tree population."

Mark shifted position in his seat, facing forward. "There was more value placed on the price of lumber by supporters of the logging industry than on the peace and ecological value others of us felt when stepping foot in that forest. For those who walked among those beautiful trees, the idea that someone would destroy those places simply to make money was beyond belief. The last of over two million acres of old growth primeval forests.

"For me," he said, "this was yet another view of how corporate power runs over the little guy. Sure there were loggers and others who had jobs dependent on the logging industry, and the workers got support from that angle, but the concern or consideration for what was right for the planet, or do we need this resource in this quantity, none of that was considered."

While driving through the Hopi town of Moenkopi, we passed several brown rectangular houses along the road and could see more houses built onto the surrounding mesas. Much more communal than what we observed on Navajoland. We couldn't help but notice, however, that large amounts of money hadn't filtered from Peabody Coal to the Hopi tribe either. The patches of green were denser than on Black Mesa and the active farms more prominent, but they were still sporadic—the water as contaminated here as on Big Mountain. Roadside homes showed signs of disrepair, tattered roofing, and a few broken windows covered by fabric.

The influence of big corporations and governmental decision making was visible in Moenkopi and on Big Mountain. Mark and Bear experienced similar interference at the Nevada Nuclear Test Site, but there was a noticeable difference between those experiences and what they saw during Redwood Summer. The forest actions were more widespread, covering a vast area from Washington State through Southern Oregon and Northern California, all along the West Coast, and the actions were more publicized. However, the money behind those representing the timber companies was significant. There was political clout and donations were plentiful.

"If you were able to piece together all the money and connections that these capitals of industry exerted," Mark said, "and what laws were passed in the midst of any controversy, you came to see what activist actions might be persecuted in favor of these corporate endeavors."

On May 24, 1990, Earth First! activists Judy Bari and Darryl Cherney were on their way to the University of Santa Cruz when in Oakland a bomb exploded under the seat of Judi's white Subaru. The blast shattered her pelvis in ten places and injured Darryl. Following the explosion, both Judi and Darryl were arrested by the Oakland Police Department at the insistence of the FBI, who claimed that the bomb belonged to the Earth First! people and had gone off prematurely by accident. The mainstream media nation-wide repeated the FBI's charge that the bomb belonged to Darryl and Judi and that they were transporting it to some unknown destination for reasons involving sabotage.

Today, the bombing crime remains unsolved. Evidence produced during the 2002 civil rights case and trial against the Oakland police and FBI agents who arrested Darryl and Judi showed that the agents only investigated environmental activists as potential suspects. They did nothing whatsoever to investigate the corporations and their representatives despite a clear, multimillion-dollar motive to target and derail Redwood Summer and create public support of Prop. 130. The rapid presence of FBI bomb investigators at the scene, virtually simultaneously with first responders from the Oakland Police Department, raised suspicion that the FBI knew about the bomb beforehand and might even have been responsible. It was later revealed that there had been a tip to law enforcement, suspected to be from the person responsible for the bomb, that "some heavies" were carrying a bomb south for sabotage in the Santa Cruz area. [58]

"When you look at the work Darryl and Judi were able to do," Mark said, "it's impressive. They drove from meeting to meeting in Judi's little car, and all of a sudden there would be 5,000 people at the gates of the lumber mill outside of Arcata. All of them recruited to support Redwood Summer. Darryl is a great songwriter and singer, so he had messages that went with it all. He was good at getting the information out there, but his activism went way beyond the organizational piece. He would go into the woods and hang out there with everyone else."

Judi was not only an activist and a musician, but she was also a labor organizer by trade. She knew how to talk to the loggers and how to discuss the possibilities of their future. Judi was known for her ability to listen as well as talk, to gently persuade as well as to pound a point home. She was a self-proclaimed virtuoso of the bullhorn but also used her music, her violin, as a call to action.

"We as activists sometimes feel that if we give people the facts, they'll change their minds," Mark said, "but it's never about that, it's about emotion. For the workers, whether it be at a nuclear power plant, or the coal mines, or in the forest, or elsewhere, it's about taking care of themselves and their families. If you're a proud person, or a working person who's been doing your job for a while, or the profession has been in your family for a while, you're not going to give this up because someone wants to save trees. There has to be a *worker paradise*, a way to

---

58 "The Bombing of Judi Bari." *Boulder Weekly.* Web. 26 Sep. 2018 <http://www.boulderweekly.com/opinion/the-bombing-of-judi-bari/>.

show that someone can change from this job to that job, without excess consequences."

Mark paused, digesting this part of the conversation. "I think this is why Judi was targeted," he said, "because she was able to make headway with the loggers, and this is a takeaway for me from Redwood Summer. You can only get so far if you don't speak to what the working people need to hear. If you can give them the message that there is an alternative way, that's how you get results. If someone would have come up to the loggers, and said, 'Hey, I'm building a solar energy plant, and I'm going to be making solar panels—I'll pay you twenty percent more than you make cutting trees,' many of them would have taken that offer.

"So all this was happening, and then one day I'm looking at the newspaper, and the headline read 'Eco-terrorists Arrested,' and this was talking about Darryl and Judi!" Mark said. "Someone had just tried to kill them, and charge them with conspiracy, yet the two of them were demeaned by the press and arrested by the police? It's was a huge story, but considering American history, California history, and activist history, it's like a little blip. Hardly anyone knows it even happened. Hardly anyone knows that the media was calling this action the Timber Wars at the time. Very few people know what an epic battle it was to save those old growth redwoods."

After taking time to recuperate from their injuries, Judi and Darryl continued with the campaign, playing their music and inspiring activists to keep up the fight. Many young hippies stayed the course for years. According to Mark and Bear, basecamps for Redwood Summer were like the Peace Camp at the test site and the activist camps at Big Mountain. People took turns with chores including cooking and clean up. Conversations remained amiable in most cases, and decisions were communal. Pertinent education and nonviolence training happened, and there was live music.

Activists could participate in different forms of direct action. Many marched and demonstrated in towns throughout Northern California. Others focused on fighting in the courts by appealing timber harvest plans and obtaining injunctions against logging the old growth forests. Just as activists walked into the test site grounds and chained themselves to PVC pipes to block the roads at the test site, in the old growth forests, some went to logging sites to sit in front of bulldozers, and some, like Julia Butterfly Hill, climbed the redwoods and camped in treetops. Many activists provided her supplies, like food and water and personal necessities by way of elevators made from rope and pulleys. Julia lived in the top of a tree she named Luna for 738 days, from December 10, 1997, to December 18, 1999.

"Julia wasn't the only one who made that choice," Mark said. "There were tons of people doing the same thing, sitting in trees, supporting. Julia was the headline as far as tree protest, but there were so many people on the ground, literally raising and lowering these buckets of her supplies and debris. People took care of her comfort needs. People brought her food, and her support people lived there in the forest or were staying nearby. And you never heard about them. There was a guy named David Gypsy Chain who got killed while protesting. A logger dropped a tree on him. By accident? Don't know.

The stage faced away from the Louisiana Pacific Paper Mill in Samoa, California, and on it, Darryl Cherney and the band Clan Dyken readied to play, setting up mics, tuning their instruments, checking sound equipment. It was Darryl's first public appearance since the bomb detonation in Judy's car. The audience was 700 strong, chanting, shouting protest slogans, and praises for Judi, and Darryl. The group warmed up the rally by singing peace songs and songs in support of Redwood Summer.

> *The trees are our caretakers.*
> *Don't bite the hand that feeds, stop cutting the trees, please."*[59]

Suddenly, a semi-truck attempted to turn into the mill, and the protesters swarmed it. In one mass movement, police crowded the protestors, a tangle of bodies, pushing, pulling, and shouting.

Recognizing the potential for violence, Darryl, Mark, and Bear turned the PA system and stage-setting around to face the mill and the truck surrounded by people. *Be non-violent,* they sang, making up words to calm the crowd down. *Be non-violent, stay non-violent. Be non-violent, stay non-violent, be non-violent, stay non-violent, be non-violent,*

---

59 Clan Dyken. The trees are our caretakers. "Not A Tree Farm." *Love is.* CD. Track 10.

stay non-violent, over, and over, and over.

"The Clan and I have always played well together," Darryl said, when I had the opportunity to speak with him by email, "even though those times are rare. They are very accommodating and happy to be my backup band for a few songs as well as take the lead, as is their norm. The point is they don't have their ego in their songs, in their heads, or on the stage. They are one of the people."

"My favorite story," Darryl continued, "is when we toured together in the weeks and days before we went to trial against the FBI in the spring of 2002. We performed on the same bill at U.C. Davis and whoever set up the marquee wrote *Cherney* on the top line and *Dyken* below, making it read: *Cherney Dyken*. Thus I officially became one of the Dykens. We all remember that one with a smile."

During the years of protests, the old growth stands of trees saw many heated exchanges between the loggers and the activists. In some instances, though, there were civil, quieter moments, when favorable exchange occurred. "A post-Redwood Summer example,' said Darryl, referring to an event in 1992, "was when about nineteen of us hiked into an old growth logging operation by Pacific Lumber. I was the first to run in right up to the faller, and I said, 'Do you know how many board feet are in this tree?' He answered. I kept asking him professionally oriented questions, displaying some knowledge of tree falling and forestry. I wasn't talking down or up to him. I was talking shop. He put down his saw and left everything there. I was pretty surprised."

"There was one time when we were drumming at a Redwood Summer action," Mark said, tapping his fingers on his knees, "and we played drums with Governor Jerry Brown and Micky Hart, drummer for the Grateful Dead. Corbin was there too. Jerry wanted to play drums with us, so we were all on this stage. Not far from where Julia Butterfly was up in the tree, Luna."

Despite the actions held during Redwood Summer, non-sustainable logging continues in Northern California. Many of the old groves are gone. "Can you imagine our relatives, seven generations out, looking back and saying, 'They did this? Corporations cut down all these giant redwood trees?'" Mark said, his eyes glazed as if his thoughts were far away.

"Redwood Summer taught me something, or maybe, I see things

a little differently now," he continued. "There is a time and place for confrontations, but using dialogue, reaching out to people who think differently than us, and finding common ground. That's what works long term. Activism, in its best form, raises consciousness. It's hard to achieve actual justice, where everyone is getting his or her needs met. Tons of people are unemployed. People live on the streets, camp under bridges and along creeks and streams. We have to find some common ground. We have so far to go.

"Sometimes I wonder if it can happen in my lifetime. We've made progress when it comes to positive growth and change, women's rights, civil rights, but there is still so much divisiveness, so much hatred and prejudice. None of this activism is over. We have to keep taking steps. Raising critically thinking and responsible children in today's world is a form of activism at the ground level. Those redwoods, they were and are something special. Activism for a reason, a cause—there we had it at its best."

"What a lovely, long strange trip it's been," Bear said, later. "All the ways we've been able to help these kinds of causes, to touch people with our music. Another such action happened in Hawaii."

Carried on a cargo ship, the components of a stage and multiple solar panels reached Hawaii before Clan Dyken did. As the band flew into Honolulu Airport, they readied to perform again, this time for an action put forward by the Homelands Hawaiian Movement in response to a major corporation relocating native Hawaiians and drilling holes in places where there was known volcanic activity, with the intention to harness steam to produce electricity for a proposed geothermal plant.

"At the time,' Bear said, "it seemed similar to what was happening at Big Mountain, where Native people were being relocated for resource extraction. So we went over there and did a similar thing, a solar-powered music concert in towns and at the farmers' market. We also provided a stage and music for an action at the geothermal plant where people trespassed and got arrested and locked themselves to the gate, and we ended up leaving those solar panels with the Homelands Hawaiian Movement."

Keeping a positive vibration and staying true to their message and vision was the motivation behind Clan Dyken's furthered efforts to make their music by solar power. "It was kind of hypocritical, at that point, to plug into the nuclear power plant when we're protesting against it, or fighting against the coal plant, but using it to power our concerts. The energy it took to cut down those redwoods, we knew we could make it better, and that's where the bicycles came in," Bear said. "But it was a guy named Bart Orlando who pointed out to me that what would be revolutionary would be if we could get everyone to ride bikes to the shows. That would save the most carbon in the atmosphere. Then came our friends, Dante Espinosa and Kipchoge Spencer, who had pipe dreams at Burning Man to make a generator that was powered by a bicycle. They endeavored to go 5,000 miles on bikes carrying all this stuff through Mexico playing pedal powered concerts on a system large enough for 300 people that was powered by the bicycles they rode."

"After the Pleasant Revolution Tour, where I first met Bear," said Dante Espinosa in an email exchange, "I got stuck in Mexico, so I started making pedal power systems to sell. Bear bought the first and only one and paid in full before I even made it. That helped me out. It was over a year before I finished it for him. Mark and Bear have done their best to make me part of their pedal power events."

"So since then," Bear added, "music-driven bike tours have been done up and down the West Coast of the United States, the East Coast, throughout Mexico, Europe, parts of Canada, and some of it has been done down in Chile. Shake Your Peace pedaled all the way from Colorado to California. Then my humble efforts at the Sail Boat Bicycle Music Tour here in the Central Valley, and we did the Emerald Triangle Bicycle Music Tour two years in a row, going from Trinity County and up into Humboldt and Northern Mendocino. So yeah, bicycle music touring. It's the next frontier in alternative powered music.

"It's uplifting to be among other riders," he said. "It is an exhilarating and revolutionary act to be having this much fun while incorporating travel and generating electricity into the art form of sustainability to produce the greenest, eco-grooviest music event imaginable."

In an interview on *Democracy Now!* Pete Seeger once described his "defiant optimism." He said, "Little things lead to bigger things. There's a wonderful parable in the New Testament: 'The sower scatters seeds.' Some seeds fall in the pathway and get stamped on, and they don't grow. Some fall on the rocks, and they don't grow, but some seeds fall on fallow ground, and they grow and multiply a thousand-fold. Who knows where some good little thing that you've done may bring results years later that you never dreamed of?"

"Bicycle music is like that," Bear said. "It is a more intimate way to bring music to people. It involves people personally. It's a way to bring bicycles to people and get everyone excited about riding instead of driving. The human-powered electric generators make a statement about the personal power of an individual, and the coming together of the ability of individuals to make something bigger and more beautiful. Bicycles as human-powered generators is a simple and powerful idea with many potential applications and exciting social implications—this is the creative edge where these ideas are being born and tested.

"I think that there is something about rolling along the earth on two wheels propelled by personal power that produces euphoria in human beings. There may be some philosophizing to do about whether or not it is a good idea to seek the euphoric experience, but it sure feels good when it happens. It might seem obvious to say it here, but, if everyone rode bicycles more often the world would be a better place."

Solar powered concert, clear-cut forest: Washington state (1989)

Nevada Nuclear Test Site (1992)

Corbin Harney

Nevada Nuclear Test Site action (1992)

Nevada Nuclear Test Site, Mark Dyken, center (1992)

12

THESE DAYS COME AND GO[60]

There will be days when you got to grieve; You go so deep to fill the need

Hoolzhish = Time is passing

"It's a third-world country out there, and most of us don't even know that it exists," Daniel Harrison had said.

Before this trip, people asked questions. Why are you going? How can the Navajo be so bad off—don't they get help from the government? Don't they get help from their tribe? *It makes no sense for them to stay where things are so complicated,* some friends would say.

Photographs might show piles of rusted cans and worn out shoes on porches, yet being on the reservation, we learned that there is no weekly garbage service and that the shoes that *Shimá* (Mom) wore last year might fit her daughter the next, so they are kept. There may be a coffee pot or a toaster in hogan kitchens, but the most prized utensils are old and handmade, some wooden or made of clay or woven, such as baskets, from small branches plucked from a nearby tree or bush. Children may snuggle in a store-bought blanket, but the most well-loved blankets are made of wool shorn from sheep in the corral just outside the front door—sheep with an ancestry as entrenched as the Navajo who care for them.

Why do they stay? The Grandmothers say it best: *My family belongs*

---

60 Clan Dyken. These days come and go. "These Days Come and Go." *Water, Fire, and Other Relatives.* CD. Track 1.

to the land. The humans belong to the land, and the land belongs to the people who live on it as caretakers.

"Everything is natural out here," Bear said. "The Blessing Way Ceremonies, the sand paintings, the Fire Dance. They are all pieces of the whole natural way of Creation. Mother Earth and Father Sky. The word *beautiful* doesn't begin to describe it."

Pedal power; musical regeneration; a connection to trees and earth and water, feet in the sand, bare toes in the garden—shared lessons of the ancestors. This night there are dreams of corn waving and sheep bleating and horses running free over open rangeland. As long as *Shìmà* sits in her cushioned armchair in her home on ancestral land, there is hope of renewal.

At Katherine Smith's house, the photographs on the wall showed her younger self carrying baskets of corn and beans and holding her famed rifle, the "don't mess with me" look in her eyes commanding respect. How her old mind must have relived those days of confusion and fear. How she must ponder over the part she played in the resistance—the time she shot her gun into the air—her standoff with BIA fence-builders and Hopi rangers; so many marches, so many speeches given in faraway places, so much suffering, and wisdom, and tenacity. Big Mountain was home, a place where she could leave her spirit with the rock, folding it into cracks and crevices where it lay protected from outside elements. The day we visited, disappointment never showed in her eyes, only an innate strength and a resolve to say her piece—but the sorrow must have been there, festering like an infection in a cut that won't heal.

The government monies received by the Navajo tribe did not manifest in her modest home. Those funds went into a reserve trust that supported parts of the reservation, but none came to the non-signers who lived on their sacred Big Mountain. Because of the terms of the agreement, the elders at Big Mountain did not qualify for help from either the Navajo or the Hopi tribes. Because they lived on Hopi Partitioned Land, the Grandmothers could not legally get assistance from the Navajo. On the flip side, according to the government, they lived on the Hopi reservation but were not members of the Hopi tribe, and so they were not qualified for any help offered to or by the Hopi people. The aging non-signers were on their own.

"Grandmother is out there now, weaving a blanket—she's lighting a fire, trying to preserve a way of life that is her birthright," Mark had said at the Williams fundraiser.

The online *Urban Dictionary* defines grandmothers this way: *any sweet old woman who will happily boost your self-esteem. She tends to know lots of neat old songs and obscure, off-color jokes. Generally, she is much cooler and less scary than one's actual mother.*

On the reservation, the word *Grandmother* would be more likely defined this way: *an old woman who will give her life to protect her home and family. She will laugh with you and boost your self-esteem, but just as quickly put you in your place. As a teacher and a historian, and keeper of the flame, she can be loving and fierce in equal measures.*

In 1996, Congress enacted an amendment to the 1974 Navajo Hopi Land Settlement Act. This amendment stated that if people signed this document, the Navajo remaining on HPL would obtain a seventy-five-year lease on three-acre home sites and the right to graze and pray freely—provided they get a permit from the Hopi to do so. Those who did not sign were given end dates—move by *this* date or get forcibly removed. The new agreement stated that after the seventy-five-year lease agreement passed, the land reverted to the Hopi tribe. To strengthen the deal, the Settlement Act authorized a payment of millions of dollars to both the Hopi Tribe and the Navajo nation, with the stipulation that eighty-five percent of the residents must sign to receive the funds. Their Tribal Council told the Navajo living on the Hopi Partitioned Land that the funds would provide them with better housing and infrastructure. Many of them signed. Only twenty-six people, including Katherine Smith, and other Big Mountain and Black Mesa Grandmothers, refused.[61]

Roberta Blackgoat, Pauline Whitesinger, and Alice Benally (all now deceased) lived in anguish during this time, knowing that some stranger, a BIA agent, might show up at any moment and tell them to leave. Perhaps a high-paneled stock truck driven by Hopi rangers would

---

61 Krasney, Zoe. "Belonging to the Land, Part III, We're Still Here." *Voices for Biodiversity*, 2 Apr. 2012, voicesforbiodiversity.org/articles/belonging-to-the-land-part-three-were-still-here.

come to confiscate their animals or someone hired by the mine, or elsewhere would destroy their crops and cap their water well, or harm their children in the process of forced removal. While the men worked mostly outside the home, either at the mine or in a nearby town or doing odd jobs wherever they could get them, the women stood their ground.

In April 1999, according to *Mother Jones*, Arizona Senator John McCain wrote to Attorney General Janet Reno and Interior Secretary Bruce Babbitt, urging them "to proceed carefully in the coming months to settle the relocation of remaining Navajo families in a timely and orderly process." He also asked them to keep him apprised of their plans for ending the twenty-year standoff. John McCain's aide, Jill Peters, said at the time, "There has to be a transfer of those areas to the Hopi tribe, and obviously the people there in that process either sign the lease agreement or relocate. There really is no in-between at this point."[62]

In 1923, the Navajo Tribe established their tribal government to help deal with the complications brought about by outside interests, including the United States Government, Peabody Coal Company, and other resource extraction industries wanting to capitalize on Navajo land. An elected president and vice president head the Executive Branch,[63] comprised of ten executive departments, identified as Divisions. The Navajo Nation Council Chambers hosts eighty-eight council delegates representing the 110 Navajo Nation Chapters.

Today, John Yazzi's son Jonathan works at the Tó Łání Lake Chapter House. Tim Johnson works at the Rocky Ridge School and at Hardrock Chapter House, helping and teaching both elders and youth.

One hundred and ten local government subdivisions, identified as Chapters, exist throughout Navajo land. Each Chapter House is a communal meeting place where residents can express their opinions to their Navajo Nation Council Delegate or decide on matters concerning their local chapter. Locals can attend offered classes and participate in events such as communal meals, game nights, and music.

At Tó Łání Lake Chapter House, there are schools, a senior center, and a residential backyard garden. Jonathan teaches the elders new ways

---

62 Bergman, B.J. "Wrong Side of the Fence." *Mother Jones*, Jan. 2000, www.motherjones.com/politics/2000/01/wrong-side-fence/.

63 *Navajo Nation*. www.navajo-nsn.gov/.

of planting, such as methods of building healthy soil and lasagna gardening—using consecutive layers of cardboard, hay, manure, compost, and topsoil to create an optimal gardening environment. During the summer when local youth participate, the elders teach the children the old methods of planting crops, grinding corn, steaming corn and making kneel-down bread. They explain the traditional ways of making dyes from native plants, water conservation, weaving, pottery, preserving the Navajo language and so much more. Elders are transported in, or those who live close to the center walk to meetings and workshops to learn, participate and socialize.

Also practiced and taught are traditional ways of healing, of staying in balance with all of the earth's people. To the Navajo, this balance is known as K'e. When feeling out of balance, traditional people seek traditional healing from native healers. Many kinds of practitioners and diagnosticians exist on the reservation including the "medicine people," who perform healing ceremonies involving herbs, balms, and purgatives, like peyote.

Tim Johnson's blessing on our first morning at Dove Springs, his voice inflections, the way he drew us in through the stories he shared, was a reflection of the way a culture is passed down from one to the other. How father to son, mother to daughter, the old ways are carried on into the future. "We don't connect to the earth the way we used to," he told us. "Our bare feet don't touch the dirt." And he told us about a man named Bahe Manybeads. "He taught me a lot," Tim said. "He was a great storyteller and was very knowledgeable about Navajo history."

There is a poem about Navajo storytelling that goes like this:

> *Then my father tells us stories*
> *Long stories made up of many words*
> *His words have power*
> *They have strength*
> *They seem to hold me*
> *They seem to warm me*
> *They seem to feed me*
> *My father's words, they comfort me*
> *His words have power.*

Fathers. Mothers. Grandmothers. Children. The young ones on the reservation are now speaking out; taught by their parents and grandparents, they are sharing their own stories. They speak about the water concerns and against fracking and resource extraction, the old uranium and coal mines still affecting the Navajo as evidenced by Facebook posts and their ongoing efforts to inform the People of health risks resulting from radiation contamination.

"Keep it in the ground," say, modern-day activists like Louise Benally, speaking of oil as well as uranium and coal.

Again, it comes around to mineral extraction, specifically uranium and coal. Uranium mining, the establishment of Peabody Coal Company, and a lack of rain—depletion of the water supply have affected not only the Big Mountain region but all the Indian lands stretching south through New Mexico and Colorado. Contaminants like lead, mercury dioxides, and sulphuric acid are present in the soil. Also, toxic pools of water, coined by some as "witches' brew," have appeared out of nowhere on parts of the reservation. Ground seepage drunk by sheep in these areas have left the animals weak and emaciated. Birthrates for the sheep have dropped, and some new lambs have a hard time walking.[64] As far as the people, instances of congenital disabilities have climbed significantly in recent years. At first, children unknowingly swam in these toxic pools. They played in debris piles concentrated around the mines.

Many Navajo have died of kidney failure, a condition linked to uranium mining. Cancer rates doubled in the Navajo Nation from the 1970s to the 1990s.[65] From 1994 to 2004, the most common cancer among the Navajo was colorectal cancer, followed by stomach cancer, kidney, and renal pelvis cancer, pancreatic cancer, and liver and bile duct cancer. A study done in 2004 showed that Navajo men were more likely to contract cancer than were Navajo women. Prostate cancer was the most commonly diagnosed cancer among Navajo men, followed by colorectal cancer and stomach cancer. The Indian Health Service estimated that 7.3% of all deaths in the Navajo Service Area was due to cancer

---

64 Pasternak, Judy. "http://www.latimes.com/news/la-na-navajo 20nov20 story.html." *L. A. Times,* 20 Nov.2008.

65 Morales, Laurel. "https://www.npr.org/sections/healthshots/2016/04/10/473547227/for-the-navajo-nation-uranium-minings-deadly-legacy-lingers." NPR. Accessed Apr. 2016.

for the period 1999 to 2001.[66] Also, exceptionally high are the rates of reproductive organ cancers in teenage Navajo girls, averaging seventeen times higher than the average of girls elsewhere in the United States.[67]

In different parts of the reservation, mounds of uranium-laden waste contaminate the landscape. The Environmental Protection Agency has identified 521 abandoned uranium mines on reservation land, ranging from small holes dug by a single prospector to sizeable commercial mining operations. The Navajo people were not told that the men who worked in the mines and were breathing carcinogenic radon gas were in danger of exposure to radiation, nor that the women washing their husbands' work clothes could spread contaminants to the rest of the family's laundry. The contaminated water looked and tasted perfectly fine. Families used it for cooking, drinking, and cleaning without a second thought.

As activist groups, many of us understood the anger, frustration, and concern on a personal level. Thinking about these statistics brought up an undeniable connection. My oldest son, Micah, was diagnosed with leukemia in 1991, and he died in 1993 at age fourteen. Bear's daughter, Rose, was diagnosed with Astrocytoma, a rare brain tumor, and she died in 2013 at age twenty-eight. The how and whys are mysteries, but there are common denominators. Bear and I live in areas where mining operations were prevalent in the late 1800s and early 1900s. I lived on a mountaintop on fifteen acres of land. It was beautiful and serene, but for years before our being there, a nearby sawmill spread debris on the surrounding roads, grading thick layers of contaminant-filled soil and gravel for miles. Mark, Bear, and I live in the Sierra Nevada foothills. As radon is a by-product of uranium, it is also a by-product of granite, the bedrock beneath many a home in our area.

Like at the local sawmill, many workers at the Big Mountain mines felt blessed to have these jobs. Byproducts of uranium are thorium, radium, and radon. Radon is a gas, but with a half-life of four days, it rapidly decays into solid products. Being a solid, it sticks to things like your lungs and studies show it as a contributor to certain types of cancer.

---

66 *Cancer Among the Navajo 1994-2004*. Navajo Division of Health.

67 "Uranium mining and the Navajo People." *Wikipedia,* en.wikipedia.org/.

According to *Environmental Health Perspectives* online magazine, "Studies have indicated that the health legacy of uranium exposure may extend to the children of exposed parents. A study of 266 cases among Navajo births suggested that children of women who lived near abandoned uranium sites were almost twice as likely to have one of thirty-three selected defects…thought to be among those connected to radiation exposure."[68]

Bear and I can never really know what caused our children's' illnesses. But to have suffered such a great loss in the shadow of poisoned land bolsters our activism. Grief can be as thick as the hope for a better world, seven generations out.

"All this, yet the humor continues," Bear said. "As you can see, these people love to play games and tell stories. Their heritage lives on, despite government efforts to silence their voices through the years."

Basketball hoops on the reservation were well used and enjoyed. Parents and grandparents bragged about tournaments won, and their pride in their children was as evident as their love for the game. The jokes told, the challenge of cat's cradle, the soft chuckles of the Grandmothers, the serious or silly stories of the Grandfathers: all evidence that the playful spirit of the people has not been destroyed.

"Leonard Benally. He was a character," Bear said, smiling. "He ran in an International Marathon in Salt Lake City. He didn't train. He said the only training he got was from chasing horses."

"He had a lot of great stories," said Mark.

"The one I love best was about Jehovah's Witnesses," Bear said. "He said they used to drive all the way out to Big Mountain wearing their suits and ties with their briefcases and knocked on the doors of the hogans. He happened to be at his Grandmother's place during one of those visits and translated for her as the Witnesses spoke. So they went on and on about the Bible and other JW stuff, and his Grandmother just patiently sat there listening, sipping coffee until it was all over, and then she had Leonard ask them, 'So hell is where the fire is, right?' And the Witnesses said 'yes.' Leonard's Grandmother then said, 'Well, that's

---

68 "Once Upon a Mine: The Legacy of Uranium on the Navajo Nation." *Environmental Health Perspectives,* 2014, ehp.niehs.nih.gov/122-a44/.

where I want to go.' And the Witnesses were like, 'We don't get it.' And she said, 'Because my son is a firefighter and when he goes off and fights a fire, he comes home with all kinds of money.' There are so many things I love about that story," Bear said, laughing.

"Leonard was also a rodeo champ," said Mark.

"Yeah," Bear said, "One time he came to visit at my house. We decided to take a bike ride, and he grabbed a bike, that unbeknownst to us, had faulty brakes, and the front wheel wasn't tight. So he got on that bike and started going downhill, faster and faster. The bike was bouncing, and then the front wheel came off, and I'm standing there watching this whole thing in horror. The front wheel came off, the forks went down in the dirt, and he stepped right over the handlebars and started running, never even fell."

Both Mark and Bear laughed. "Yeah, and he loved riding on the bus," Mark said.

"Yep. The bus is a part of the legends," Bear said. "We come out here, and they say, 'we heard you guys were on the bus, and the drums are going, and everyone's smoking weed and no one is driving the bus!'"

"That's all Leonard," Mark said, still chuckling. "He's the one who started *that* rumor."

Back at Dove Springs, the sandstone bluffs appeared as caricatures of elder men with prominent noses and deep-set eyes, standing guard, watching the moon as it rose in the sky. Their masculine energies coiled like invisible snakes, twisting, worrying over the fate of their people. The Grandfathers were there, still and always—singing, praying, beating their drums. They have lived here for a very long time. They are rooted here.

As we exited the truck, the wind whistled through the wash, a noise like a whisper of voices, the chants of the ancients. Across the way was the hogan of our hosts, our main camp, the clearing where we shared Tim Johnson's morning prayers. While on the reservation, the days were mild and the nights cold. Mittens helped. Hats, shawls. Even now there was a fire in the firepit. There was a pot of soup cooking. The hint of oregano and basil, perhaps, wafted across the sandy wash— squash, beans, and maybe corn tortillas alongside, cooked hobo style, warmed on the grill. Bear's shift pod gleamed silver in the evening light;

the bus stood ready as Mark stowed gear and did his nightly walkabout, and bus-check, readying for tomorrow and our trip home.

These Days Come and Go 243

"Buster" (the bus) stuck at Dove Springs: Big Mountain, Arizona (2014)

"Buster" (the bus) stuck at Dove Springs:
Big Mountain, Arizona (2014)

©Roberta Blackgoat carrying a protest sign.
Next to her is Dorothy Lew Deal, also from Big Mountain, ca. 1981
Photo by Dan Budnik

©Big Mountain resistors, carry signs in protest, ca. 1981
Photo by Dan Budnik

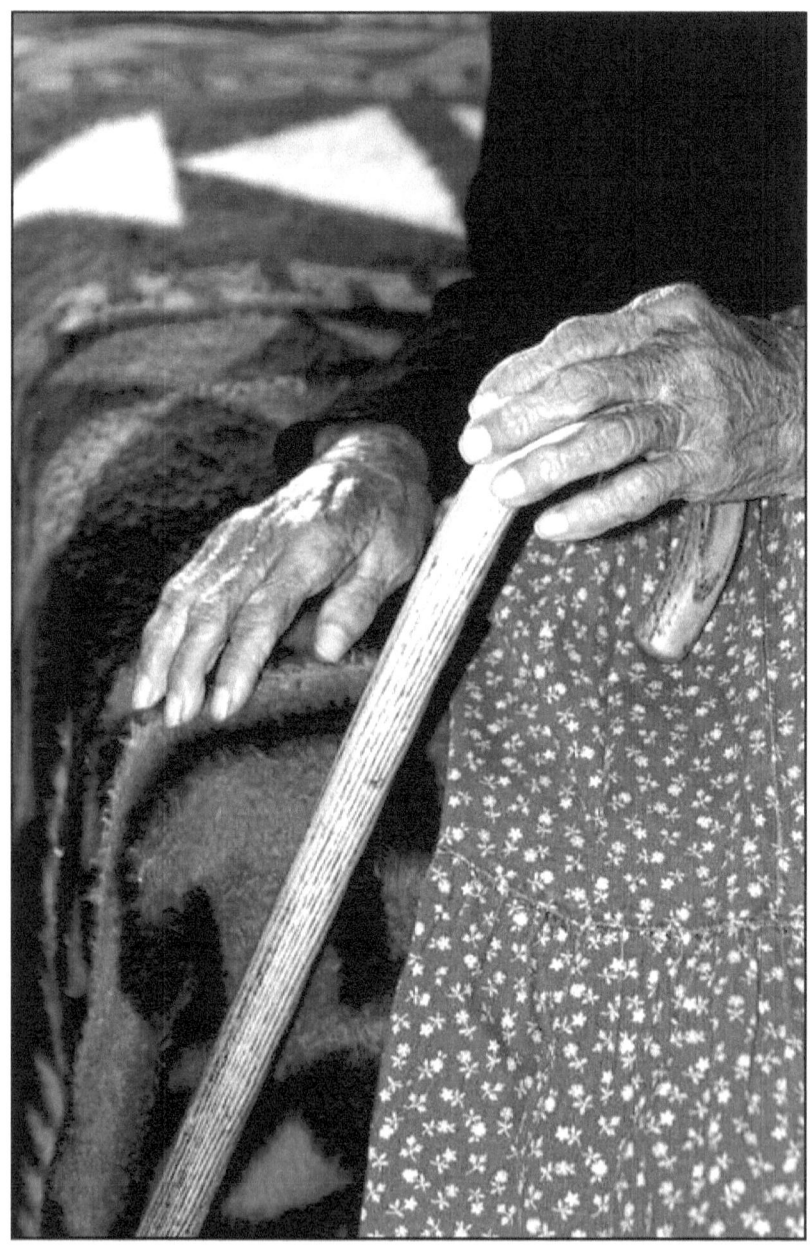

Grandmother, Mary McCabe: Big Mountain, Arizona (2003)
Photo by Daniel Harrison

Shucking corn: Big Mountain, Arizona

Daniel Harrison (2008)

John Yazzi Sr. and Mark Dyken (2001)

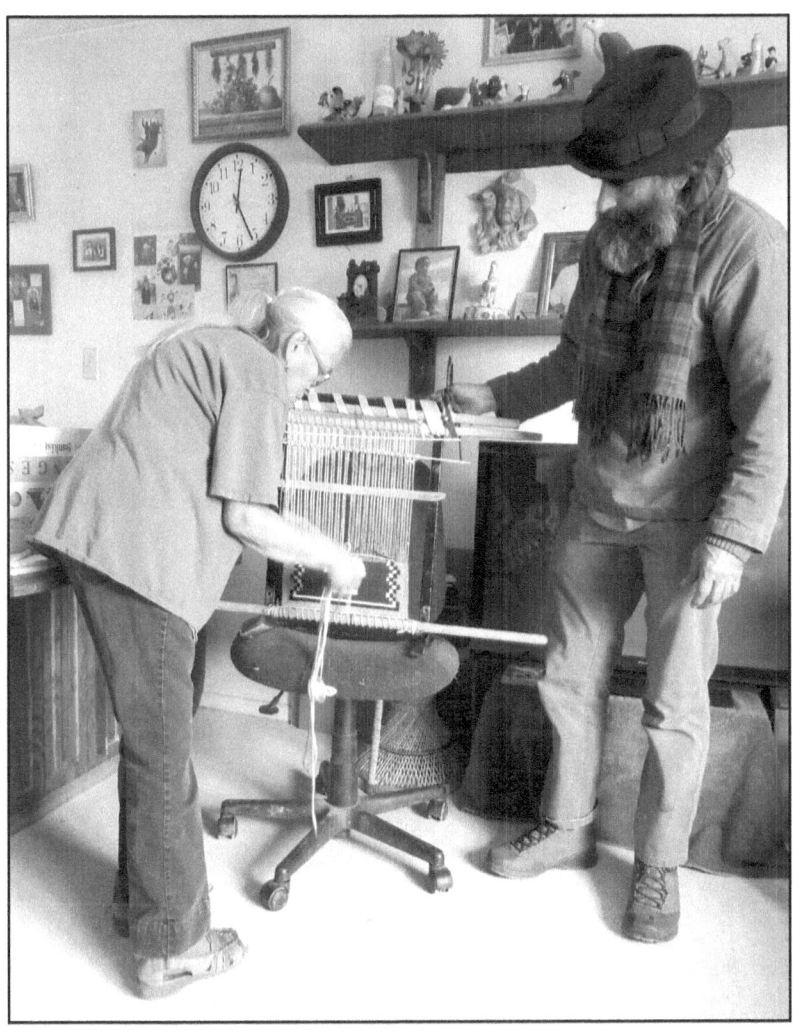

Grandmother's weaving (Helen) with Bear Dyken: Low Mountain (2016)

These Days Come and Go   251

Grandmother (Dolly), making fry bread (2010)

A load of coal, Coal Mine Canyon (2016)

Catherine Lambie and Shelley Muniz:
Coal Mine Canyon (2016)

Coal Mine Canyon (2017)

Bear and Mark (2016)

Coal Mine Canyon (2017)

Leo Yellowhair's place (2016)

Leo Yellowhair and Bear (2016)

Anna Begay's horse (2016)

Anna Begay's homestead: Coal Mine Canyon (2017)

Anna Begay and Shelley Muniz with Anna's last weaving (2017)

Anna Begay and Louise Benally (2017)

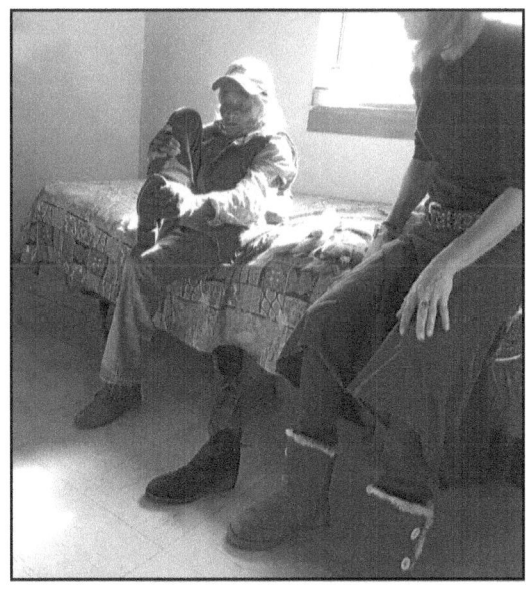

Anna Begay, trying on shoes

A child building a mud hogan:
Anna Mae Camp (2017)

John Benally, Karen, Mark, Tzaddi

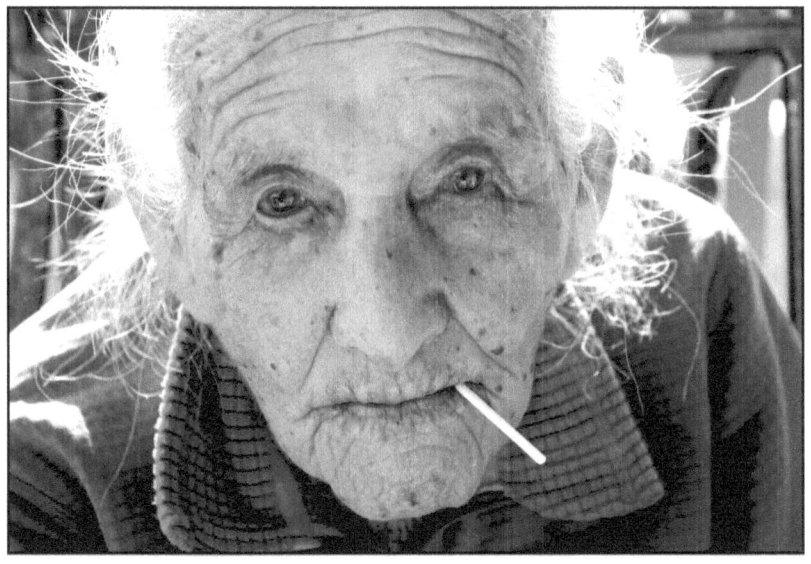

Katherine Smith (2016)

Katherine Smith (2016)

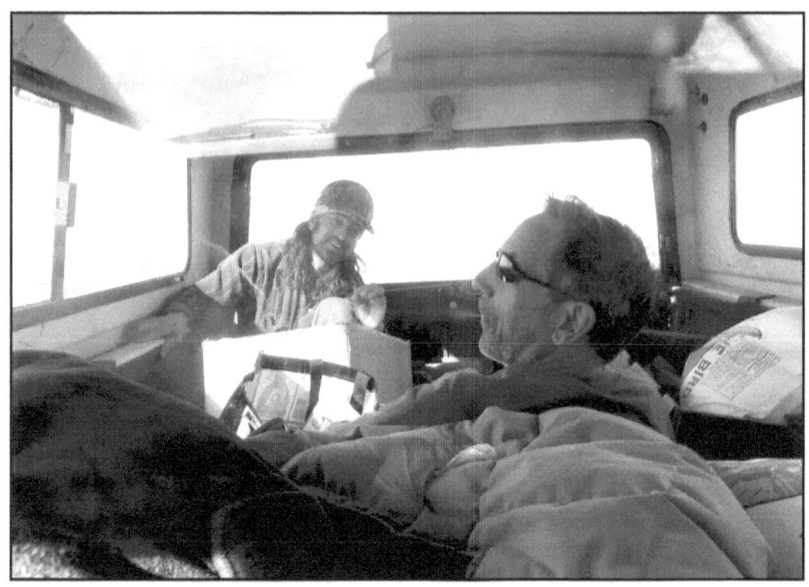

On the way to the Yazzi's: Sand Springs (2017)

Yazzi compound: Sand Springs (2017)

These Days Come and Go

Sand Springs, Yazzi compound

Jim Lundeen and Kaleb Yazzi

Bear Dyken and Lanora Percy (2017)

13

WORLD I IMAGINE[69]

Strengthen the things that remain; be strong where the truth is plain; this is something to believe in; we need something to believe in; In the world I imagine.

Náá'ahideeltsééh = Farewell

As the Silver Eagle left its resting place at Dove Springs, echoes of goodbyes filled the void inside the bus. The bays, closets, and hallways lay empty of donated clothing and boxes of fresh food, all distributed now to Navajo families. Only a partially-filled bin of persimmons remained, smelling a bit musty, ready to be recycled into compost.

Glancing back, I saw Tzaddi's camper and Bear's truck still at our campsite. Brian and Michelle had left the day before, as did Mike and Dar. Jim Lundeen was off to visit relatives in Sedona. Mark, Catherine, Kim, Lotus, and I were bound for California, tired and a bit weatherworn. Everyone agreed that it was hard to leave people and a place we had grown to love.

"All too soon it's time to go home," wrote Mark on the Clan Dyken blog. "This place that once seemed foreign and remote has become familiar and comfortable. The trip back to another reality seems even farther than the one to get here. It will take a while for re-entry. The artificial

---

[69] Clan Dyken. Strengthen the things that remain. "World I Imagine." *Green Prayer.* CD, Track 5.

colors of the chain store signs, the bright lights of twenty-four-hour convenience stores, the hard, smooth pavement, the chatter of radio and television, the speed of cars and pace of life all seem out of balance now. No matter where the traveler goes from here it's a long way. The comfort zone doesn't seem to fit so well anymore. Perhaps it should be left behind more often."

I couldn't have expressed the enigma of traveling to and from Dineh Bikéyah (Navajoland) any better. Leaving felt strangely sad and heavy-hearted, yet I was grateful to be with my friends, together on a bus that had become our rolling home. Returning to a world of supermarkets and well-paved roads—the constant chatter of busy lives and syndicated news would be awkward at first. I knew this from past experiences. Leaving by choice is one thing—moving on at the end of some impactful life experience is something else. In the grand scheme of things, however, this type of transition was nothing.

At the beginning of our journey, Mark had said, "You and I know what it's like to leave somewhere, to be somewhere else. We don't know what it is to lose our ancestral homeland, our language, and our ceremonies by force."

For as far back as the Hog Farmers first trip to Big Mountain, the appreciation for the Navajo culture, the unfairness of their situation, the passion for acting or reacting, has remained, as has the desire for a bit of fun. Somehow being on the bus again and traveling the highways demanded a sequence of play-listed songs, some old Sixties stuff from Jefferson Airplane and The Band, and more conversation about early activists and hippies—those bands of colorfully-clothed freethinkers who marked the same path we drove this day.

Mark wore his mesh fingerless driving gloves, his fingers circling the steering wheel as he relaxed into the driver's seat. Someone joked that we needed a mood adjustment and that this trip was over, but it would never be over—there was next year and the next in our future. We laughed about the old story that Leonard Benally told and that so many others repeated: "We heard you guys were on the bus, and the drums are going, and everyone's smoking weed and no one is driving the bus!"

Mark's stories blended with previous ones that he and Bear had shared along the Beauty Way Tour, eventually rounding back to Wavy

Gravy. "Wavy says that 'churches can be built anytime, anywhere, but Navajo land *is* their church, and their ceremonies are their services.' Can you imagine," Mark said, "what would happen if a church, any church, closed its doors because the government or some agency of the government denied its parishioners the right to worship? It would be all over the newspapers. It would be a major headline, yet it happened here at Big Mountain and elsewhere on Native land with little or no recognition."

Wavy Gravy was known for speaking his mind. In 1968, he and the Hog Farmers joined the Youth International Party (Yippie) and ran Pigasus the Pig for President. Wavy is also believed to have nominated Nobody for President at the Yippie National Convention outside the 1976 Republican National Convention in Kansas City. Every election year since, the Hog Farmers have presented their candidate, Nobody, to the United States and the world, using his Nobody statements as campaign rhetoric. *Nobody is perfect*, banners and signs read.

Wavy was a stand-up comedian when he first started out, but eventually, he got into music. Though he and his friends settled on the hog farm in New Mexico, he was on the road a lot, working gigs for Bill Graham, introducing name bands and acting as MC. "Wavy has a way of directing energy, synthesizing whatever is happening around him," Mark said. "He was perfect for all of these things and became famous at Woodstock for quips like, 'What we have in mind is breakfast in bed for 400,000.'"

Mark's imitation of Wavy's gravelly voice was stellar. He had it down.

Wavy's trail of activist activities is extensive. He played a part in many charitable events, either by acting as MC or recruiting notable performers to raise money for their cause. Not only did he and the Hog Farmers establish Camp Winnarainbow, but they also assisted in founding Seva,[70] a global nonprofit eye care organization. Even in his eighties, Wavy remains active as a member of the Board of Directors of Seva, and is a spokesperson, highlighting the group's mission: "selfless service to others."

And Wavy is a good friend to Clan Dyken.

---

70 *Seva.* www.seva.org/.

"It's like every cool thing that ever happened back in the day, Wavy was the MC. He's just a consistent love being throwing it out into the world," Bear had said earlier. "After we met Wavy at the Rainbow Gathering in West Virginia, we started doing our festival thing. We were kind of the house band at the Whole Earth Festival in Davis, and back in those days, Wavy was the MC. He liked us, and he invited us to be the house band for his Nobody for President Tour in 1992 when Clinton was running against George Bush, Senior."

Above the windshield of the bus, the picture of Buddha, his belly wrapped with the words *Suffering Sucks,* was now bordered with desert flowers and a sprig of fresh sage. A new collection of rocks, including small pieces of chert gathered at the Yazzi place, lay on the dashboard next to the boxes of incense, the Blue Meanie, Yellow Submarine figurines, and the miniature replica of Sgt. Pepper's bass drum—not unlike what likely decorated Wavy's hippie-filled bus way back when.

"Wavy calls himself the Temple of Accumulated Error," Mark said. "His body has been through a lot, but his wit never fails him."

By 1992, Clan Dyken had done a few Bill Graham shows. They once opened for the Garcia Band and Paul Kantner of Jefferson Starship, both for which Wavy was MC. Wavy had seen them often at the Whole Earth Festival in Davis, California, at the Hundredth Monkey Festival, and the Nevada Nuclear Test Site. The Clan had played music at the Hog Farm Family picnic, so by this time, had built a relationship with Wavy and others at the Hog Farm. "These guys, the Hog Farmers, were people that we looked up to regarding idealism," Mark said, "and the artful way that they expressed points of view and politics. We were so stoked when Wavy asked us to be his band on this tour."

In mid-September 1992, the Dykens drove their bus to Berkeley and picked up Wavy to begin their Nobody for President Tour. Wavy had just finished his book, *Something Good for a Change,* so the tour was to be his book launch, as well. For six weeks, the group traveled the United States, stopping at pre-determined sites set up and maintained by Wavy's manager. Starting in San Francisco, they then drove north to Eugene, Oregon, where they played with Rambling Jack Elliott and stayed overnight at Ken Kesey's house. From there, they headed down to Los Angeles and on to the test site. Vegas. They went to St. Louis, and Kentucky, and Kansas City, New York, Boston, Connecticut, Vermont, and then to

Washington DC.

"The thing with Wavy," Mark continued, "is that he knew people everywhere. Every place we went, people came out to see him, I mean, this was Wavy Gravy, the guy who'd been there through the whole thing. He's the person who had introduced every band we knew at venues all over the country. Everybody has a Wavy story."

As a beat poet, and comic, a Merry Prankster, friend and roommate to Bob Dylan, boyhood friend of Albert Einstein, acting coach, and activist, Wavy has a unique perspective eighty-plus years strong. He is a master storyteller and has a story for every experience and situation. "Wavy knows how to hook you with a lead," Mark said. "He has a catchphrase or two throughout and uses character and voice to hold his listeners. Wavy showed me, by observation, how to hold an audience."

Mark's storytelling prowess became evident during the Beauty Way Tour. His skill at capturing and holding his audience was aided by voice fluctuations, body language, and facial expressions in combination with his use of Grandmother Drum, uniquely his own but inspired by Wavy.

"All of our kids were on board for the Nobody Tour," Mark shared. "Leon's son, Sierra, was just a baby. Wavy wanted Sierra's first words to be Wavy Gravy, so he would sit back there and say, 'Wavy Gravy, Wavy Gravy, Wavy Gravy.'"

"We're all bozos on the bus," Wavy was known to say, "so might as well sit back and enjoy the ride."

In New York City, Wavy directed the Dykens and their bus through narrow streets, Mark *bending metal* as he is known to do, negotiating corners in midtown Manhattan. The entire group climbed the Empire State Building with Wavy dressed in full clown regalia, red nose, big hat, and floppy clown shoes. The "Clown Prince of Hippiedom," as he is known, a big man with a bad back, no less, negotiating the building with the Clan and friends, twisting this way and that to fit into the seat of a cab when done, made quite a spectacle. "It was great," said Bear. "An epic Wavy adventure."

"The best part about being on the East Coast with Wavy was playing music on the steps of the Federal Hall," Mark said. "We were right across from the Wall Street Stock Exchange. A thousand or more bankers were out there in their three-piece suits tapping their feet. Mark sliced the air with a sharp slap to the steering wheel. "We had no permit, no nothing," he said. "I parked the bus in a blue zone, which means no parking anywhere, for anyone—ever. We pulled right in, parked, and ran electricity from our inverter to hook up the sound. We didn't have a permit for any of this, nothing. We just did it," he recalled, shaking his head. "I don't know how this could have happened. We set up on the front steps of the museum on a Friday afternoon. The cops were helping us. They formed a perimeter, right across from the New York Stock Exchange.

"In front of the building, there was a statue of George Washington with his hand up as if he was taking an oath of office. Our saxophone player hung a sign over George's hand that read 'I grew hemp.'"

At each stop, Wavy would come out and do his speech: "Who bakes better apple pie than your mother? NOBODY. Who lowers your taxes? NOBODY. Who keeps all their campaign promises? NOBODY. Who should have that much power? NOBODY." Then he said, "Wait, wait, NOBODY is going to speak!" and he would pull fake chattering teeth out of his pocket, wind up the teeth and hold them up to the microphone, *da-da-da-da-da*, the teeth would chatter. "Vote for NOBODY!" he would scream, or in the case of the 1992 tour, "Vote for Hillary's husband!"

"Wavy would finish his speech," Mark said, "and then introduce us. We played a lot of activist songs, like 'Shut the Test Site Down.' We were right in the middle of all of those actions at that point, the test site and Big Mountain. The band, at the time, was me, and Laura, Bear and Harmony, Leon, our bass player, Jeff, and our saxophonist, Darrin. Plus we had a lot of support people with us."

After the gig at Federal Hall, Wavy stayed in New York with family while the Dykens headed south. The goal was to meet up in Washington on Election Day to do a "goodbye George party," celebrating the end of the Bush presidency, right across from the White House. There were no shows booked for several days, so it appeared that the Clan could take a leisurely trip and enjoy the scenery. Ben Cohen, of Ben & Jerry's Ice Cream, had come to the show in Burlington, Vermont and loved it, so he invited the gang to tour his ice cream factory. Afterward, Ben loaded them up with ice cream, which they stocked in the small freezer on the bus. The first significant mishap of the trip happened just after this, on the Connecticut Turnpike.

"We were eating a lot of ice cream," Mark said, "just cruising down the road. We had just finished smoking a joint, and Jeff Jones, our bass player, was driving the bus. This bus was our third—one we called *Big*. It was a City of Seattle Metro bus that we got from the *Seeds of Peace*."

It was a sunny day, bright sky. After the hustle and bustle of New York City, the urban areas of Connecticut were a pleasant change, still congested, but there were green byways and plenty of trees, the highway running west to east along stretches of shoreline. Big pressed along, moving at a comfortable speed. Taped to its side, barely rippled by the airflow was a large banner that read, *Nobody for President*.

"Jeff was driving the bus, and we're going along," Mark said, and suddenly, he said, 'Oh man, I think we're getting pulled over.' Behind the bus was a Connecticut State Police car, lights flashing.

"'Oh, okay, I think we're good,' I told him. So Jeff pulled over and right away, it was evident that this was not a typical traffic stop.

"The officer parked alongside the bus and climbed out of his car, giving the bus a once over. As Jeff opened the door, he stepped inside. 'You've got the wrong kind of license plate for this vehicle,' he said.

"So we opened the door for him, which we should never have done," Mark said, voice cracking, arms launching skyward. "So he came in, kicked over a trash can we kept by the door and spilled garbage all over the road. 'What's this?' he asked.

"'Um, a trash can,'" I answered.

"He was tripping from the first second he got on the bus. So he pulled Jeff and me off, saying that he wanted to talk to us. All of a sudden, all of these cop cars pulled up, parking on the grass and all around the turnpike. There were cops in front of us, cops behind us, the whole place was filled with cop cars, and I'm thinking, *What the hell is going on?*"

People in the support vehicles jumped out of their cars with video recorders. The policeman who initially pulled the bus over grilled Mark. "Who's on the bus? What are you people doing here? Where are you headed?"

Laura watched from inside the bus. Officers were inside now, as well. "Stay still," they said, as they rummaged through the crew's belongings. Mark and Laura's son, Peta, slid onto her lap. Their daughter, Kiri, was in a support vehicle behind the bus.

"So I'm outside with this cop," Mark said, "in my socks, no shoes, wearing jeans and a sweatshirt. I felt something in my pants pocket and reached in to see what it was. We'd just finished eating ice cream, and I'd forgotten I shoved a spoon in there. I pulled it out slowly, remembering then that it was a spoon, and the cop knocked it out of my hand. 'You have any other weapons?' he asked me.

"'What's the matter with you?' I said. 'It's a spoon!'

"And that was it. The cop spun me around and threw me against the bus. 'What's this about, are you arresting me?' I asked. "He's patting me down, and I'm saying 'What's going on here?' Then I looked to the side. One cop had Bear, another cop had Jeff, and I started to lose it. 'What the fuck is going on here?' I asked.

"He put me in handcuffs and started asking questions about the kids on the bus, and I'm telling him that he needs to tell me what's going on. 'Have we broken some law?' I asked. 'I don't understand what's going on here!'

"Jeff stood up. 'I don't recognize your authority,' he said to the cop and walked away.

"As I demanded to know what was happening and got no answer, I became increasingly agitated. At one point, he put his hand on my chest and a leg behind me, pushed me over on my back on the ground with his knee in my chest and said, 'You calm down!'

"'Me calm down? What the hell is the matter with you guys?' I asked. He pulled me up on my knees. 'Have you ever heard of a document called the Constitution?' I asked.

"'Yeah, I wipe my ass with it every morning,' said the cop.

"'I don't know what the fuck is the matter with you guys,' I said, and more and more of them were showing up. They were crawling around in the bus. One of them took the video recorder from our support crew, shouting, 'This isn't *America's Funniest Home Videos*!'

"'I don't want you on my bus,' I shouted. 'I have a right to know what's going on!'

"'We have reason to believe that you are transporting weapons, narcotics, and abducted children,' one of the officers finally said.

"And I looked at this guy and said, 'Are you fucking kidding me? If we were carrying weapons, and narcotics and abducted children—would we be driving around in a red, white, and blue bus with an itinerary posted on the side, with *Nobody for President* written all over it? I wish I could afford to make the kind of mistakes you jackasses make with tax-payer money.'

"I just lost it. I couldn't help it. I lost it. About this time, another cop, a Sargent DeSanti, showed up. He looked at the cops on the bus and told them to get off, and he looked at the trash on the ground and instructed them to pick it up. Then he went on the bus and asked the kids some questions. When he came out, he told the other cops to take the handcuffs off me and said, point blank, 'I want you to know, you haven't been harassed.'

"'Well, that makes me feel a lot better,' I told him. I mean, I had tears of rage. He had just embarrassed me in front of my kids, and now he was telling me that everything was fine? By that time, he'd backed the other cops off and sent them to their cars. So obviously, he'd realized that what he thought we were or thought about us wasn't true.

"He told me that the United States Department of Justice sent him, and I'm like, the United States Department of Justice? 'Great,' I said. 'We're going to Washington DC. I'll check it out.'

"'Go ahead,' he said, and I did. When we got to Washington DC, I went to the Department of Justice. The guy in the lobby allowed me a phone call, and the official on the phone told me that the whole thing was ridiculous. If they had wanted us, they would have sent a federal marshall. My next call was to the sergeant, and I told him the Department of Justice had never heard of him. He told me he'd send me the teletype, which of course he never did. I tried to call him several times after, and he never answered my calls. The whole thing never got resolved. We still have no idea why we were pulled over. It's still a big mystery."

Despite everything, the show went on in Washinton DC.

"It was a Goodbye George party in Lafayette Park, right across from the White House. Wavy was back with us at this point," Mark said. "He did his thing, and we did ours. Once again, you could never get away with this kind of activity these days. We were plugged in and playing music directly across from the White House.

"What Wavy has done, what the Hog Farmers have done as a

collective, is extraordinary," Mark said. "When you think about it, they were responsible for so much of the hippie culture, let alone all the good they've accomplished with their charity work.

"At Big Mountain, they did their activist bit, and funny thing, Wavy taught some of the people out there how to roll a joint," Mark said, laughing. "That guy proved handy to have around, as some will say."

For non-natives, the Navajo word for *clown* seems challenging to pronounce: *Łąʼátʼíinii*. For all Wavy has done, for the stories he's shared, it's a moniker by which he will be remembered. As the buses roll, as the drum beats, as the teeth rattle, and the love light shines, the Seva motto, Compassion in Action—combined with his wacky approach and humor—will stand out as his rally cry.

14

Mother Ocean Carry Me[71]

When you left, the big wave tumbled;
that's the way I was washed back out to sea
Mother Ocean, carry me

Ahéhee' t'áá ánółtso = Thank you all

--Navajo Prayer--

We are staying here now and tomorrow and forever,
all four seasons, forever.
We are staying for the land, the song, and the prayer.
All my sweat comes out of Mother Earth,
and our Great, Great Grandmothers had to use this land,
they were born here, died on the land,
the soil we're walking on came from their dust.

I was home now, and Bear was visiting. We were in my kitchen, and I was preparing a meal of vegetable bean soup and whole grain bread for friends who would soon join us. The room smelled of basil and oregano, and the yeasty tang of sourdough. Outside, the rain came down in continuous sheets, overfilling the gutters and storm drains, and as we

---

71 Clan Dyken. When you let the great wave tumble. "Mother Ocean." *Water, Fire, and Other Relatives.* CD. Track 4.

listened to the pelting *drip, drip, whoosh* we wished for the same at Big Mountain. Water to refill the aquifer, water for the animals, water for the trees and plants. Water for the Dineh.

Whether on a rainy night or a clear night, the sky at home was different from on the reservation. In my neighborhood, the darkness held a glow, a reminder of the power grid that serviced countless houses. On the reservation, there was mostly darkness, a black "beyond" harboring billions of stars, no streetlights or neon signs to dim the show. In my neighborhood, houses were within sight of each other, and in every home were multiple light switches, easy access to electricity. In most of these homes, forced-air blew from electric or propane heat units, but mine offered little comfort—not as it had in past winters. There is something about what I now know and caring so much about all I saw—something about wishing it could be different for those we left behind.

Home was a word that held new meaning. A home can be comfortable and sufficiently sustainable, or it can be a source of stress. It is a place you feel grounded, or from which you are *ungrounded* or forcibly removed. Whether that connection to "place" happens in a hogan or on a vehicle with four wheels, in a stick-built house or in a tent in a park or under a bridge, all are tangible expressions of human existence. We move to them. We move from them. We lose them to disasters like fire, but nothing can prepare us for the kind of loss the Navajo suffered.

I had written a children's picture book that was set in the Grand Canyon. It was about a family of squirrels who judged one another by their differences rather than loved one another for their similarities. And Bear was illustrating it. He dipped a paintbrush in water, adding a wash to the watercolor drawing he'd started. "Nothing is what it seems," he said. "You think you have a home that will house your family forever. And then something happens, and it's gone."

Whether at the test site or Big Mountain, or elsewhere, we saw what happens when decisions are taken out of the hands of the people involved; loss of land, deterioration of families—and what happens when the government or other entities impose upon the rights of others. I experienced loss in my way as well, loss of land, home, the family I thought was forever.

Stories Repeat.[72] As a writer and a child of the 1960s, I had witnessed love and loss, hate and prejudice, overconsumption, the mismanagement of natural resources, forced occupations, and the devastation of war. This track on *Water, Fire, and Other Relatives* was a reminder that all of life's missteps, mysteries, and even family sagas can play out in a myriad of ways. Choices and events can feed or burn our souls, nourish our lives or transform them.

> *Christmas*
> *Alone*
> *Water for lunch and dinner again*
> *Darkness only.*

Nearly a year had passed since the Butte Fire, but Bear's accumulated losses still burned. In the solitude of the moment, a feathered memory as palpable as a heartbeat, the frenzied grief of those still living caused me to sigh. Both Bear and I had experienced the death of a child by cancer—his daughter, and my son. For me, it had been twenty-three years, and for Bear, only three, but still, we grieved.

Darkness only—a refrain that sunk in my gut like an irradiated stone. Everyone knows loss: loss of parents, a home perhaps—the umbilical cut to a place, a person. For Bear, the losses came bundled together, igniting a bomb of debilitating sorrow. In 2011, he, Mark, and the other Dyken children lost their beloved mother, Dorothy. In 2013, he and Harmony lost their daughter, Rose, and in 2015, the Butte Fire, one of the most devastating in California history, destroyed Bear's home, along with many others throughout the Amador and Calaveras County areas.

"It started as a little wisp of smoke," Bear said, recalling the force of the blaze once again. He paused for a moment, clearing his throat as if smoke still lived there. "The fire went from zero to sixty in no time at all. There was a giant mushroom cloud, like the kind that happens with a nuclear explosion, a 200-foot wall of flames."

The air took a while to clear within the burn-scar area, but the stench is finally gone. Bear's house burned to the ground, but carcasses of trees remain, and his sauna came through unscathed. The idea that reju-

---

[72] Clan Dyken. Too many tears, heart of night. "Stories Repeat." *Water, Fire, and Other Relatives*. CD. Track 5.

venation might occur came by way of a fig tree and a few smaller shrubs and bushes that survived the inferno, followed by the birds, the animals, sprouts of green poking their heads through the ash.

During these times of loss, Bear's sailboat, the Delta Hobo became his refuge. "I'm a self-taught sailor," he said. "You get on the boat, let the wind blow you around and figure things out as you go."

Movement in a vehicle—be it by air, land, or water—seemed to be in the family genes. Richard Dyken loved flying planes and was partially self-taught. Mark learned to drive his first bus without any bus driver's training—just by hopping in the driver's seat and shifting into go mode. Bear honed his sailing skills by steering into the wind, rather than in a classroom somewhere, or at the hand of professional sailors. "I read a lot and watched a lot on the Internet. I've got some friends who are more versed in sailing than I am. I've been to San Francisco and back three times and to Sacramento and back twice. Mostly, I go for day trips around the delta, just hoboing around."

Bear's ocean songs, "Mother Ocean, Carry Me," and "Good Ship Starfinder"[73] come from an experience sailing with a friend on a thirty-six-foot boat. "We sailed under the Golden Gate and 100 miles out. You can't see any land, buildings, nothing but water. Out there, I realized that the ocean is always changing, but that it will always be primordial landscape. This view is as ancient as the earth. It never changes and yet it's always changing, and somehow that knowledge gave me perspective and helped me deal with my grief."

Unlike at Big Mountain, there are no fences on the open sea. There are no lasting boundaries nor finite rules for the way the waves crest or when a storm should arise, or how a sailor might behave should he lose his bearing. Like at Big Mountain, there is the lure of an ancient life-giving body, a tie to primitive ways of being that seem to ground body and soul. At Big Mountain, and at sea, undulating currents create an age-old dance, music played out on rocks and sticks, lyrics written and modified—real-life experiences guiding the art of knowing what works and doesn't work, the laws of men acting only as a placeholder for what is real.

"I didn't go to the sea to intellectualize," Bear said. "But then there was this moment, this experience that drew that out of me. There was

---

73 Clan Dyken. "Good Ship Starfinder." *Water, Fire, and Other Relatives*. CD. Track 10.

phosphorescence in the water. The boat seemed to be gliding on this trail of sparkling green light, and the dolphins were playing with the boat, shooting around. The experience was so encouraging, rejuvenating, to see these dolphins, hundreds of them, playing in the light."

As often happens, time spent on a voyage can influence future endeavors. A few years after Bear first set sail on the Delta Hobo, and following his experience on the high sea, he purchased a second boat, now christened *The Soul Journey*. His plans are many, including trips to Guatemala and sailing with friends throughout the Caribbean. Recently, Bear sailed *The Soul Journey* to Cuba, where he and his companions played music and sang songs, both in Spanish and English—including some songs he has written for the Big Mountain Dineh.

Our trip is barely over, and the pleas continue, over the Internet, on activist websites and underground newspapers: *URGENT, URGENT, URGENT. Many of the signatures on Relocation Agreements were obtained illegally and by fraudulent means. Some people, who thought they were signing documents to release their animals from impoundment, found out later that they had signed these leases (these people could not read or write English). Many considered as "signers" are people as totally committed to resistance against loss of their ancestral land as anyone.*

URGENT, URGENT, URGENT. We need sheep protectors and water warriors!!! Grandmas' risk having their sheep stolen by Rangers! We need your help! Law enforcement has been driving around, and helicopters have been flying overhead. If you're willing to serve as a human rights witness, please get in touch. Aheheh'! Thank you!

URGENT, URGENT, URGENT. I am sending out this urgent appeal for hay and feed for the two donkeys and one horse that have to remain penned inside a corral to avoid confiscation. The impounding of animals cost money, and Ella and Anna Begay, as you know, have no money.

I wonder—can renewal happen at Big Mountain as it has in the heart of the Butte Fire burn area?

"The trees are burnt up," Bear had said. "The landscape ruined. Homes destroyed but people are coming back. Resettling. As are the frogs—they came back right away. We saw a bear about a week after the fire, walking around out there. Gophers didn't miss a beat; they never left. Hummingbirds, moths. There are a lot fewer squirrels. We see some deer, coyotes, raccoon. There are lots of birds now, more than before. I think they like the openness and continuity of home."

For as long as the Grandmothers live on Big Mountain, supporters will aid the Native activists who belong on this land. The struggle is theirs; they lead and others follow. The intimidation and efforts toward the forced removal of the Navajo people continue. Livestock-related harassment by law enforcement is still a regular occurrence for families resisting federal relocation policies. Public Law 93-531, the Navajo-Hopi Settlement Act of 1974, remains intact despite four decades of indigenous resistance and international petition for repeal.

In 2005, the Mohave Generating Station shut down because of a Clean Air Act lawsuit, and the Navajo and Hopi tribes both passed a resolution ending Peabody's use of the Black Mesa aquifer. According to the EPA, the coal plant was the dirtiest in the western United States, emitting up to 40,000 tons of sulfur dioxide per year. Since the plant was the sole customer of the Black Mesa mine, and because Peabody did not have an alternative source of water, the operation of the mine and slurry line ceased as well. The Kayenta Mine remains a working plant. People continue to suffer the ill-effects of mining pollution, including chronic lung ailments such as bronchitis and pneumonia, and there are elevated cancer statistics in both children and adults, particularly for those living close to the mine.

Peabody Coal Company, now called Peabody Energy, has never taken responsibility for its role in creating and exacerbating the conflict between the Navajo and Hopi, nor have they admitted responsibility for any environmental hazard resulting from their mining operations on Navajo land. Instead, the company takes credit for the creation of jobs and bringing billions of dollars of revenue to the Navajo and Hopi tribes.[74]

---

74 "Belonging to The Land, Part Three: We're Still Here ..." 26 Sep. 2018

Peabody Energy's website boasts: "Peabody is the leading global pure-play coal company, serving power and steel customers in more than twenty-five countries on six continents. The company offers significant scale, high-quality assets, and diversity in geography and products. Peabody is guided by seven core values: safety, customer focus, leadership, people, excellence, integrity, and sustainability."[75]

Yet today, water extraction in the Black Mesa region and from the Colorado River continues to feed generating plants that service the southwestern United States. Due to extreme drought and Peabody Coal Company's thirty-year practice of pumping millions of gallons of water out of the aquifer, the windmills on Big Mountain can no longer draw enough to sustain the Dineh. There are six wells located on mine property, and residents travel there to get water—but the fear of contamination remains. There are no springs. There are seven functional power plants, yet residents of Big Mountain have no power, no running water—simply because they say NO to relocation.

---

75 *Peabody Energy*. www.peabodyenergy.com

Solsbury Hill, England (1994)

Clan Dyken, Glastonbury Festival: England (1994)
Fantuzzi, Quiltman, Hannah Suncloud, Bear Dyken, Mark Dyken
Photo Credit: Annika Forester

Clan Dyken, Whole Earth Festival: Davis, CA (1994)

Clan Dyken, Geothermal Plant Action: Pahoa, Hawaii (1992)

Nobody for President Tour with Wavy Gravy (1992)

Nobody for President Tour, Ken Kesey's house near Eugene, Oregon (1992)
Beth Wittke, Kiri Dyken, Trevor, Peta, Silas, Moses, Dave Millington, Bear, Mateo Fierria, Jeff Jones Wavy Gravy, Ken Kesey, Rose Dyken, Harmony Dyken, Mark, Laura

Clan Dyken, Nobody for President Tour, Federal Hall, New York (1992)

Mark and Bear in handcuffs, Nobody for President Tour: Connecticut Turnpike (1992)

Nobody for President Tour: Lafayette Park, Washington D.C. (1992)
Photos by Kerry Rice

Clan Dyken, 1st Gulf War action: State Capitol, Sacramento CA (1994)

Clan Dyken, Redwood Summer action, clear-cut forest:
Northern California (1995) Left to right: Mark Dyken, Bear Dyken,
Hannah Suncloud, Zazmo Deex

Mark Dyken and Wavy Gravy, Camp Winnarainbow: Laytonville, CA (1996)

Emerald Triangle Bike Tour: Hwy 101 near Garberville, CA (2012)

Bear, Emerald Triangle Bike Tour: Blue Lake, CA (2012)

Mother Ocean Carry Me

Mark, Women's March: Sacramento, CA (2017)

Rise for Climate Change: McKinley Park, Sacramento, CA (2018)

15

WAKE UP THE SKY[76]

The light, the light, the holy moonlight; the light, the light, the ancient starlight;
Wake up the sky tonight, wake up the sky.

Ak'ijidí = Blessings

"Living with a traveling band of gypsies is how I remember my childhood," Silas Dyken says, referring to times on the bus with his parents and the various and ever-changing members of their band. "We were always on the road, always playing shows and doing lots of cool sightseeing. I didn't live the typical life, but it made me who I am today, and if I could go back, I wouldn't change a thing."

At age ten, Si picked up his first bass guitar, and at age fourteen, he wrote his first rap song. Using the stage name S-One Freshperception, he dropped his first CD, *Cali Life*, in 2014. Silas's music preferences are rap and reggae, but Bear's influence is undeniable. Though Si travels and plays with Clan Dyken, he maintains his schedule for solo gigs. Aside from being a bass guitarist and lyricist, Si has created a clothing and merchandise line and is building a business using his *Mountain Motivation* logo. The family's musical genes show up in Mark and Laura's grandson, Benjamin, as well. At age fourteen, he expresses a natural rhythm and his grandpa's

---

76 Clan Dyken. The light, the light, the holy moon light. "Wake Up the Sky [Big Drum Songs]." *Love is*. CD. Track 14.

love for a variety of music. Benjamin plays the violin and is no slouch when drumming on Grandmother Drum, adding his unique beat and sound with accompanying instruments.

"It all happened because of the Beatles," Bear had said early on.

Though the fondness for 1960s music prompted the Dyken brothers' artistic growth, those early jam sessions with aunts and uncles playing various instruments, firing it up and raising the roof were the seeds that germinated their passion. Richard and Dorothy played a part, encouraging independence and creativity in their children. And the Dyken family has now grown to include seventeen grandchildren and five great-grandchildren.

I can envision the look of concern on Dorothy's face when Mark announced that he intended to hitchhike across the country and the same with Bear when he embarked on a similar journey a few years later. Dorothy's boys *left* but were never *gone*. You can hear traces of a mid-Western accent in both of their voices. Their eyes soften as they reflect on family and when they speak of their parents, their youth in Wisconsin, the home where they grew up—their childhood antics, the forest, the river, the cemetery—and even Freeman Chemical, the site of their very first activism. Though they have moved on, the connection to *place* is still there. Their ancestral home lives in their bones.

> *The Voices of Wisconsin were whispering to me*
> *Saying something about life long ago.*[77]

We watch through Mark and Laura's kitchen window as a hummingbird drinks from a glass feeder. Its tiny wings move at a rate unfathomable to the human eye, holding the small bird airborne while we take pleasure in observing this small blessing. The bird's graceful movements, the way he accepts this human-made offering, is a reminder that all things change, that adaptation and evolution are constant. The hummer's coloring, bright green and brown with a hint of red, resemble the surrounding oak trees, the winter grasses in the yard, and the foothills in which he lives. There is continuity here in Vallecito, as there is at Big Mountain

---

[77] Clan Dyken. The voices of Wisconsin. "The Voices of Wisconsin." *Water, Fire, and Other Relatives*. CD. Track 7.

where the Grandmothers use the earth's color pallet as their muse.

There is a fire blazing in the woodstove. Laura's handiwork decorates the walls: small quilts and lovely applique. Old family photos are magnet-bound to the refrigerator, and on the dining room wall is the framed menu from Nathy's Restaurant in Durango, Colorado. On the pantry door, Mark's brother Greg painted a mural of two Native women, resplendent in traditional dress, colored in turquoise, red, and brown. Over their heads flies an eagle, solitary, ever-present.

Mark's music studio is filled with radio equipment, band equipment, and piles and drawers filled with Clan Dyken memorabilia. Outside, the yard speaks to years of settling down in one place, the well-established flowerbeds blooming one flower or another year-round. There are fruit trees, barren now, but they soon will be laden with fruit. The words *family* and *nested* come to mind, yet across the road, mere feet from the house, there stands a bus—the Silver Eagle, aptly named Smokey, waiting, calling for that next adventure.

Much has come to pass since Mark first hitchhiked across the country and since Bear rebuilt that old guitar given to him by his friend's mother. Children are grown and married. Two were lost to tragedy, Adom—Gary and Linda's son, who died in a car crash at age fifteen, and Bear and Harmony's sweet Rose, who lost her battle with brain cancer at age twenty-eight. Since Rose's death, her daughter, Bella, has lived with Mark and Laura, amid all of her treasures: collections of hand puppets, small miniature crafts made by her and Laura, multiple Littlest Petshop characters, and her newly acquired trumpet—the latest and fondest of her musical instrument choices.

Bear and Harmony are no longer together. The Butte fire happened, destroying everything on the Land Trust in Calaveras County, including both Bear and Gary's homes. The old bus, Sahabi, was charred to its bones behind Bear's house, as was Gary's bus, Betty Lou. Most recently, brother Leon, passed on—leaving behind, a plethora of musical memories and Leon-esk vocabulary like *skiddly-bob*, and *spliffy* and *bam*!

Splayed across the table are collections of old photographs, childhood pictures of family and friends, snapshots of travels and gigs and buses and musical happenings at activist actions. Many included Corbin, the man who brought so much to Clan Dyken as a group, and Mark and Bear as individuals.

"Meeting Corbin was fate," Mark says.

"I came to understand that one time at the test site," says Bear. "Some people wanted to film him, and so he told them to meet him at his sweat lodge. Corbin sat cross-legged in front of the lodge and talked about his animals and other things, and then, as if something happened, he began saying, almost chanting, 'You're putting a bomb inside my mommy. You're blowing up my mommy.' Tears ran down his face, and everybody there just hit the ground. I fell to my knees."

"Right then was when I knew that whatever we could do for Corbin, whatever he needed from us, we'd be there," Mark says. "And we were. We kept going back to the test site and going back to his place. We were friends for many years."

"In many ways, he's still with us," says Bear.

When invited to the Glastonbury Festival, Mark, Bear, Laura, and Harmony took Corbin along to England. Near the village of Batheaston in Somerset, a protest was underway when they arrived. The issue was a proposed by-pass highway through Solsbury Hill, a small, flat-topped hill rising above the River Avon and the site of an Iron Age fort and one of the last great battles between the Pagans and the Saxons. The concerns and actions of protestors resembled those at the test site and Redwood Summer.

"Many people wanted to preserve the area as an indigenous sacred site, and a development corporation was putting a highway right through it," Bear explains. "They had knocked down some old buildings, and when we got there with Corbin, there were activists buried in the rubble, and people camped out between rocks and trees—more ways of locking down and stopping progress or construction work. These people had buried themselves. They dug themselves in with the plan to stay. They were not going to move."

The land was historic. It was a place where families went to enjoy the beauty of the countryside, to picnic, and to celebrate special occasions. The Solsbury Hill actions were the last resort because the Council and Department of Transport were not listening to the local people. "We're not going to take this lying down!" protesters yelled. "You're destroying the public land. You're destroying people's lives."

When Mark and Bear arrived, Mark pulled out Grandmother

Drum. Corbin began to drum and to sing, and the activists danced around him. "The drum activated them," Bear says, "and they just took off with it, chanting and doing this round dance. They *felt* the beat and were into it. The effectiveness of the round dance is part of what Corbin taught us. We learned that from him. Corbin told me many times, 'It's not the words I'm saying, it's the vibration I'm putting out. The sound that's going out from me here—that's what I doctor people with.'"

"At first," Bear says, "Corbin would go on the radio and talk about himself, his life, and would get off track. He got frustrated that he couldn't get his message across, and so he learned very quickly to bring his drum with him, so that no matter what questions an interviewer asked him, Corbin said what he wanted to say, and it was the same thing over and over. 'We only have one earth, we only have one air, we only have one water. We live on one planet. We're one people. We have to stop dividing ourselves by race and language. We're all red on the inside, and we have got to come together.' He learned to ignore what the interviewers were saying and kept putting out the message he wanted to put out. I mean, how were those interviewers, no matter who they were, going to interrupt a Shoshone elder, playing his drum?"

The Dyken brothers' time spent with Corbin provided constant inspiration, both personally and professionally. "I became aware, hanging out with Corbin on that trip to Glastonbury," Bear says, "that he saw the world differently than I did. After Solsbury Hill, it was a race to get to Glastonbury Tor by solstice, and when we finally got there, everybody was drunk. Corbin kept trying to get a round dance together, and the participants couldn't do it. They were too drunk, and they couldn't do it, and so Corbin said, 'Let's get out of here.'"

"Corbin said that that wasn't an accident," says Mark. "It was a sign."

"So we left," Bear says, "and we walked over the hill and down the other side where there were these two ancient wells. The red well and the white well. The people there believe that the water in these wells can heal them. So there was a guy with a crippled wrist, and he was putting his wrist in the water, and Corbin was sitting there looking at him with his beady eyes, and he was intent on it, and he goes, 'That water is not helping that guy.' Then he went over to the well, and he said all these prayers in his native language, and he was doing all these things with his hands, and then he stepped back for a little while, and he said, 'That's not good enough.' He went back to the well, and he did it some more, and he stepped back again, and he said, 'There. Now it's good enough.'"

"I still have some of that well water," says Mark.

"There were other times in his ceremonies at the test site where he would say, 'The smoke told me this,'" Bear recalls. 'At today's action, you need to be careful. Something is going to happen.'"

"There was one time in England," says Mark, "where we went to this house, and there was a big Celtic mandala on a tapestry hanging on the wall, and Corbin took one look at that thing and told the entire story of the mandala."

"It was a story about the seasons," Bear says. "And Corbin said, this represents the moon, and this represents the sun. He said the same thing about the dancing that happened at the Glastonbury Festival. 'They have one dance where they are poking holes in the sky, and that's a rain dance,' he said. 'They have another one where they are poking holes in the ground, and that's a fertility dance,' he said. 'The dancers are going through the moves, but they've forgotten what it's about.'"

"Yeah," says Mark. "He could see those things, as clear as day. He went to Stockholm and understood what the city was about—he understood just by the lay of the streets."

"He came to Mark's house, and Mark took him up 6-Mile Road, and Corbin said, 'Oh, there were Indian people here,'" Bear says.

"He did that," says Mark. "He just walked out the front and looked up at the bluffs up there. He held his hands up like this, and he said, 'Indian people used to hide up there.' Later on, I checked with one of the local Me-Wuk, and sure enough, the Me-Wuk elder said, 'When the government came for us kids, we used to run up to those bluffs and hide.'

"Corbin didn't know anything about that, well, he did, but nobody told him about it. He just stood out the door of my house, and he had this bent thumb, and he put his hands up and said, 'Indian people used to hide in those bluffs.' Just like that, and this was before I told him what was around here." Mark waves his arm and gestures outside. "At one time, this whole place was part of the Rancheria. There are people buried under the buckeye tree over there. Corbin just felt it."

"He had bent thumbs because someone in his past had tortured him," Bear says.

Neither Bear nor Mark knew for sure what happened to Corbin's thumbs. There was mention of someone abusing him with a thumbscrew while he was at Indian Boarding School, but that was never substantiated. Corbin also mentioned injuries sustained when cowboying, but not in direct association with his thumbs.

"Talk about a guy who knew what it meant to be a human being," Bear says. "Corbin knew he was responsible for the animals and the plants at his place. He said that saying thanks is what they need from us. They need our gratitude, and they need our appreciation, and he always said, 'You got to take care of what you got.' Part of his prayer was to the darkness. 'We need the darkness to hide from the enemy. Without the darkness, I wouldn't be here today,' he would say."

"He used to say that Clan Dyken helped him come out from behind the bush," says Mark.

"I was thinking about that," Bear says. "When he first started coming with us, he'd carry our gear and do our dishes, and we'd ask him not to do that, and he'd say, 'No, no I got to carry my weight.'"

"We had his first birthday party," Mark says, softly. "He didn't know how old he was, or when the real day of his birth happened."

"He was like a little kid," Bear says. "So excited. I remember, he asked my daughter Rose, 'How old are you?' She said, 'I'm four years old.' And Corbin said, 'I'm four years old too.'"

There is a place called Big Mountain. It exists and lives and breathes. There, Hopi Community Radio, KUYI—meaning water in Hopi, and owned by the Hopi Foundation—provides on air entertainment. It broadcasts from a trailer outside Keams Canyon deep inside Navajo land, population, 260 as of the 2000 census. The Navajo word for Keams Canyon is *Lók'aa'deeshjin*. The Hopi word is *Pongsikya*. In the last quarter of the nineteenth century, in Keams Canyon, there was a trading post. The post served both the Navajo and the Hopi offering a year-round opportunity to exchange goods between the two tribes.

"Hopi Community Radio reaches all over the reservation," Mark says. "They play a great diversity of Native music, both traditional and contemporary. Their programmers share stories, information, and news from a Native perspective. They maintain their independence by not asking for support from either the Hopi or the Navajo tribes. That way they can freely represent many tribal affiliations.

"There is a strange relationship between the Hopi and Dineh people," he continues. "As we've discussed, as individuals, especially among traditional people of both tribes, there is mutual respect, understanding, and solidarity as indigenous neighbors. I have met many Hopi, including respected elder Thomas Banyacya. They speak of cooperation and a need to stand together against the forces that created the supposed land dispute between the two nations. Many friendships and marriages cross tribal lines. I have seen and heard Hopi people speak out against the forced relocation of Dineh, yet the Hopi tribal government, backed by the BIA, is openly hostile to the Dineh who have not signed the Accommodation Agreement. It always calms me a bit to hear the radio station playing music representative of both tribes. It gives me hope that, in the future, these two tribes can find some peace."

Before we had left Sand Springs, Angelita Yazzi presented each of us with a beaded necklace—treasured pieces because—aside from the beads and the stones or the effort it took to make them—they were given out of friendship and trust. On our last trip to Anna Begay's house, we gave her shoes. The look on her face was the gift of the day. Before leaving, Anna showed us the last rug she wove with turquoise and gray yarn—one she is not selling, and that she will keep as a reminder of her skill on the loom.

On the Clan Dyken website, Mark once wrote, "I have sat in wonder as Grandmothers tell stories about their lives as young women. Sometimes I miss part of the story because I forget to listen to the interpreter. Grandmother's voice, even though it's speaking in a tongue I don't understand, gives me a special feeling. She is speaking of the fire and how her Grandmother told her always to keep it burning, for her relatives live in that fire. I watch the flames dance among the logs in her dilapidated wood stove while the music of her language entwines with the high desert wind blowing the sand up against the hogan and get a sense of what she means without understanding the words.

"Yes, we are all like that fire. Here, only in this moment, yet connected to every previous flame. Her ancestors, my ancestors, and all the ones gone before have become fuel for that fire and will soon be ashes waiting to return to the earth and start over again. Grandmothers are keepers of the sacred fire. They will share this wisdom if the world listens. They are watching their culture die, and I can see it in their faces. Faces that remind me of the desert with eyes that shine out like stars in the early morning on Black Mesa.

"As always, when we arrive, the place is buzzing as workforces dig into their tasks of dividing and delivering more than five tons of goods, twenty-five cords of firewood and loads of love to the 110 families. From Big Mountain to Blue Canyon, Teehsto to Jeddito, Sand Springs to Coal Mine Mesa and beyond. The names of the places start to tell the stories, and every year we add a few more chapters.

"One thousand miles is a long way to travel, or it's just a few blinks of the eye, depending on your perspective. World leaders, business tycoons, and diplomats criss-cross the globe in jets and a thousand tiny miles zoom past far below, as a family walks from the homeless shelter to the food bank in one of the towns that dot the landscape. Somewhere between the speed of a 747 cutting through the sky and the measured pace of a well-worn, too-large tennis shoe shuffling down the cracked sidewalk, a caravan rolls through time and space to a land out of time. You supporters were on that caravan. You loaded it with food, warm clothes, firewood, and kindness. You delivered the message of hope and connection to elders and families that live beneath the chemtrails and wide open skies of the high desert in the land of the Dineh. You put smiles on the faces of the people who Walk in Beauty through the land the Creator put them on so many years ago. They were glad to see you."

Magic—*'Alííl*. Even around Mark's kitchen table, hundreds of miles from Big Mountain, you can feel it. You know it is there. It's more than a memory or a spot on the map. The relationship between people here and there is tangible, a thing you can hold onto in the dead of winter and when summer sun parches the land. Elsie, Louise, Angie, Jonathan, Tim, and Belinda, and others are a text away. Often now, mornings are started with a *Yá'át'ééh*, or *Hello my friend, hope you are well.*

"Thinking of names and faces reminds me why we go to Big Mountain," Bear says. "It makes me think of how the government bulldozed the Sundance grounds and built a chain link fence around the site.

It reminds me of how they have been blowing up Black Mesa, burial sites and all, and how they are digging up the coal to power Las Vegas and L.A. The truth is that renewables are cheaper and safer. It's time for the fossil fuel nightmare to end and humanity to step into more profound compassion about our consumption of energy and the Native people of the earth. This is what spurs us on to do the work, to go out to the reservation. The vibration that the community pulls together at fundraisers raises our vibration, and suddenly we're ready to go. There's nothing that warms our hearts more than to be invited into the homes of a Dineh family and share their food and talk and hear news of what's been happening over the last year."

The sun sets at Mark and Laura's place, as it sets at Big Mountain. As with any journey that comes to an end, there is a bit of sadness, but also there is the wonderment that comes with knowing that the next trip is bound to happen. There is music to play. There are actions to support. There is a family that continues to grow, day by day. Bear's granddaughter, Bella, cuddles on my lap. She pats my cheek. "I love you," she reminds me. Family—it's a good thing—and by now, it's comfortable and lasting. My email pings with a message from Elsie Benale, letting me know that she has finished a new rug. Continuity, connections; they happen for a reason. Today, and every day, I feel blessed. Such blessings are, no doubt, part of the transformation Mark spoke of, the one he promised would occur if I were to go on the trip to Big Mountain.

"People used to tell us we were crazy back then," Mark shares, as he rummages through his decades of family photos. "Now I look back and think, man, we were a little crazy. I mean, in all those years of driving around in the buses, we had our vehicles registered, insured, legal, tags and all of that. Sometimes they could have been in better and safer mechanical condition—but we did take care of things so that we would have less of those kinds of hassles. We did keep that all together, but the rest of it was wide open. Anything could happen.

"Because we were living in buses, we were spending time out in nature. Even in the years before we started doing activism, we were visiting National Parks. You put people out there in warm hot springs, or at the ocean, or on a mountaintop, their stress level will go way down. If you take this away, you are causing human illness. It all connects.

"All these places, the test site, Ward Valley, Big Mountain, all connect with the beauty of the land," Mark says. "Maybe it's related to being older, being a grandparent and wondering what kind of planet will be left for future generations. Elders I looked to for wisdom and perspective are gone. I have to squint a little harder to find the light. Then it hits me—it's up to me to change the way I'm looking at things. To find hope, I have to be hopeful. To see the light I have to turn my own up. When a child smiles, when a song rocks, when the next generation of activists make their voice heard, when the brilliance of what humans are capable of reveals itself in art, dance, scientific innovation or inspired revolution—hope grows. When loving displays of compassion reveal themselves in scientific innovations or inspired revolution, hope grows. When loving displays of compassion happen in the middle of a disaster, my resolve is renewed. I simply have no choice. I have to believe we can make it better.

"Now more than ever, it's time to be in touch with the creative mind, the moral imagination, the source of the light. Time to come together and feel our power. That's what the Clan Dyken Revive the Beauty Way Tour has been all about for all these years. In our small way, we connect in community and bring that collective goodwill in the form of food supplies, firewood, labor, and witness in a spirit of solidarity to true Earth Protectors and Wisdom Keepers of the Dineh Nation in the Black Mesa region of the Navajo Reservation in Arizona. Remembering how we act every day, how we treat each other, how we use our energy and where we direct it is far more important than whom we vote for in Washington."

Amá sání, my dream Amá sání, it is hard now to keep her quiet. Even at Mark's, I can see her in my mind's eye. She is cold and wet standing beside the sea. Her body aches. She is tired. Travel has been tedious. Amá sání has experienced much in her lifetime, some things for which she should be glad, but her heart is heavy. Even now, breathing in the salt air and feeling the rush of each wave as it breaks she finds life difficult. Her children have moved away from Dineh Bikéyah. Her grandchildren are scattered, each with their demons to fight.

Amá sání's struggle has brought her here to speak in front of strangers. She is too old now to wander the high desert in search of plants for the dyes or for medicine. Rangers took the last of her sheep. They kicked down her hogan door and told her she must leave. "No, she told them. My feet will wither in the hot sand before I move. My body will waste with no water, but I will not go. Dineh Bikéyah is my home. I will not leave."

Soon they will call her, the ones who brought her to this place. She likes the little activist with the long dark hair. The girl has a good heart and a loud voice, sharp and clear. For her, Amá sání will talk. She will tell them about her loom, which sits idle. How there are no sheep to shear, no wool with which to weave a rug. For the Dineh, seven generations out, she will tell all that has happened since the coal mine came and the rangers and government agents began terrorizing her relatives.

Someone *must* listen. If Amá sání talks loud enough and long enough, someone, somewhere will hear. Maybe there will be more like the little dark-haired activist. Maybe then, someone will help her rebuild. So Amá sání can rest. So she can go home. Maybe then, she can plant a garden and make kneel-down bread and even, maybe then, she can get more sheep. Only then, will she dream peacefully and sleep soundly, and for the first time in a long time, be able to say her prayers of thanks. To give blessings for all that is good while standing in front of her hogan door facing east.

The day we left Big Mountain, our hearts cried out to stay on the reservation, to remain with the elders, yet the fact remains that the Navajo survived before us and they will survive after we leave. These people *survive*, as did Katherine Smith after Mark first saw her work her loom; as did Anna Begay after Bear saw her leaning over the hood of her old truck; as did John Yazzi after Catherine first spoke to him in his garden of corn and beans. Through it all, these elders stayed, and they lived to the end with pride in their souls and courage in their veins. Still, they *live*. In the hearts of their children, grandchildren, and those, seven generations out, they *live*. Their struggle continues.

Nizhóní yee' – Beautiful

Peace.

"When the Creator moves me, I will go."
--Katherine Smith

Walking in Beauty, a Navajo Blessing

Today I will walk out; today everything unnecessary will leave me,
I will be as I was before. I will have a cool breeze over my body.
I will have a light body. I will be happy forever;
nothing will hinder me.
I walk with beauty before me. I walk with beauty behind me.
I walk with beauty below me. I walk with beauty above me.
I walk with beauty around me. My words will be beautiful.
In beauty all day long may I walk.
Through the returning seasons, may I walk.
On the trail marked with pollen may I walk.
With dew about my feet, may I walk.
It is finished in beauty.
It is finished in beauty.

Photo by Dan Budnik.
©Katherine Smith, Big Mountain resistor. Her basket holds sacred objects symbolizing her land and life, ca. 1981

The most important thing is that we must come together as one people.
We must continue to work together to provide for our future generations
to protect Mother Earth. By ourselves, we are not so strong,
but together, as one people, nothing can stop us.
Our Mother Earth is relying on us.

—Corbin Harney

Photo by Dan Budnik
©Katherine Smith on horseback with rifle, ca. 1979

Afterword

Heal These Global Wounds

by Bear Dyken
performed by Clan Dyken

Let the food I eat give me strength to do the work of the one Great Spirit
who animates all the universe from the smallest creature to the farthest star,
heal, heal, heal these wounds, heal these global wounds
Let the water I drink give me strength to do the work of the one Great Spirit
who animates all the universe from the smallest creature to the farthest star,
heal, heal, heal these wounds, heal these global wounds
Let the air I breathe give me strength to do the work of the one Great Spirit
who animates all the universe from the smallest creature to the farthest star,
heal, heal, heal these wounds, heal these global wounds
Let the fire I burn give me strength to do the work of the one Great Spirit
who animates all the universe from the smallest creature to the farthest star,
heal, heal, heal these wounds, heal these global wounds.

Timeline
Navajo/Euro-American History

1863: General Carleton, Commandant of the Military Department of New Mexico, ordered Kit Carson to move the Navajo from their homes to the Bosque Redondo.

1868: The Navajo return from a forced walk and incarceration at Fort Sumner (the Bosque Redondo). The United States Government entered into a peace treaty with the Navajo Tribe and established a 3.5 million acre reservation for the Navajo people.

1882: Executive order established a 2.4 million acre reservation for use and occupancy by the Hopi and "such other Indians as the Secretary of the Interior may see fit to settle thereon."

1901-07: The Federal government continued to expand the Navajo Reservation until it completely encircled the 1882 Hopi Reservation.

1909: The U.S. Geological Survey discovered eight billion tons of coal at Black Mesa.

1921: Oil was discovered on Navajo land.

1923: Formation of the Navajo Tribal Council.

1930: The U.S. Senate Investigating Committee revealed findings of systematic removal of Navajo children from their parents by Indian Administration school officials.

1934: Legislation added and changed the boundaries of the reservation in Arizona.

1936: Formation of the Hopi Tribal Council.

1936: The Department of the Interior and the Hopi Council established nineteen grazing districts on Hopi and Navajo reservations. District Six, a 499,258-acre area within the 1882 reservation, was recognized as encompassing all of the lands exclusively occupied by the Hopi.

1941: District Six was expanded to 631,194 acres. Navajo families were told to move.

1947: John Boyden applied to Navajo Tribal Council for the position of General Council but was turned down in favor of Norman Littell. The Hopi Tribal Council hired Boyden as their General Council.

1952-57: Boyden and Littell petitioned the Secretary of the Interior to partition lands outside District 6.

1958: Congress authorized Navajo and Hopi tribal councils to participate in a lawsuit to determine their respective rights and interests.

1962: Healing vs. Jones: It was ruled that the Hopi Tribe have exclusive title to District Six and both tribes had joint, equal, and undivided rights to 1.8 million acres of the 1882 reservation outside of District Six. A federal court ruled that only Congress could partition Indian lands and declared outside District 6 a Joint Use Area to be controlled by both Hopi and Navajo.

1965: Interior Secretary Stewart Udall embarked on a plan to develop water and mineral resources in the Southwest.

1966: Despite Hopi Traditional Spiritual leaders' objection, the Hopi Tribal Council granted a thirty-five-year lease to Peabody Coal Company, to develop Black Mesa.

1966: Commissioner of Indian Affairs, Robert Bennett, issued a series of administrative instructions restricting any development in the 1934 Act reservation. This became known as the Bennett Freeze.

1971: The Native American Rights Fund filed suit on behalf of sixty-two members of the Hopi tribe to stop strip mining on 100 square miles of the Hopi Reservation, including the area known as Black Mesa.

1971: Livestock reduction was mandated. Navajo people living on "disputed land" were ordered to reduce their livestock by ninety percent to control overgrazing.

1972: United States vs. Kabinto: more than fifty Navajo families were evicted from District Six without relocation assistance.

1973: Navajo people living on "disputed land" were ordered to reduce their livestock by ninety percent to "control overgrazing."

1974: The Navajo-Hopi Land Settlement Act (PL 93-531) became law. Congress authorized partition of the surface rights in the Joint Use Area. Relocation Commission was established and given responsibility to move those Indian families living on the wrong side of the partition line.

1975: Navajo efforts to select relocation land were blocked by Non-Indian ranchers and the Interior Department.

1976: Hopis accept 5,000,000 dollars from the United States for aboriginal land claims concerning Hopi Lands outside District 6.

1977: Fences were erected around Hopi Partitioned Land. A resistance movement supported by Hopi and Navajo traditional and religious leaders sprung up around Big Mountain.

1979: Navajo traditionals declared their Declaration of Independence, disassociating themselves from pro-development Tribal Council and pledging total resistance to relocation.

1980: Peabody Coal Company announced that there was enough coal under Black Mesa to be mined for the next 100 years.

1980: P.L. 96-305 authorized Navajo selection of "new lands" and amended the Relocation Agreement, adding seventy-five-year leases to certain applicants otherwise required to relocate.

Afterword

1982: The Big Mountain Defense Committee was formed in Flagstaff, Arizona to fight for the repeal of the Navajo-Hopi Land Settlement Act.

1985: President Reagan designated former Interior Secretary William Clark to encourage the tribes to settle the dispute over HPL. Clark determined it unlikely the tribes could negotiate a settlement because the Hopi Tribe was unwilling to negotiate. July 8, 1986 was set as the final date for all residents of Big Mountain to relocate. The families who chose not to move would, at that point, be forced to move by the National Guard, as mandated by President Ronald Reagan.

1986: Congressman John McCain and Morris Udall drafted an amendment to PL93-531 calling for an end to the relocation of residents and exchange of lands between the Navajo and the Hopi. July 6 deadline for relocation of Navajos from Hopi Joint Use Area Land passed; approximately one-half of the Navajos certified for voluntary relocation benefits were not relocated.

1987: Manybeads vs. the United States. A lawsuit challenging forced relocation based on the Freedom of Religion Act of 1978 was first filed.

1988: Obligations and funding for home construction by the BIA under P.L. 99-190 were transferred to the new Commissioner of the Office of Navajo and Hopi Indian Relocation under P.L. 100-666.

1989: Secretary of Interior Lujan imposed a new policy that no relocation benefits should be provided to Navajos who have voluntarily left the Hopi Partitioned lands until all eligible Navajos currently residing on HPL were resettled.

1996: Accommodations Agreement Law Passed. This law provided a seventy-five-year lease for all families of Big Mountain area who had not relocated. They had to sign a lease with the Hopi Tribal Council which made them subject to the jurisdiction and laws of that council. Some Navajo families signed others did not.

2001: Manybeads vs. the United States was denied a hearing by the U.S. Supreme Court.

2001: On July 14, 2001, Navajo resisters from Big Mountain were arrested by the Hopi tribal council. They included elder Pauline Whitesinger, Ruth Benally, and her daughter Elvira Horseherder. They were held in jail and charged with criminal trespassing.

2001: On August 17, 2001, the Hopi Tribal Council accompanied by Federal Marshalls destroyed the Sundance Ceremonial Grounds at Anna Mae Camp on Big Mountain.

2002: The Big Mountain women were acquitted by the Hopi Tribal Council.

2005: Peabody Coal Company announced plans to expand their mines on Black Mesa.

2006 to the present: The Navajo continue to resist relocation.

Afterword

Aside from Big Mountain, the Nevada Nuclear Test Site, Ward Valley, Livermore Lab, and the rest, Clan Dyken has been inspired to keep the music flowing as a part of activist actions during both Gulf Wars. Clan Dyken supported the Occupy Movement and played pedal-powered music for the Oakland General Strike in 2017. They regularly add their vibe to actions regarding climate change, such as the Climate Fest/Rise for Climate Rally in September of 2018 in Sacramento, where the band played their music via a pedal-powered groove. They have also played music for the annual LGBT Pride in the Park event, held in Murphys, California, and the Rise Against Monsanto Rally in Oakland. Wherever they play, Clan Dyken has consistently brought their funky, magically meditative combo of drum, bass, lead guitar, harmonica, flute, and mouth harp, to stages throughout the United States, and other parts of the world, their multi-genre beat lending to folk, blues, rap, reggae, world music, and floor-shakin' rock.

The band has persisted beyond the limitations of relationships and members coming and going. They fraternized with Utah Phillips, who mentored and encouraged them. Clan Dyken has also been active in the medical marijuana movement. The songs on their CD *Green Prayer* came out of that effort. There is a rumor that when a group of activists was brutalized with pepper spray during the fight to save old-growth forests in Northern California, they chanted *Heal those global wounds.* A fitting tribute to a band who not only has kept the music coming all these years but who lead their lives as living endorsements of all that they fight to support.

Clan Dyken Timeline

1978

- Beech Street Band
- Place: Grafton, Wisconsin
- Members: Bear Dyken, Mark Dyken, Phillip Fellenz
- Music: Rock n' Roll cover tunes, original tunes

1979

- Search and Rescue Band
- Place: Lake Tahoe, CA and Durango Colorado
- Members: Bear Dyken, Mark Dyken, Laura Hardin, Phillip Fellenz
- Music: Cover songs and some original tunes

1982

- Allright Family Band
- Place: California
- Members: Bear Dyken, Mark Dyken, Laura Hardin, Judy Hardin, Bill Rogers, Marilyn Rogers, and others
- Cover songs and some original tunes

1982

- Band's first Whole Earth Festival
- Place: Davis, CA.
- Band members: Bear Dyken, Mark Dyken, Laura Dyken, Harmony Suncloud, Gary Dyken, Raymond Jennings, Ken Nahan
- Music: Original tunes and some cover songs

1986

- Clan Dyken
- Place: California

- Band members: Bear Dyken, Mark Dyken, Gary Dyken, Leon Dyken, Laura Dyken, Harmony Dyken
- Music: Original tunes and some cover songs

1988

- Rancho Seco
- Place: Sacramento, CA
- Band members: Bear Dyken, Mark Dyken, Laura Dyken, Harmony Dyken, Gary Dyken, Leon Dyken
- Music: Original tunes, some cover songs

1988-1992

- Nevada Nuclear Test Site
- Place: Mercury, Nevada
- Band members: Bear Dyken, Mark Dyken, Laura Dyken, Harmony Dyken, Leon Dyken, Jeff Jones
- Music: Original tunes, some cover songs

1990-1991

- Redwood Summer
- Place: Arcata and other locations throughout Northern California and Oregon
- Band members: Bear Dyken, Mark Dyken, Laura Dyken, Harmony Dyken, Leon Dyken, Jeff Jones
- Music: Original tunes, some cover songs

1991

- First trip to Big Mountain
- Place: Black Mesa, Arizona
- Band members: Bear Dyken, Mark Dyken, Gary Dyken, Leon Dyken
- Music: Original tunes, some cover songs

1991

- Gulf War I Peace Marches
- Place: San Francisco
- Band Members: Bear Dyken, Mark Dyken, Laura Dyken,

Harmony Dyken, Leon Dyken, Jeff Jones
- Music: Original tunes, some cover songs

1991

- Lawrence Livermore Lab Actions
- Place: Livermore, CA
- Band Members: Bear Dyken, Mark Dyken, Laura Dyken, Harmony Dyken, Gary Dyken, Leon Dyken
- Music: Original tunes, some cover songs

1992

- Nobody for President Tour
- Place: Berkeley, CA to Washington DC.
- Band members: Bear Dyken, Mark Dyken, Laura Dyken, Harmony Dyken, Leon Dyken, Gary Dyken, Jeff Jones, Darren Houser
- Music: Original tunes, some cover songs

1992

- Hawaiian Geothermal plant protest
- Place: Hawaii
- Band members: Bear Dyken, Mark Dyken, Laura Dyken, Harmony Dyken, Leon Dyken, Gary Dyken
- Music: Original tunes, some cover songs

1994

- 1st Beauty Way Tour
- Place: West Coast
- Band members: Bear Dyken, Mark Dyken, Rick Matteson, Zazmo Deex,
- Harmony Dyken, Leon Dyken
- Music: Original tunes, some cover songs

1994

- Glastonbury Festival
- Place: England
- Band members: Bear Dyken, Mark Dyken, Jeff Jones,

- Laura Dyken, Harmony Dyken, Fantuzzi
- Music: Original tunes, some cover songs

1995

- Hog Farm Pig Nic
- Place: Laytonville, CA
- Band members: Bear Dyken, Mark Dyken, Zazmo Deex, Rick Mathisen, Lisa Beane
- Music: Original tunes, some cover songs

1995

- Ward Valley
- Place: Ward Valley, California
- Band Members: Bear Dyken, Mark Dyken
- Music: Original tunes, some cover songs

1996

- Volcanic Rock Festival
- Place: Bend, Oregon
- Band members: Bear Dyken, Mark Dyken, Zazmo Deex, Rick Mathisen, Lisa Beane,
- Jan Peters
- Music: Original tunes, some cover songs

1997

- First Trinity Tribal Stomp
- Place: Hayfork, CA
- Band members: Bear Dyken, Mark Dyken, Harmony Dyken, Zazmo Deex, Rick Mathisen, Lisa Beane, Fantuzzi
- Music: Original tunes, some cover songs

1999

- Mountain Aire Festival
- Place: Calaveras County
- Band members: Bear Dyken, Mark Dyken, Zazmo Deex, Rick Mathisen, Lisa Beane, Fantuzzi
- Music: Original tunes, some cover songs

2001

- Spirit of Woodstock Festival
- Place: Italy
- Band members: Bear Dyken, Mark Dyken, Gary Dyken
- Music: Original tunes, some cover songs

2002

- Afghan War Resistance
- Place: San Francisco and Sacramento, CA
- Band members: Bear Dyken, Mark Dyken, Gary Dyken

2003

- Gulf War Resistance
- Place: San Francisco and Sacramento, CA
- Band members: Bear Dyken, Mark Dyken, Gary Dyken
- Music: Original tunes, some cover songs

2004

- Kate Wolf Music Festival
- Place: Laytonville, CA
- Band members: Bear Dyken, Mark Dyken, Laura Dyken, Gary Dyken,
- Andrew Christian
- Music: Original tunes, some cover songs

2009

- Pleasant Revolution Bike Tour
- Place: West Coast to Mexico
- Band members: Bear Dyken, Somer Moon, Ginger Ninjas
- Music: Original tunes, some cover tunes

2011

- Oakland General Strike, Occupy Movement, 2nd Gulf War Action
- Place: Oakland, CA
- Band members: Bear Dyken, Mark Dyken, Silas Dyken, Somer Moon
- Music: Original tunes, some cover songs

2012

- Emerald Triangle Bike Tour
- Place: Northern CA
- Band members: Bear Dyken, Mark Dyken, Silas Dyken, Somer Moon, Kris Osward
- Music: Original tunes, some cover songs

2014

- 20th Beauty Way Tour
- Place: California and Oregon
- Band members: Bear Dyken, Mark Dyken, Silas Dyken, Somer Moon
- Music: Original tunes, some cover songs

2015

- Butte Fire
- Place: Central California
- Bear, Gary, Somer Moon, and the Cedar Creek community lose everything

1999-2018

- Annual Earth Day Festival
- Place: Angels Camp, CA
- Band members: Bear Dyken, Mark Dyken, Silas Dyken, Somer Moon (2005-2015),
- Kris Osward
- Music: Original tunes, some cover songs

2009-2018

- Kate Wolf Music Festival, Kid Zone
- Place: Laytonville, CA
- Band members: Bear Dyken, Mark Dyken, Somer Moon (2010-2015).

2018

- Soul Journey, Sailboat/Bicycle, Music Tour
- Guatemala to Cuba and back again
- Crew members: Bear Dyken, Lanora Percy, Dante Espinosa, Obo Martin (aka Martino), Miguel, Adriana Bautista.
- Music: Original tunes, some cover songs

2018

- Rise for Climate Change Rally
- Place: Sacramento, CA
- Band members: Bear Dyken, Mark Dyken, Silas Dyken
- Music: Original tunes, some cover songs

2018

- Pride in the Park
- Place: Murphys, CA
- Band members: Bear Dyken, Mark Dyken, Silas Dyken
- Music: Original tunes, some cover songs

2018

- March Against Monsanto
- Place: Woodland, CA
- Bear Dyken, Mark Dyken, Silas Dyken
- Music: Original tunes, some cover songs

CLAN DYKEN DISCOGRAPHY

Clan Dyken

- Released: 1987
- Format: CD
- Label: Clan Dyken
- Mastering: Jeff "Fingers" Crawford
- Sound Engineer: Jeff "Fingers" Crawford
- Producer: Clan Dyken
- Notes: *Clan Dyken* was the first recording made under this name. Bear Dyken, vocals, guitar, Laura Dyken, guitar, vocals, Harmony Dyken Vocals, Mark Dyken, Drums, Gary Dyken, bass. Songs include: Into the Night, New Day, Pay the Fiddler, Help You Bear Your Load, Techno Voodoo, Roots, Still Jammin', The Tough, and Positive.

Song Catcher

- Released: 1989
- Format: CD
- Label: Forward Productions
- Mastering: Gary Dyken
- Sound engineer: Bear Dyken
- Producer: Clan Dyken
- Notes: Recorded live in New Mexico

Family Values

- Released:1989
- Format: CD
- Label: Forward Productions
- Mastering: Dave Millington
- Sound Engineer: Dave Millington
- Producer: Clan Dyken

Notes: *Family Values* is dedicated to future generations. The songs are about the issues of the day: the closing of Rancho Seco Nuclear Power Plant, the sinking of the Greenpeace flagship, the war in Central America, and more...Mark Dyken, drums, Laura Dyken, guitar, vocals, Harmony Dyken, vocals, hand percussion, Leon Dyken, percussion, Bear Dyken, vocals, guitar, harmonica. Songs include: Seven Generations, To All My Relations, Wild Country, Dry Ranch, summer, Ain't We New?, We Got the Groove, Rainbow Warrior, Medicine People, What Kinda Vibe?, Telegraph Avenue, War On the People, Let the People Live, Ho brother, and Happiness Is Up To You.

Shundahai

- Released: 1992
- Format: CD
- Label: Forward Productions
- Mastering: Dave Millington
- Sound Engineer: Dave Millington
- Producer: Clan Dyken

Notes: *Shundahai* was recorded independent of grid power, using solar panels, batteries, and a full sine wave inverter. The songs were inspired by Clan Dyken's involvement with the Western Shoshone elder and spiritual leader Corbin Harney, and their trips to the Nevada Nuclear Test Site. These songs belong to the folks who fought to stop nuclear weapons testing on Indian land. Bear Dyken, vocals, guitar, Laura Dyken, vocals, guitar, Harmony Dyken, vocals, hand percussion, Jeff Jones, bass, Leon Dyken, percussion, Mark Dyken drums. Songs include Spirit Trail, Shundahai, Stand By My Watch, Song For A Nation, Love Conspiracy, Search Of enemies, Stolen Land, and Dear Friends.

Clan Dyken Live

- Released: 1993
- Format: CD
- Label: Forward Productions
- Mastering: Dave Millington

- Sound Engineer: Dave Millington/Sonora Fairgrounds, Sonora, CA.
- Producer: Clan Dyken

Notes: *Clan Dyken Live* is the documentation of a show done on New Years 92-93. The year saw Clan Dyken record the world's first solar-powered album, "*Shundahai*, take Corbin Harney, Western Shoshone spiritual elder, on the road and bring his message to new audiences and participate in the 100th Monkey concert, Walk and Action, to end nuclear weapons testing. Clan Dyken traveled coast to coast with Wavy Gravy on the Nobody for President tour. Bear Dyken, vocals, guitars, harmonica, flute, and djembe, Harmony Dyken, vocals, hand Percussion, Laura Dyken, vocals, guitars, Leon Dyken, percussion, Mark Dyken, drums, Jeff Jones bass. Special guests; Darin Houser, saxophone, Kim Angelis, violin, Nathan drum and vocal. Songs include: Drum Prayer Intro, Into the Night, Precious, Sister Colorado, Dear Friends, Ain't We New, Raise the Morning Star, AIM Song/Leonard Peltier Honor Song, Tohono O'odham Reggae, Seven Generations, and a gospel medley with drum accompaniment, which falls into Auld Lange Syne at the stroke of midnight.

Green Prayer
- Released: 1996
- Format: CD
- Label: Forward Productions
- Mastering: Alex Stephens
- Sound Engineer: Alex Stephens
- Producer: Clan Dyken

Notes: *Green Prayer* definitely has a botanical thing about it. These songs are mostly about the relationship between humans and the plant world. Recorded at Enharmonic studio in Sacramento California by Eric Broyhill. The entire collection of songs was performed live in the studio at one time, very little production after that. Mark Dyken, drums, Bear Dyken, guitars, vocals, harmonica, Rick Mathisen, guitars, Zazmo Deex, bass, Harmony Dyken, vocals, Moku, Carla Campbell, and Warren Jones on percussions. Songs include: Let My Seed Grow, Johnnies Seed, Harvest Song, Something Comes Our Way, World I Imagine, Shamans Drum, Walk On Two Feet, Planting Party, Herb Doctor, and Can't Touch the Herb.

Revive the Beauty Way.
- Released: 1998
- Format: CD
- Label: Forward Productions
- Mastering: Dave Millington
- Sound Engineer: Alex Stephens
- Producer: Clan Dyken

Notes: *Revive the Beauty Way* is dedicated to the native Dineh people of Big Mountain Arizona who are resisting forced relocation from their homeland to make way for coal, uranium, and oil mining. Many of the songs were inspired by the experiences on the annual Thanksgiving Food and Supply Run to Big Mountain. This project was powered by using thirty-four solar panels, a 4,000 watt Trace inverter with grid interface capability. Rick Mathisen, guitars, Jan Peters, keyboards, mandolin, bouzouki, vocals, Zazmo Deex, bass, Harmony Dyken, vocals, Lisa Bean, vocals, Bear Dyken, vocals, guitars, accordion, harmonica, flutes, Mark Dyken, drums. Songs include: The Dhange, Coal Carriers, Good Thing Comes, Revive the Beauty Way, What Are We Doing?, Reach Up For the Healing, Thank You For Music, Whatcha Gonna Do With That Stuff, Find Some Room, Shining Like the Sun, Runner, and the drum chant, Heal These Global Wounds.

Love is…
- Released: 2002
- Format: CD
- Label: Forward Productions
- Recorded: Emeryville CA at Ex'pressions Center for New Media
- Sound Engineer: Students at Ex'pressions Center for New Media
- Producer: Clan Dyken

Notes: *Love Is*...Featuring Mark Dyken on drums and vocals, Gary Dyken on the bass, Bear Dyken on guitars, vocals, harmonicas, and hand drums, Andrew Christian on congas and percussion. Songs include: Indestructible, 911, Flying Dream, Free Form Jam, On the Way To Big Mountain, Five, Feel Good Music, Meet You In Paris, Go For The Good, Not A Tree Farm, Burn It Down, Truth Is God, More Jam, House Of Song, Big Drum Songs.

Bush League Hits

- Released: 2003
- Format: CD
- Label: Forward Productions
- Mastering: Alex Stephens
- Sound Engineer: Alex Stephens
- Producer: Clan Dyken

Notes: *Bush League Hits* is a collection of twelve original acoustic songs by Bear Dyken. Also featuring guest vocals from Windsong, Kat Del Rio, and Alice DiMicele. Songs include: New World, Bush League Prima Dona Blues, The Ballad of Steven "No Nukes" Willard, Full Moon Hotsprings, Smile Big, It Ain't Me, Cryin', Leaky Faucet, Ship in the Sky, Red Calaveras Clay, Peach Pie, Dance with Me, Sing to Me, and Realms of Mystery.

Spell Breaker

- Released: 2004
- Format: CD
- Label: Forward Productions
- Mastering: Dave Millington
- Sound Engineer: Dave Millington, Jeff Crawford
- Producer: Clan Dyken

Notes: *Spell Breaker* features socially conscious songs, all relevant in an election year, full of hope, a touch of anger, a bit of humor and of course danceable grooves. Flute and drum songs break up the familiar while the

Burning Man Techno influence and the life of musical activists are all found in the songs.

Retrospective

- Released: 2008
- Format: CD
- Label: Forward Productions
- Mastering: Dave Millington
- Producer: Clan Dyken

Notes: 3 disc set depicting Clan Dyken's career span. All songs ©Dyken Music 1987, 1989, 1992, 1993, 1996, 2002, 2003, 2004, except for *Stolen Land*.

I'm a Mystery

- Released: 2011
- Format: CD
- Label: Forward Productions
- Producer: Clan Dyken
- Notes: *I'm A Mystery* - A Collection of Very Personal Songs by Bear Dyken

Last Ride at the End of the Old World

- Released: 2011
- Format: CD
- Label: Forward Productions
- Sound Engineer: Jeff Crawford
- Mastering: Dave Millington
- Producer: Clan Dyken

Notes: *The Last Ride at the End of the Old World*, is one-and-a-half hours of Clan Dyken Music. Songs include: This Is My Soul Journey, Human Power, Can't Breathe, Wings For My Birthday, Ritmo y Flautas, To Be So Blessed, The Whole World, Going Ballistic, New Orleans, Dos Yantas,

Gypsy Song, Mother Lost Her Son, Strawberries and Cream, Harpos Ladder, Federal Reserve Gang, Hands of Grace. Bear Dyken, words and music, vocals, harmonica, guitar, grand piano. Mark Dyken, drums, vocals. Gary Dyken, bass, vocals. Somer Moon, vocals. Silas Dyken, bass. Thomas Spellman, vocals and guitar, Rick Moore, sax.

Water, Fire, and Other Relatives

- Released: 2017
- Format: CD
- Label: Forward Productions
- Sound Engineer: Wind River Studios, Santa Cruz, CA. Engineered by Keith Greeninger
- Mastering: Dave Millington
- Producer: Clan Dyken

Notes: Fourteen songs with an outstanding cast, including Keith Greeninger, Dayan Kai, Tammi Brown, Heather Normandale, Thomas Spellman, and Warren Jones. Combined with their world-class vocal and instrumental performances, the strength of the material, and the magic of the Wind River Recording Studio, Clan Dyken produced something special. The CD features a range of musical styles and unique crossover sounds. From the stark and introspective duo of Mark Dyken on cajon and rattle being the only accompaniment to the vocals and acoustic guitar of his brother, singer-songwriter, Bear Dyken on Stories Repeat to Vietnamese Don Moi mouth harp and Silas Dyken thumping the bass in *Good Morning Grandmother*. From the transforming influence of the Butte Fire in *Grandfather Fire* to the expansive and powerful *Good Ship Starfinder* every song hits the mark. There are no fillers.

More Notes from Friends

"I've had the pleasure and honor of crossing paths and joining forces with Clan Dyken in service of their missions to bring support and solidarity to Diné grandmothers and make a difference through music, lyrics, and community. I'm continually impressed with their resilience and deep caring for what matters most."

—Thomas Spellman, Musician

"I have known Mark and Bear for over twenty years and have always been inspired by their bone-deep dedication to social and environmental justice. From protesting at a nuclear test site, delivering supplies to the folks at the reservation or helping under-served youth in our community, they have always worked tirelessly for the good of All. And, despite the many challenges they have faced personally, they continue to be humble, joyful, endlessly creative and, most of all, completely genuine paragons of true leadership for our time."

—Erin Ross, Passionate Earthling Songstress

"What Clan Dyken is doing is beautiful. They have dedicated themselves to a yearly giving ritual that makes a difference in people's lives. That is admirable and worthy of much praise. This story is an inspiration, and I'm glad to see it written. We must continue to find ways to connect with our elders, to this land's history, and find ways to fight back against the greed that is destroying people's homes and livelihoods."

—Heather Normandale, musician/vocalist/songwriter

"Back in the day, I often played percussion for Clan Dyken. I'd arrive at an event and hear them doing a sound check, then run to the stage. It was as if I was the adopted Dyken brother, and it was always an honor and a pleasure to play with them. At the Glastonbury Faire in England, we ended up with Native American activist and musician, John Trudell.

Other times we worked with Native American Medicine Men like our elder, Corbin Harney. Both of these men had the highest regards for Clan Dyken, as did all of us. Mark and Bear walk their talk like no other. One of my favorite things we did as a band and a family was to parade to the center of the audience and form a prayer circle often beating on a big Native American drum. We sang 'Heal These Global Wounds.' It was so powerful."

—Fantuzzi, performing artist, percussionist

"The Dyken family band and activism are the circus I ran away with. In that motion, I feel, my future brightened. The Beauty Way Tour to support the Navajo/Dineh resistance rocked my soul in the bosom of Abraham! And Bear's songwriting heavily influenced my writing, I am sure, and my continued activism.

"I'll never forget Mark stopping our caravan on the way into Four Corners to see an extraordinary petroglyph spot. I hope it's still quiet and unbothered at that sacred site. Forever. And I'll never forget witnessing the Dineh grandmother resisters, herders, weavers, forced to settle but still raising their animals and turning toward the sun every morning. Sometimes I think it's only their prayers that are holding together the good stuff of this world as we know it.

Thanks for the ed-u-ma-cation, Clan Dyken! Thanks for the true friendship and heart connections across the miles with the people and the land at Big Mountain and all Black Mesa."

—Diane Patterson, folk activist

Special Thanks to Dan Budnik and Joel Grimes

For noted interior photographs:
Dan Budnick: http://danbudnik.com/

Dan Budnik is a photojournalist who has documented social, political, and cultural change in the world for the past fifty-five years. In 1958, Dan shot pictures of the revolution in Cuba. He was at the heart of the civil rights movement, with photo credits including the March on Washington in 1963 and the 1965 Selma to Montgomery March. Since 1970, Dan has been a fervent advocate for the traditional Navajo and Hopi tribes at Big Mountain. He was awarded photography grants from the National Endowment for the Arts (1973) and the Polaroid Foundation (1980) to aid in his documentation of the culturally destructive collision between industry and corrupt tribal and government officials.

For the cover photograph:
Joel Grimes: https://www.joelgrimes.com

Over the years, Joel Grimes has sought to be an ambassador for the photographic process. Joel's assignments have taken him to every state across the USA and over fifty countries across the globe. In 1992, he produced his first coffee table book *Navajo, Portrait of a Nation*, which received a number of photographic and design awards. In addition, this project produced an eighteen-month sixty print solo exhibit at the Smithsonian American History Museum. Joel feels that by being an open book with his process, he has an opportunity to inspire others to follow their dreams and passions to create.

Acknowledgments

We have been fortunate to have wonderful people around us all of our lives. If we tried to name them all, we'd struggle to stop and would still leave a deserving person off a list of those who helped create this book and the stories on the pages. Thank you to all the flame keepers, language holders, storytellers, culture stewards, ceremony masters, earth defenders, sheepherders, patrons, photographers, radio DJs, journalists, activists, healers, artists, musicians, teachers, poets, farmers, dancers, writers, actors, laborers, athletes, lovers, mothers, fathers, sons, daughters, grandparents, sisters, brothers, ancestors, aunts, uncles, cousins, friends, travelers, seekers, finders, dreamers, community builders, and celebrators of life. We are here because you care.

We'd like to offer a special acknowledgment to our book editors, Dr. Kate Evans, Anne Pawlak, and Daniel Harrison, and our graphic artist, Melody Young. We thank you deeply.

—With love and respect, Mark, Bear, and Shelley

Afterword

If you are interested in supporting Clan Dyken's Beauty Way Tour in support of the Dineh, please go to their website: clandyken.com and click the Donate button.

Ahéhee'
Thank you

To download a copy of the songs mentioned in this book
go to this link:
http://www.clandyken.com/cd/store/
Click on the link for *When the Creator Moves Me*
Click the CD download link

www.ingramcontent.com/pod-product-compliance
Lightning Source LLC
Chambersburg PA
CBHW030302080526
44584CB00012B/415